YAHOO ANF-849

The Thread That Binds

Interviews with Private Practice Bookbinders

The Thread That Binds
Interviews with Private Practice Bookbinders

Compiled and with introductions
by Pamela Train Leutz

*The paths that led
20 bookbinders to
private practice bookbinding,
including a special interview with
bookbinder Don Etherington*

Oak Knoll Press
2010

(C
Z
269
.T47
2010

First Edition 2010

Published by
Oak Knoll Press
310 Delaware Street
New Castle, DE 19720
www.oakknoll.com

© 2010 Pamela Train Leutz
All rights reserved

ISBN 978-1-58456-274-0 (paperback)
ISBN 978-1-58456-276-4 (hardcover)

Publishing Director: Laura R. Williams
Cover photo by Pamela Train Leutz
Typeset in Berkeley Oldstyle
Book design by Sunlight Graphics, Colorado Springs, CO

No part of this book may be reproduced in any manner without
the express written consent of the publisher, except in cases of
brief excerpts in critical reviews and articles. All inquiries
should be addressed to the publisher.

⊛ Printed in the United States of America on acid-free paper meeting
the requirements of ANSI/NISO Z39.48–1992 (Permanence of Paper)

Library of Congress Cataloguing-in-Publication Data

Leutz, Pamela Train.
  The thread that binds : interviews with private practice bookbinders / compiled and with
introductions by Pamela Train Leutz. -- 1st ed.
     p. cm.
  "The paths that led 20 bookbinders to private practice bookbinding, including a special
interview with bookbinder Don Etherington."
  Includes index.
  Summary: "A collection of 21 interviews with modern private practice bookbinders,
exploring both their challenges and successes in the business as well as the common 'threads'
that connect their stories. Illustrated in grayscale with photographs of the binders and their
studios"-- Provided by publisher.
  ISBN 978-1-58456-276-4 (acid-free paper) -- ISBN 978-1-58456-274-0 (pbk. : acid-free
paper) 1. Bookbinders--Biography. 2. Bookbinders--Interviews. I. Title.
  Z269.L48 2009
  686.30092'2--dc22
  [B]
                                                               2009047868

LOYOLA UNIVERSITY LIBRARY

WITHDRAWN

Dedicated to all people who work to keep
bookbinding alive in the world.

Contents

Introduction

*B*ookbinders tend to be diverse and likable people. They are quirky, earthy, unconventional, traditional, innovative, intelligent, and creative. Most bookbinders today make a living by working at an institution—a library, museum, university, or one of the few large binderies in America. Some, however, are independent bookbinders in private practice: general bookbinders, book conservators, book restorers, book artists, designer bookbinders, edition bookbinders, and box-makers. It is a life of hard work and perseverance, and it holds the risk of uncertain finances. On this variable income, bookbinders have to pay themselves a living wage, maintain a workspace, equipment, supplies and tools, and provide their own health insurance. "You have to be a little bit crazy," was Czech master bookbinder Jan Sobota's reply when I asked him what advice he would give to someone interested in making private practice bookbinding a career.

Each independent bookbinder has a "story"—significant, fascinating and unique, that reveals the path that unfolded, leading them to bookbinding and sustaining them as they continue their craft. What was their life path that brought them to bookbinding? Where did they learn the craft? What made them choose private practice? How do they ensure a living? How hard do they work? After years of bookbinding, do they still like what they are doing? What do they really like about being a bookbinder? What do they dislike? Where do they get clients? What advice would they give to someone interested in becoming a bookbinder? What common threads do these folks share? I was curious about the lives of independent bookbinders.

Why did it interest me to find out about the life of private practice bookbinders? Whenever I went into my studio to bind I found myself in a joyful place, and time had no meaning. Teaching bookbinding energized me and introduced me to fascinating people. I was in a transitional period in my life. Could I try bookbinding as my livelihood instead of as the supplemental income it had been for the last 20 years? I knew that the life of private practice bookbinding was hard work, in addition to being financially risky. Would I have the skills and character to create a successful business? I decided to make some discoveries about the life of bookbinders. I would call it the *Aunt Jessalyn Project*, after my great aunt who had just passed away and left me some money that would fund my project.

I would interview independent bookbinders, taking a human-interest angle. Much has been written about certain bookbinders' techniques and bindings. I wanted to know about the people themselves and the lives they led. I asked independent bookbinders I knew and respected if I could visit and interview them. In addition to hearing their responses to my questions, I also wanted to see where they worked, to get a fuller sense of their lives—and to record my images and impressions as I interacted with these people and their work.

I was warmly welcomed by every bookbinder I approached. Not only were the visits themselves remarkable and moving, the process of revisiting each bookbinder, as I listened to his or her interview, and transcribed it into text, was almost as inspiring as the face-to-face interaction. Time-after-time I was motivated by their optimism, caught up in their joy in the creative process of bookbinding, celebrating the fact that they live life, doing work that they are passionate about. This, I think, is the strongest thread that links them all—they are passionate about the work they do.

The *Aunt Jessalyn Project* reinforced my perception of bookbinders as amiable, interesting people—intelligent creative, passionate and skilled. These people are an inspiration—their work helps keep alive the art and craft of private practice bookbinding in America. I extend my respect and gratitude to these fine bookbinders and fascinating individuals.

Eleanore Ramsey:
Exquisite Precision and Sophistication

Sausalito, California
March 2005 & March 2008

The first interview took place in March 2005, at the studio of Eleanore Ramsey, a designer bookbinder working in Sausalito, CA. My friend and fellow bookbinder, Judy Thompson, who lives in California, accompanied me on that visit. Eleanore spoke softly and my audio equipment was weak. We left after a fabulous interview, only to later discover that the interview was not audible above the faint music that played in the background. I immediately recorded my memories from the interview, horrified that this long trip to California and to my first interview was a disaster. Because Eleanore's interview was not successfully recorded, it is written in a different format from the others. It is summarized in my words with quotes from her that I added from a later phone interview. I regret not having the complete interview in her voice, but I am grateful to include this remarkable woman in the collection.

We found Eleanore's studio on one of the small, hilly streets of Sausalito, a quaint house bordered by lush plants. We rang the doorbell but there was no answer. As we peered around the picture of the dinosaur that was stuck to the windowpane in the door, Eleanore's car pulled up behind us. Her studio comprises the lower level of the house; the cartoonist Phil Frank and his wife Susan occupy the level above.

Off a small entry hall is a large storeroom. Work surfaces, presses, and tools fill the main workroom of the studio to the left. At the end of the hall is a tiny kitchen with a sink, refrigerator and microwave; a white enamel stove, with knobs removed for safety and topped by plywood, supports a Kwikprint. Eleanore explains it is rarely used because, "I want students to tool their titles directly onto their books."

The kitchen doubles as a storage room and houses two handsome wooden paper drawer units, a wall of type holders, stacks of type, a miniature printing press and piles of book projects under boards and weights.

Everything was arranged to fit the wee room like pieces of a jigsaw puzzle. Beyond the kitchen, in what would have been a small bedroom, is another workroom.

A photo of Barbara Hiller, Eleanore's teacher for ten years, looks down on more tools and a huge, antique French wooden standing press made by Bertram Frères & Cie. Eleanore told me the story of three San Francisco couples who were interested in binding and printing at the turn of the century. Equipment was hard to find in the States, so they ventured to Europe and returned with three Bertram Frères presses.

Eleanore treasures this beautiful piece of equipment. She finds the percussion feature (permitting the platen to ratchet down tightly) especially important. "When I'm 90, I'll still be able to get good pressure." She also has a more modern Italian standing press, with percussion, in her main workroom.

Each room in the studio was crammed full of bookbinding paraphernalia, including the bathroom, which houses sewing frames. Thoughtful planning was necessary to find space for everything. Each piece of equipment had to be numbered and moved in that order. "If I had made a mistake, something would not have fit."

A guillotine is set up outside the main space in a little storeroom just off the porch. A tiny door opens to reveal its perfect fit. When Eleanore moves her studio into the home she and her husband (the book collector, Dr. Andrew Nadell) recently bought, she will have a larger space. She looks forward to finally replacing her Kutrimmer with a good board shear, a luxury she had to part with when she moved here.

As I interviewed her, we had a lovely tea party—Eleanore brought delectable pastries from a local bakery that she served with red bush tea, a tea that has been made more popular by the books of Alexander McCall Smith (*The #1 Ladies Detective Agency*), favorites of us both. Eleanore put on the white lab coat that she wears when she works. Her brown hair, now streaked with wisps of grey, was high on her head in a loose bun, her signature look. Middle aged, she is pretty and her smile still youthful. Eleanore possesses all the characteristics I find so attractive about bookbinders—she is intelligent, passionate about her work, creative, inspiring, positive and personable. She is a hard working, skilled, design bookbinder.

Eleanore graduated from college with strong interests in philosophy and art but not knowing what she wanted to do for a living. Undecided, she moved with her roommate to Rockford, Illinois. There she wandered into an antiquarian bookstore, The Bookstall, and got a job. She had always been passionate about books. The owner, John Kuehn, was a second-generation rare book dealer. "It was perfect work, researching books and reading, then meeting people with fascinating stories," she explained.

One day while arranging books, an exhibition catalog of French design bindings fell to the floor: *La Reliure Originale Francaise,* Museum of Contemporary Crafts, New York, 1964. She had never seen bindings like those pictured in the catalog; on turning the first page she recognized this would be her career. She researched where she could take bookbinding classes, but quickly discovered they were not so easy to find.

"I started writing letters, trying to find classes. Much later I learned of Laura Young and Gerard Charriere in New York."

Meanwhile, Eleanore married and moved to Washington, DC, where her first husband had been assigned to Walter Reed Army Medical Center. Determined to follow her interest in bookbinding, she sought out bookbinding books and equipment. While living in the Washington area, she learned of an auction where a "bookbinding press" was to be sold.

"In a moment of blissful ignorance I purchased the handsome wooden press, moving it across country when relocating to San Francisco, only to discover it was actually a linen press."

It turned out to not be a total loss. She found the beautiful, large, pressboards useful in bookbinding. Through her letter writing, she discovered bookbinding classes with Barbara Hiller in San Francisco. After studying briefly with an English bookbinder, she began to study with Barbara Hiller in 1975. After Eleanore divorced, she and Barbara decided to share studio space. They rented a large Victorian flat, which had many rooms all on one side of a long hallway.

"Barbara had the first two rooms where she worked (she also had an apartment where she lived in San Francisco), the next room was a shared workspace for students to work on their own, and then I worked and lived in the back half."

Barbara taught a traditional French style of bookbinding, a Bradel binding, and half and full-leather bindings, as well as tooling. Although she executed the designs on her work, she preferred to have it designed by an artist whom she credited, not unusual in the French tradition. She was a formal lady and a very demanding teacher, but Eleanore has fond memories of the years spent with her.

"Over the years we became great friends. Living in the "bindery" was truly an adventure full of humor and feats of bookbinding." In order to pay her bills and buy equipment, Eleanore kept her job.

"I worked as a social worker while sharing space with Barbara. I worked full-time and later, part-time, a rare privilege then. I eventually quit (to do bookbinding full-time) and later learned that I was replaced by three people! I worked all the time [between social work and bookbinding]."

After many years teaching her, Barbara told Eleanore that it was time for her to teach—that it was her responsibility to share her knowledge, and that teaching would provide a dependable way to pay bills.

"I was dead set against it. I told her, 'I'll never teach,' " said Eleanore.

Barbara, however, had her own plan. "Two days later, she informed me that my 'first student, Mr. X, will arrive Saturday at 10:00 a.m. and this is what you'll say ...and this is what you will do...,' ending with the advice: 'good teachers teach with their hands.' Barbara was an extremely intelligent and serious sort of person that did not accept 'no' for an answer. I felt fortunate that we were close friends."

"I worked manically for years and years. It would have been a shame not to teach what I had learned, particularly because it had been so difficult for me to find a teacher." After ten years of sharing space together, they were evicted. Rent control laws had changed, and they couldn't find a big enough place that they could afford. Rent had more than doubled in those ten years. "We looked everywhere. It was a terrible time."

Barbara decided to retire. She moved near family on the Virginia coast. Before leaving, she stayed to help Eleanore move.

"She gave me some rather neat things: tools of course, but also paintings and a Colt pistol, which turned out to be a collector's item. I had never had a gun in my life. I can only assume she wanted me to be able to protect myself and to be sure that I was properly started. She did not leave until I was settled. She was happy with her decision to retire but died about two months after she left." Eleanore regrets that she didn't get a chance to visit her.

Eleanore was grateful she was "forced" to teach. She believes that bookbinders should share their knowledge. She still relies on teaching to pay the studio rent. Sometimes students fly in for one-on-one instruction, spend a long day with Eleanore, and leave in the evening. Most students come once a week. Every Tuesday morning and afternoon, and every Wednesday morning, afternoon and evening she teaches bookbinding, taking two to three students in each class.

It is important to her that she is available and watchful so her students learn properly. Since simple structures can be learned at the local Center for the Book, she starts students off with a more complex curriculum. She teaches a millimeter binding with leather, a Bradel binding, half-leather and full-leather bindings, box-making, and paper decoration.

On an ongoing basis, students work on plaques (simulated book covers) practicing design work, tooling and onlays. These can later be design models for their full-leather bindings. After completing these bindings, students work on their own projects. Camaraderie develops between students, and they also learn from each other. The class often brainstorms solutions for structure, designs, and for correcting errors.

"Students need to make errors. Errors are hugely valuable; they pave the way to advanced work. As a consequence, to brainstorm with students in order to work out their problems, I think, is a necessity. Errors help them think about the process in a logical way. Curiously, the solution seems to always make the work better than it would have been otherwise."

Eleanore is an enthusiastic and devoted teacher. "I can't think of a student I didn't like. They have been serious and worked hard. They ask great questions. This is important because it lets me know how they are thinking about their work. Unfortunately, there are many specialized tools necessary in hand bookbinding. This is a problem for students, as they can be difficult to find, and expensive. It took me years to accumulate the tools and equipment necessary for my studio. Many of the tools are venerably old with interesting provenance, making them a special pleasure to work with. I have all the tools students need, and because much has been handed down to me in the way of supplies, I try to be generous to students. I also make a lot of my own tools and teach students to make them. I think it makes their work more their own. I try to encourage their work as much as possible."

I asked about what her students do with their bookbinding skills after studying with her.

"Some do commissions. Some work on their own books. Several have started their own businesses and are very successfully selling their work. Some teach at the Center for the Book in San Francisco and other schools. Then also I have had students that are book collectors and work on their own libraries. Of course I go to exhibitions, and I am always gratified to find accomplished work done by my students. This actually is a great pleasure I did not anticipate."

On Mondays, Thursdays, Fridays, Saturdays and Sundays, Eleanore works on design bindings, often late into the night. She showed us one of her current commissions, a miniature book titled *A Desert Tale*. The design uses very strong, embedded magnets to secure the head of a camel that wraps around from the back of the book, onto the front cover. The work seems perfect and beautiful, with very fine, detailed onlays and tooling.

Next, she showed us her *Alice in Wonderland* design binding. She was borrowing it for a photo-shoot from the client who commissioned it. The cover displays leather onlays of the rabbit hole in profile with other distinctive characters and motifs that Alice encounters on her adventure. The skilled workmanship, choice of color, and design are stunning.

When I asked Eleanore what her favorite parts are of being a bookbinder, she replied that developing the design is most important to her. "And then to build a working structure in order to support that design. In bookbinding this means it must operate both in two and three dimensions. It is to 'work' aesthetically and literally to function as a book. Also, it is interesting and feels playful to test designs with new materials and then, subsequently, techniques."

Presently, she is accepting fewer commissions to allow more time to

The studio is spread throughout the house.

work on projects and books of her own choice. There is more freedom in doing uncommissioned work, and Eleanore sometimes worries about taking too much time on her roster of commissioned bindings, some of which take up to two years. Clients discover her by having seen her work in exhibitions or by her reputation.

Clients include book and art collectors, members of the (California) Roxbourghe Club and other book groups, and libraries. With part of the profits from her work, she has bought books to bind later and has accumulated an impressive collection.

Her favorite binding was for the Southern Methodist University Bridwell Library's 50 X 25 invitational exhibition where she was given two copies of Ladislav Hanka's, *Scripta Naturae: Leaves of Organic Verse* to bind. The library kept one binding, and she kept the other. Her binding showcased an engineering marvel—on the front and back covers were hinged cutouts, camouflaged in the designs, that were held in place by tiny concealed magnets, that when opened, became easels to display the open book.

In developing designs for her bindings, she looks at the book as a whole—the printing, the text, the illustrations—and then a design emerges in her mind. She researches her design thoroughly and creates a mock-up of it on paper before executing it. For example, in one project she wanted to include an onlay of a loon. This required a visit to the Academy of Science where a curator brought 19th century, preserved loons to a little room where Eleanore could photograph and draw them. They didn't have eyes, so she had to research further. She was led to a bird specialist in Chicago who explained the eye was the color of blood. She enjoys the diverse steps of creating the whole binding for each one-of-a-kind binding.

I asked Eleanore what abilities and gifts she has that contribute to her being a good bookbinder. "The obvious one is patience. Bookbinding has a long process. I like to put the design on the book; it seems to materialize in front of your eyes."

Only the best bookbinders achieve the level of perfection she executes at gold-tooling. When only tooling occasionally, one cannot become a really good finisher. It requires extensive practice. Early on, she got a job tooling a series of titles on a set of books. Although the books were many different heights, the client wanted all the titles to be aligned when shelved. She said she made every mistake possible but learned to title (as well as to correct errors) and was comfortable with tooling after that project.

When individuals express an interest in pursuing bookbinding, she invites them to come to her studio to see what it is about. She offers very small classes so they can learn the process of bookbinding and see if it works for them. Having students at various levels in a class allows them to see work besides their own and observe different techniques so they learn from each other as well. "Students learn more from classes on an ongoing basis as opposed to only attending workshops."

Eleanore admits that it is not easy to make a living by bookbinding, and dealing with business matters is difficult. Nevertheless, she supported herself by bookbinding for many years. The solution was simple. "I worked an unbelievable number of hours per week."

Looking forward, Eleanore doesn't think she will ever retire completely from bookbinding. She continues to be stimulated by the work.

"Each book is different. I really like working it out; it's a nice process. Every book requires new design solutions and it keeps me interested. It can also be challenging to resolve technical problems. Our basic materials are flour, water, leather and paper—the complexity of objects we can make out of these simple materials is amazing."

For more information about Eleanore Ramsey, and to see examples of her work, go to www.EleanoreRamsey.com.

Tini Miura:
Bold Designs of a Peaceful Woman

Long Beach, California
September 2005

A place of beautiful sunsets over a peaceful ocean, a city of energy, a contemporary home-studio filled with art and Asian accents. This is Tini Miura's home in Long Beach, CA. My good friend Judy Thompson met me in Long Beach to celebrate my 50th birthday and join me in visiting Tini. Judy had traveled through Europe with her many years before when Tini and her Japanese husband, Einen, led a trip there, so for them this was a reunion. Tini's studio is located in the main room of her high-rise home in the city, a part of which is a sitting area separated from the workspace by a long table lined with book presses, jars of brushes and stacks of weights. On a clean worktable are a litho-stone, a textblock and a skin of leather, cut and pared. Soon this table will also hold a bottle of champagne and three fluted glasses for a toast we make to life.

Under a bank of windows on the far side of the room stands a guillotine and standing press. A polypress and board shear line an adjacent wall. All the pieces of equipment are painted a peaceful shade of turquoise blue.

The opposite side of the room opens to a modern kitchen. Vintage drawings of Parisian women line the hall that leads to a bedroom and bathroom. Asian art and decorations accent the sitting room space. Though this room holds all the equipment and supplies of a bookbinding studio, it still has clean lines and a feeling of Zen-like spaciousness. Tini's distinctive "oleaugraph" marbled papers are framed and hung on walls throughout the space.

Tini greets us warmly and invites us into the sitting room. Her straight blond hair, cut to chin-length with bangs, frames her dazzling blue eyes. Her complexion is flawless. Tini's gentle demeanor reflects peace and compassion.

Her bindings have an unmistakable signature look—bright, bold, intricately and perfectly executed onlays, her own contemporary oil-marbled paper endsheets of equally brilliant colors, finely sewn headbands, and classic French-style bindings. She learned bookbinding first in Germany, continued her studies in Switzerland with Hugo Peller, and also studied in Paris. In Sweden, she marbled paper with the distinctive patterns of Ingeborg Boerjeson at the artist's studio. Later in Tokyo, together with her husband Einen, she developed "oleaugraphs," a mixed technique of marbling.

Tini is an exceptionally positive, accepting, and spiritual person. Her design bindings reflect this joyfulness through her use of bright colors and artistry. Tini takes her appreciation for life, her positive nature, her intellectual and intuitive abilities, and her skills, and pours them into bindings that manifest beauty and passion, much like her.

Did you always want to be a bookbinder?

No, my first choice was to be an archeologist because I grew up near a Viking dig. I was so fascinated that I taught myself to write runes. Then at the age of ten, when my family moved back to my town of birth, I was singing in an opera choir. The first set design I saw made me understand that I wanted to work with colors. But the atmosphere, all those hectic people screaming, some crying, was not for me. Close to graduation from school, I had to think hard and decided to combine my two hobbies, reading and painting, into becoming a book illustrator. My father taught art; he suggested I study bookbinding first before entering art school. He said that a fashion designer needs to know how to sew and understand materials. I should take a similar approach. My grandfather was shocked that I was not going to get a PhD like my cousins, but I had my father for moral support. Later, when newspapers wrote about me, my grandfather softened his stance, but he didn't live long enough to see the first book published about my work. My father, who pointed me into the right direction, could see it on his deathbed, and I was grateful for that. He had always supported me.

Tini Miura paring leather.

Now I was on my way to enter adult life. I thought three boring years of apprenticeship were ahead of me, but I started and was pleasantly surprised. Each year was divided into nine months of training and three months of theory, design, and history. The first book I ever bound and designed was a novel by my literature professor. I was thrilled and thought that I invented designer bindings. I did not know how ignorant I was. I lived in the most northern state of Germany, which had a castle, a shipyard, a great university, and a well-known institute for global economy; the countryside was farmland. The books I saw were from book clubs, a little more attractive than ordinary editions. That was the extent of my knowledge of the world of books.

But designing and binding my first volume, I realized how perfect this profession would be for me. Physically, I am creating something that I can watch grow into an object. Mentally, I am engaged when I try to understand the content, and my soul or emotions convey my interpretation onto the cover by using colors and forms. What could be better than using body, mind, and soul, which make us human? The next step for me now was how to get the best education that was available. I had the advantage to have studied several languages at school. I was advised to go to Switzerland and study with Hugo Peller, a great technician and teacher. With the money won by having the best exam works in the whole of then West Germany, I bought two suitcases and left for my 14 months with Hugo Peller. I learned a lot and preferred the French technique to the one I had used before. I decided I would go to the source, Paris, where Hugo himself had studied. While in Switzerland, I received an invitation to a conference held by the German Association of Master Binders in Paris. I went, and my eyes were opened to the beauty of limited edition books, with illustrations by famous artists like Picasso, Rouault, and Matisse, who often signed the original prints. I had never heard about nor seen anything like it. I was hooked.

A wonderful gentleman, Monsieur Altermatt, who lived in Montparnass with many of his artist friends and who was a walking encyclopedia on private press books, suggested that I should study at the Ecole Estienne, a college for graphic professions. Monsieur Altermatt introduced me to professor Raymond Mondange, and he agreed to take me in the future. Only four students per year could enter. I was very happy and had to make plans to earn and save so I could go.

But first I landed in Stockholm, Sweden and worked for a while for the royal binder G. Hedberg and later had my own studio, Atelier Bremer, with my first husband. In Sweden, I was fortunate to do some very prestigious work, the Nobel Prize Diplomas, gifts of state to other states, the king of Sweden's gifts to other royalties, etc. Later, moving to Japan, this showed to be a big advantage for my profession and me.

While I was in Paris, my professor, Raymond Mondange, who was one of the two main gilders who executed Paul Bonet designs, took good care of me. He knew how difficult it is to survive and pay for your training, rent, living costs for two places (Stockholm and Paris), and study other techniques on the side. One time I saw a small sketch by Paul Bonet on thin and crumpled paper, like the paper used for wrapping a sandwich, with the size [of the design] indicated by centimeters. He worked it out to full scale and the job was done. Professor Mondange told me, his eyes shining with joy and pride, that he had met Paul Bonet when both of them were poor, before Bonet became famous, and helped him with the execution of the designs, charging friendship fees or nothing. Years later I was told by a fellow student that some of Professor Mondange's students thought that when he died suddenly, that he had died of a broken heart. There was a huge Bonet exhibition in Paris with Paul Bonet's books, with no mention of the friend who had helped him. Professor Mondange lost interest in life and died.

While discussing that life sometimes is a struggle, Professor Mondange pointed out that his chin was at an angle because he was still growing when he entered his training as a gilder. To push the handle of a big roulette, he needed the strength of his arms, while also pushing with the side of his jaw.

Through Professor Mondange, I got to know other fantastic professionals, like Monsieur Koch, the master of edge gilding on uncut deckle edged paper. I was fortunate enough to take classes from him as well as visit and work on my own books in the studio of Semet & Plumelle on some occasions, because I needed advice. Monsieur Plumelle, the sole survivor of that studio, was very generous in sharing his knowledge. He was the gilder for his studio and a friend of mine was the employed binder.

Soon I realized that all the great masters were 70 years old or older. Two world wars and a depression had made the demand for luxurious books scarce, and I understood that a whole generation was missing. I had to learn as much as I could now and was never refused an answer to my questions. Later I heard that my male peers were not as lucky with studios in the city. I don't know if being female and a foreigner was helping me. French men of all ages were very charming towards women—or they thought that a woman could not be competition; she would marry and take care of the family. Whatever it was, I am eternally grateful, and ever since I have tried to pass my knowledge down to the next generation. It is not my private possession; there is a very long line of people who were before me. Looking back, it was financially difficult, but I did what I wanted to do, and it never felt hard. I am lucky to earn a living by doing what I love.

The most interesting thing that I observed in France was that the bookbinding profession there is divided into seven sections. Seven people would work their specialty on a binding. Techniques and tools have evolved differently compared to what I was used to. Today my binding technique is 98% French.

An interesting story from my time in Paris is from an incident that occurred during a collective bookbinding exhibition on Boulevard St. Germain, with all known French binders present at the opening. My father attended; he had come to Paris with a group of his art students. After his death, my sister showed me my dad's papers relating to the trip. I was so in awe of George Crette, a giant in the bookbinding profession, and just to be in the same room with him is still one of my highlights, that I totally forgot what else had happened to me.

Jean Paul Sartre saw the show, liked my work, and talked to me, while shaking my hand to congratulate me. It took me a while to remember; all that was important to me then was seeing George Crette while he was still alive. But having shared a handshake with Jean Paul Sartre now seems miraculous to me. Who hasn't discussed existentialism at one point in life?

My journey to learn and study binding techniques and design was a long one. Normally one needs eight years of study to get a master diploma. Only then is one allowed to teach others. You may open a bindery any time you like, but if you want to take apprentices, you need to hire a master binder. I had studied in Germany, Switzerland, and France, and was fortunate enough to become one of Emilio Brugalla's friends. During his visit to Sweden and mine to Barcelona, Emilio was very generous with his knowledge every time we met and showed me a few of his "tricks" which helped me with my gilding. I am so grateful to have had the chance to see or study with the greats of the twentieth century. My mother always said that I was born under a lucky star on a Sunday. Looking back on my life, I have learned that bad situations experienced in life turned out to be a blessing, when put into context.

Three weeks before my divorce was final, I had decided never to marry again. I would go to the United States, work, and find out who I really was (I had gone from my father's hand to a husband's, not knowing myself). I met Einen Miura while volunteering in an open-air museum on weekends. He traveled in Scandinavia on his summer vacation from London University. Had I escaped my first marriage earlier, I would not have been at the right place at the right time to be found by Einen. We married after I finished my obligations to my clients, and I followed Einen to Japan. I thought I would be a housewife and he would follow his dream to have an impact on people who could not fend for themselves.

When we left Europe and said goodbye to my friends and clients, they were happy for me but regretted that I would not work again. After a few weeks in Japan, Einen told me that the words of my clients were still ringing in his ears and that I should continue because what I do makes people happy. Einen helped me, studied with me, got interested so much that he is now more book crazy than I am.

We worked together and developed a special technique for decorated paper we coined "oleaugraph." Einen wrote a book, *The Art of Marbled Paper,* which was published in five countries and is used in many libraries to date a paper by looking at the pattern. Visiting Argentina and Brazil to lecture and teach, I was very surprised to hear a librarian at the University of Belo Horizonte in Mina Gerais, Brazil, tell me that he had my husband's book.

Arriving in Japan, New Years 1976, we soon moved to Tokyo and taught conversation and mathematics to pay our bills until we started our own Atelier Miura. In 1980, we founded Japan Bibliophile Binding Society. We would meet once or twice a year, help and answer questions about bookbinding, give lectures and slide shows, teach, and every second year, arrange a trip to a foreign country to see the treasures in their libraries.

Einen and I visited the United States for the first time in 1980, the same year my first book was published in Japan. We were introduced to many colleagues. Mel Kavin and his family have a special place in our hearts. He has done so much for our profession, inviting designer binders from various countries to share their knowledge with others who want to learn more. Even after his death, I can call and ask advice from Bruce Kavin in matters of machine binding of which I know next to nothing.

I have been coming to this country annually and feel at home here. Einen always wanted me to have one foot in the West, in my own culture, in case something happens to him.

After studying politics and economics at Waseda University in Tokyo, Einen went to study at the University of London. He wanted to understand the Western mind and culture better and wanted me to have the best of two worlds. He is very strong and knows who he is; as an Asian man, he studied under a woman.

We work on many projects together and have become such a team that we don't have to ask, "Will you do this?" It is just done. We love the same music and art and support each other always.

After 20 years of travel, my energy level to continue traveling was diminishing. We decided that I should open a studio in the United States in a place easy to reach by airplane. I settled for Long Beach, California and have two more years to citizenship, if all goes well. My studio, in which I work and live, is only a few blocks from the ocean, and the ocean smell makes me happy. It seems familiar after having had the Baltic Sea near where I grew up. But my wish to live here goes back many years. I really have this special feeling about people in this country.

When the war was over, my family crossed Germany in cattle wagons and lived in refugee camps and bombed out homes of relatives, from the French sector to the American, and finally the British in the North. The only soldiers I saw on the newsreels after the war, hunched down eye-to-eye with the frightened children, were the Americans. Their soothing voices were calming, and gentleness was in their eyes. Still now I have not forgotten.

Another wonderful thing that happened to me also came from the United States in a care parcel in the spring of 1946. Like most people I knew, I too was wearing mended hand-me-downs from grown-ups or things made with material my mother could find. In the parcel was this pale blue dress with little puffed-up sleeves which had little flowers embroidered on them as well as on the pocket. It was the most beautiful dress I had ever seen, and I felt like a princess when my teacher chose me to wear it. I thought, "Who is this mother who is giving such a beautiful dress to a stranger who is living in the country that just a little while ago was the enemy?" At age six, I was very aware of this situation because my father, a prisoner of war, had not returned by 1946.

In 1999, when I was visiting China for the first time to see one of the biggest libraries in Shanghai, NATO bombed the Chinese Embassy in Kosovo. There was an angry demonstration by students, an understandable reaction. If it had happened to my embassy, I probably would have demonstrated too, as I did as a student for Hungary and later for Czechoslovakia. We could not get into the building and did not meet until the next day. An official asked me what my nationality was. When I answered "German" she called me a liar. But all my other visits were wonderful experiences, both the meetings and our treatments by officials and private Chinese citizens. I have very good memories and am grateful. In the same week, I was interviewed for a magazine, and I could tell the Chinese public why I like Americans. I said that they are the most generous people in the world. If there is a disaster, the Americans are there to help without asking your nationality or religion.

It is about the big three "Ts." When asked what I meant I explained. The first T is for treasure. If you are rich you share your treasure. Look at Bill Gates—he has made it possible to immunize all children in Africa. The second T is for time. You can give of your time and volunteer, for example in a hospital, feed babies or take care of lonely people and read to them. The third T is for talent. You share it with others to make their life better and happier.

The winter of 1945-46 was very, very cold. People in the neighboring village who had survived the escape from the East froze to death inside a barn. We were forced on another villager who owned a house. She was not happy about it. The winter right after the war found my mother and her three daughters in one little room without electricity, water, and heat. We had been given a pile of straw and a large army blanket. Once a day, we went to be fed in the schoolhouse. At night we huddled under the blanket wearing all our clothes, and my mother would tell us Greek, Roman, and Germanic mythology. Everything I ever learned about morals, ethics, faithfulness, action, reaction, and the consequence of deeds was then.

I still can recapture these feelings of awe and wonderment and even though I am a grown woman, somehow I still expect something wonderful to happen. If I just turn around quickly enough in a forest or meadow, I might see an elf. I still remember my mother asking me if I knew why the October evening sky was so pink. Her explanation was that, "Christmas is not far and the angels have started baking cookies for all children in the world, and when they opened the oven, the reflection of the light from the fire inside colored the evening clouds." When looking at the evening sky (and it looks like it did then), my feelings are that of the six-year-old.

I thank my mother, and wherever she is I hope she knows of my gratitude. I am who I am now because of my mother and her way to make me reflect about everything I encounter and see or feel beauty. I never felt poor. When we were hungry, my mother would distract us with songs she taught us until we forgot about our empty stomachs. I have no bad memories; there was nothing to compare to. Our nanny was gone; no other children had one now. We were all living a similar existence. So did Einen, my husband. After 1948 things changed for us. My father came home. Life in Germany began to get better for most people. It took many more years for circumstances to change in Japan. There was no Marshall Plan.

As a five-year-old, the youngest of four, Einen had never met his dad. His father died going down with his ship in the Pacific War. His mother would disappear occasionally, never telling them if or when she would be back. She suffered from deep depression and sought help in temples. To help himself as a five-year-old, he found a job for one meal a day. He sat next to a lorry driver on an eighteen-hour drive. His duty was to keep the driver awake. There he was, this little five-year-old in his father's sweater that reached to his ankles, sleeves rolled up, clowning around. This experience made him strong and taught him self-reliance. He would get up before dawn, go to the riverbank behind his house, wait for the sunrise, and dream about going to another wonderful place. Later this longing turned into wanting to go to America, the land of hope. We both were very emotional, standing next to each other in 1990 in Telluride on the fourth of July. We both feel that our freedom was made possible through the courage and sacrifice of the American soldier.

Did you like those years teaching in Telluride at the American Academy of Bookbinding?
Yes, every minute of it. It was wonderful. What my husband and I were doing was worthwhile. To teach and see the students' responses is very gratifying. I never wanted to be a teacher; several in my family were. Their students had to go to class; mine wanted to be there. It is very different. In the first years, before the school became known, I would be there at 9 a.m. and often late into the night. Later when the classes grew, I tried to be home before 6 p.m. I observed how the students communicated, helped each other, and how they gave advice. It was a wonderful thing to see. To have played a part in this gives my life more meaning. I was able to do it for many years. When we had the first graduates, I could retire with a good conscience.

What are your favorite parts of being a bookbinder?
Opposite things. One is to be alone with my music and books.

The other is being with book people anywhere in the world. I like teaching too. It sounds awful, but I like coming up with solutions for problems I have never encountered myself. But when a student needs help, and I can come up with new ideas to correct the mistake, it feels very satisfying.

Before I start a class, I always tell my students that everyone will make mistakes. I will call them to the table and explain the why and how to correct the situation. It is easier to remember a problem than a smooth work sequence, especially if one is not doing this kind of work for a whole year [day in and day out].

When I went to Switzerland, a new world—a world of beautiful books—was opened up to me with the help of Hugo Peller. I was his fourth student, and he was my teacher for 14 months. He was a great teacher and spread enthusiasm for books everywhere he went. He transformed my mistakes into something beautiful to look at. I am grateful to my teacher in Flensburg, Rolf Steffen, who recommended I seek out Hugo Peller. To meet both of these men was a big gift to me.

What are your least favorite parts in bookbinding?

Sanding, because I have to vacuum afterwards. It is the dust, not the sanding in itself. Dust is everywhere. In Tokyo I can go outside. Here I can't. It is not really fair to say sanding. It is the cleaning up. Sanding is the shaping that makes a book snuggle into your palm. It makes holding a book feel good. So it is the cleaning and the cardboard dust in the hair and nose, despite wearing a mask, that I don't like.

Who are your clients?

I have clients in several European countries, Asia, and North and South America, as well as libraries and other institutions.

How do people hear of you?

So far I have never advertised. It has always been word of mouth, through my exhibitions, or books about my work. But I have to get a web page. I have not put the text together yet, but have chosen the images. As soon as I get time, I will start doing it. People started paying attention to my work because of my decorated papers. My main work was on books printed in the 20th century, and I did not feel good about putting marbled patterns from past centuries on my bindings. I wanted some connection to the content, even if it only was through colors, which I love to use to create a certain mood. Through these small, decorated paper bindings, collectors became aware of my work. I did not start out making full-leather designer bindings. To win the trust of a collector, you have to win local and international competitions more than once. If they trust you with their prized possessions, they want to know if you got lucky once or if you are really good. And of course you have to be honest with the jury and let them know if you had help or if you did everything yourself.

In my early years, when I was 25 years old to around fifty, many serious collectors of fine bindings were alive. Now we have a different generation with different interests. But there will always be people who are passionate about collecting the beautiful book.

I have two nice stories to tell that fall into this category: When I was working for the royal bindery, Gustav Hedberg in Stockholm, Sweden, I received a letter from a young man. I never met him, but I could read between the lines that someone whom he loved had disappointed him. He told me that he loved poetry but did not have a lot of money. I remembered how poetry was my medicine for my growing up pains, and I wanted to create special papers for his small, delicate volumes. After receiving the books, he wrote a beautiful letter to thank me. He told me that when he opened the parcel and held the book bodies in his hands, he had moments of total happiness. When I am attacked for my work, I remember these words and then feel moved and grateful. Praise for your work means so much.

My second story tells of a collector, T.H., whose work place was only two stations away from my studio. He and his wife were government-employed lawyers. They owned a one-room apartment and had a bottle of red wine delivered every evening at the right temperature to drink that night. My client collected what he called "the pearls of Swedish literature" beginning with the 16th century. His wife let him spend all his money on his collections, but demanded a first-class holiday in Italy once a year, first-class flight, five-star hotel and first-class treatment.

Whenever a book was in my studio and he could see the empty space in his bookshelf, he truly suffered. For me, his books were always a priority. When he had waited for 11 years for one of his "pearls" to show up in a good condition at auction, he decided to buy it. It was almost 200 years old and moldy. I explained what needed to be done to save the book, and he agreed to it. T.H. dropped in often for tea or lunch and when he showed up while his pages were swimming in the vat, he almost fainted. He turned greenish/purple, and I sat him down and gave him a stiff drink.

That winter, T.H. caught a really bad case of influenza and was hospitalized. He had internal bleeding and was near death. His worried, loving wife visited every morning and evening, but he was lethargic, showing no interest in anything, had the curtains drawn and lost his will. When his wife told me about his condition, I dropped everything I was doing and started on his book. I called to give the book to her. Later she told me what she was thinking at that moment: "My husband is dying, and Tini thinks about books."

When she brought it to his hospital room, he sat up and asked to open the curtains to look at his treasure. He recovered soon after. T.H. was the most passionate collector I have ever met. If you feel such passion, what capacity to feel joy!

That is why I want to do this project, The Thread that Binds. *There is something about that story—a thread that brings aliveness to us in how we touch others and fulfill our own lives. I think that thread is passion.*

That story means a lot to me. I was always very private, and as a teenager thinking I was the only one who cared and understood misery, injustice and suffering in the world. I helped myself by reading poetry and listening to music. Many wonderful things have happened to me because of books and people who love them.

I think you are very open to allow things to happen in your life.

You may be right. I expect something wonderful to happen. And when it does, I feel humbled and grateful. This attitude is my mother's gift to me. Every day I think that something wonderful is just around the corner.

I feel the same way. But I think it is something I've developed as an older person that I blocked as a younger person. I can't tell you why it has changed.

That is lucky that you have found it. You are aware of it. And when you are aware, it happens more and more. Even the bad things that happen to you, when you look back, they have taken you to a better place.

Yes, even though it has been painful.

This afternoon I was talking to a friend on the phone and said that I will not allow myself to think of the bad things that happened to me in the past few years. I have lived a very sheltered life, protected by people who love me. My number one rule in life is to never hurt anybody on purpose. I am sure I have, but not knowingly. I am at peace with myself. Of course I heard or read about bad people. If someone looks at me with an honest expression, I believe him or her. It hurts when it is someone you trusted. So I learned my lesson late in life, but I move on. I will not spend my energy on negative things. I guess not everybody has a conscience that bothers them. This experience just makes me appreciate my friends even more.

You think the best of everybody.

Yes, I do. I don't want to use my energy for negative things. It just is not me. Only once in my professional life was I annoyed by a critique. If people don't like what I am doing, I really don't care. I like what I am doing; if not, I would be dishonest with my clients. Tastes are different. But if a critique says that I overload my covers to show off my various skills, I get upset. Integrity is very high on the scale of my vocabulary.

When people give a critique, they are only seeing through their own eyes.

Yes, I don't mind if they say, "You are too colorful or you are too this or that." I don't mind at all. I know that I am colorful—for many people too colorful. But color and music make me feel so very much alive—I need both in my life. If you feel, you know you are! You feel good! I don't have to study to find out why I am happy. To analyze it would be for me like pulling petals from a daisy and being left with nothing. I don't like that. I want a bit of mystery left in everything. That makes me happy.

What do you feel are your gifts and abilities that make you a good bookbinder?

I think to translate the story into colors and shapes, and also to teach.

Do you read the story before you bind it?

Yes, while reading the design "swims" into my mind's eye. Most literary works I bind are known to me, but the typeface, layout, and illustrations demand different approaches. Sometimes, when touching a text unknown to me, I feel the design.

Later, while I read the story, understanding comes. I cannot explain this, but I say a silent thank you to wherever it came from and accept the gift. I never change a design that has happened to me in my one-of-a-kind bindings. It is different for edition books. I take advice and may use it.

What would you like to achieve in bookbinding that you haven't done yet? Is there anything?

I want to write another book that explains the technique that I am using now.

So you have changed technique?

Yes. I have learned a lot in 25 years, and many things I am doing now I think are better.

I'll buy that book.

Years ago, I was fortunate to talk to a gentleman in a Scottish library. The collection there had everything I could think of. I want to make a picture book for beginners in book collecting and binding. I want to show the different styles developed over the centuries in various parts of the world, with explanatory texts. But honestly, I cannot afford to take a year off from work to do so. I have to find out what funds are available for such a project and where to apply. But right now I don't have the time to look for these scholarships. It would be a good tool for book lovers who want to learn more.

Is there anything you would like to tell someone who is interested in becoming a bookbinder? Do you have any words of advice?

Just don't give up. If you want to do it, do it, and it will not feel hard to give up things you like to be able to get that special education. I went to three different countries to do so. A famous musician got asked once by a potential musician if he should study to become one. The answer was, no, if you feel the need to ask, then it is not for you. If you feel bookbinding is what you want to do, then you can do it.

Frank Lehmann:
From Rocket Science to Restoration

San Diego, CA
(interviewed in Portland, OR)
October 2005

Though I wasn't able to visit Frank Lehmann at his bindery outside of San Diego, I very much wanted to include his story in the collection. I interviewed him at a Guild of Book Workers Standards of Excellence conference in Portland, OR with the hope of visiting him later. My friend and fellow bookbinder, Judy Thompson, joined me for the interview.

Frank has a very endearing and funny personality. Judy had met him in Telluride while taking classes from Tini Miura at the American Academy of Bookbinding. They became good buddies. Judy had told me about this guy, Frank, and how he was a real rocket scientist-physicist, but wanted to pursue his love of bookbinding. I was intrigued by her stories about him.

I finally met Frank at a Standards meeting. This was before he started attending the conference as a vendor, selling fine, old, European decorative tools and well-crafted wooden book presses, ploughs, and other bookbinding equipment made by craftsman Frank Wiesner, in Australia.

As a child, Frank loved books. He started binding books when he was ten years old, using instructions from a book he bought with the money he earned doing yard work. He continued learning bookbinding as he grew up and even took classes during his lucrative career as a physicist.

Eventually he left the corporate world to focus intensely on the craft of bookbinding, full-time. He was fortunate to get the opportunity to study with John Mitchell in England for four years, refining his skill at restoration binding, until his savings were depleted.

It was quite a risk for Frank to leave a profitable career and use all his money to hone his bookbinding skills and become a full-time bookbinder. He opened Lehmann Bindery outside San Diego in the community of Vista, CA. Through referrals from other binders, and a strong work ethic, he consistently has jobs coming in.

He carries out the old traditions of book restoration, conservation, and fine bookbinding, and he shares his knowledge by teaching students. His connection with the book world in Europe has given him the opportunity to buy the old, skillfully made decorative tools that he uses on period bindings. I admire his total commitment to doing what he loves. I still hope to visit him and finally see where he works—and meet his two dogs, Pogo and Chip, who accompany him to work each day.

Have you ever had a job other than bookbinding?

Yes, or as I like to say, I took a slight detour in my bookbinding career. Although bookbinding had been a hobby for me since I was a kid, I didn't see it as a viable career path after graduating from high school. At the time, I didn't know of any professional hand bookbinders in the States. So instead, I entered University and eventually graduated with a PhD in Physics. I had no Idea at the time, that when I graduated from high school, I was only halfway through my schooling.

I worked as a physicist for about ten years. In many ways it was very interesting. Either directly or indirectly, I worked for the Department of Defense. The type of projects we were working on were far beyond anything I had experienced in graduate school. It also took me to interesting places and involved me in projects that otherwise I would never have known about. I still have fun thinking about the things I worked on that are now either flying in the sky or zooming through outer space.

The part of physics that I loved was building something with my hands that had never been done before. I also loved it that, as a physicist, it only had to work once. Thereafter it was an "engineering problem". As my career developed, I rapidly rose up the hierarchy. In the end, this is what made me leave the field. I was no longer working with my hands, working on really neat things. Instead, I was moving paper from one side of my desk to the other.

How did you become interested in bookbinding?

I grew up in what was then the small town of Issaquah, Washington. (We had only one stop sign, at the time, on Front Street.) There we had Wessex Books. It was run by Derek Lowe and his wife, Felicity. Mr. Lowe was a Boeing engineer who had emigrated from England. His great love was book collecting, especially Thomas Hardy and Samuel Johnson. He and his wife ran Wessex Books as a hobby.

Wessex Books was a small shop on a side street in Issaquah. It dealt primarily in used and antiquarian books. I had always loved reading (something I inherited from both of my parents) and had become something of a book collector, without realizing it. I wanted the editions with the best pictures, which usually ended up being first editions. With Mr. Lowe's help, I started collecting in earnest, first with $1.25 first editions of Edgar Rice Burroughs (no dust jackets) and then, much later, with Dickens firsts, going for a whopping $25 each.

On one of my frequent visits to the shop (I was around ten years old at the time), I found a beautiful full-leather calf binding. I think it was done by Zaehnsdorf. I fell in love with it. To this day, I cannot remember what the book was, but I can still see that binding. At $18, it was out of my price range at the time. As luck would have it, a few shelves down was a used 1950's copy of Douglas Cockerell's book *Bookbinding and the Care of Books* for 35¢. That I could afford! Being ten years old, I was convinced that I would be turning out beautiful full-leather bindings in a matter of weeks. Well, it took a bit longer.

One of the first things I did was write to all the advertisers in the back of Cockerell's book. Since the edition I had was about twenty years old, many of them were no longer in business, but it did put me in contact with such companies as Whiley and Sons for gold leaf, H. Band for vellum, Barcham Green for handmade paper, and Sydney Cockerell, first for marbled paper and then later for general supplies. I finally met Sydney Cockerell in 1979 when my father and I went to England for a vacation. I had his address but didn't realize that it was for his home and not a shop. My dad and I showed up unannounced. He was very gracious. He had kept all of my old letters to him, including the ones I had written in pencil as a kid. My dad and I spent the day with him.

He showed us how the marbled paper was made, his blocking "press" made from the hydraulic piston from an airplane's landing gear, and he taught me how to pare leather.

I also ordered a lying press, plough, and sewing frame from Dryad's ad in the back of Cockerell's book. These came by ship. When my dad and I went to the Port of Seattle, they had a hard time finding it. When we did find it, there was my tiny package on a huge wooden pallet. It was surrounded by other huge pallets carrying spools of wire thicker than my arm and piled to the warehouse's ceiling. I was glad we didn't have an earthquake at the time. I still have these, along with the tub my dad and I made. The "lying" press is actually smaller than the finishing press that I now use, but I didn't know better at the time.

The first "formal" training I had was while I was working in Los Angeles as a physicist. I had been buying books from Heritage Bookshop for years by mail, and now that I was in the LA area, I started taking weekly lessons from David Weinstein who ran Heritage Bindery behind the bookshop. The building had originally been built for a funeral home. The front part, which housed Heritage Bookshop, looked like a midlevel cloister. The back part, where the bindery was, had been where they prepared the bodies. In a storage closet there was a large, six foot plus long sink where I was told many Hollywood personalities had dressed for their last performance.

The first thing that struck me, once I started taking lessons from David, was that I wasn't half bad. I wasn't a great bookbinder (yet!), but I had learned something from all those books I read and the stubbornness that had kept me going even when I didn't really have a clue what I was supposed to be doing. At Heritage, I also met two other students who became two of my best friends: Tom Blue, who shares my love of books and sleight of hand magic, and Katy Carter, who later worked at Heritage Bindery and then went on to private practice where she specializes in cloth case repair and paper and dust jacket restoration for most of the top dealers in the country.

My physics job took me next to Washington, DC. There I started taking weekly lessons from Tom Albro, who at the time was the head of the Conservation Department at the Library of Congress. Up to this time, I had mostly learned trade practices from the books I read and from David Weinstein, who had been trained at LCP. From Tom, I started learning the conservation side of bookbinding. I think my physics background really helped me out here. I was able to analyze the information that was given to me by both camps, look at the evidence found in old books, and even try a few experiments on my own. All in all, I'm a better binder having the blend of the two. I also discovered that some of the scholarly papers I read in conservation journals would not have passed in the undergraduate laboratory classes I had taught.

Tom was also a very kind and thoughtful person to me. He could drive me crazy when I showed him something to see if it was correct, and he would find a flaw that even I, being very near-sighted, could barely make out. But this was good for me since it forced me to focus on things that few, if any, people would notice. After two years in Washington, DC, I was going to move on to another job in physics. I had the choice of either LA again or San Diego (I had discovered that I loved Southern California—growing up in Washington, I figured if you are going to be stuck in one season all year long, summer wasn't too bad). I decided on San Diego once I learned from Tom Albro that David Brock was there. David had worked for Tom at the Library of Congress, and Tom had only wonderful things to say about him.

Once I was in San Diego, I immediately called David Brock, but he didn't have any room in his class for me. I was devastated. Every month I would call David to see if there was an opening. It seemed like it took forever, but finally David had an opening, and I started taking weekly lessons from him. What he taught me blended very well with what I had been learning from Tom Albro about the conservation side of bookbinding.

Most of the finishing David did with a Kensol. From him, I learned many tricks with it that I still use today. Unfortunately, David rarely did any finishing, something I really wanted to learn. I decided to take a one-week course in finishing from Tini Miura in Telluride. I had admired Tini's work and had hoped to gain an insight into why gold finishing wasn't working for me. At the end of the week I came to the conclusion that even though I had learned a lot from taking a one-week course once a year, it would take me forever to become proficient at finishing.

By this time, I had also decided to leave physics as a career. One of the good parts of my career as a physicist was that it paid very well and gave me no time to spend it. (I can't remember how many Christmases I worked through.) This left me with a substantial savings. I quit my job, not knowing exactly where I would be going next, but it would be to learn gold finishing. I started writing letters to English binders who I knew did finishing to see if they would take me on as an apprentice. Jim Brockman had just taken on his son Stuart as an apprentice, so he wouldn't be able to take me on. Then one of the luckiest things in my life happened. Bernard Middleton wrote back that, though he does not take on apprentices, he suggested that I contact John Mitchell who had just written a book on finishing. Things then just started cascading into place for me. John was going to give a presentation on edge gilding at the Guild of Book Workers Standards Seminar in Alabama that year. I contacted him, and he agreed to meet with me and look at photos of my work and decide if he would take me on as a student.

The meeting with John went well and I arrived at Heathrow Airport at 5:30 a.m. on October 19th, just a couple of weeks after I had met John for the first time. I had expected to take the tube and train to Woking where John and his wife Gwen had set up accommodations for me. Instead, I found John waiting for me. He was standing against a pillar, sound asleep. I ended up staying at the YMCA in Guildford.

John had also made arrangements for me to use the equipment and supplies at Guildford College, an easy walk from the Y. He taught finishing there once a week and for the rest of the week, I would either practice at Guildford or work with John in his bindery at home. There I would do anything from advancing my finishing skills to sweeping up. I stayed with John for about four years. By then, my money was running out, and John was about to retire from teaching. I am so fortunate that I had not waited any longer to pursue bookbinding; otherwise I would have missed the golden opportunity of learning from him. Both John and Gwen have become a second set of parents to me.

When I finally returned to San Diego, I had a dilemma. I wanted to set up shop, but I also did not want to take work away from David Brock. Again my luck was holding out. I contacted David and found out that he had accepted a position at Stanford University. Not only did this remove my concerns, but also David very graciously referred his clients to me.

Since 1999, I've been working out of my home in Vista, which is just North of San Diego proper, as a book conservator/bookbinder in private practice.

What are your favorite parts about being a bookbinder?

Gold finishing. I'm convinced that the whole reason God invented books was so that I could do finishing on them. There is something about the flow of the gold leaf, the heating of the tools and resulting brilliant impression that is fantastic. To me it is also a way of connecting with the history of bookbinding. Many of the finishing tools I use are anywhere from 100 to over 200 years old. I also think that part of the appeal is that it is not easy to do. I was very fortunate to have the opportunity to apprentice under John Mitchell in England. Not only is John one of England's best finishers, but he is also an excellent teacher.

Being a professional bookbinder also gives me the chance to see books that I wouldn't have otherwise. I have worked on Dashiell Hammett manuscripts, Mark Twain items, WWI original aerial photography and 19th century seaman's journals.

I also like that my two dogs, Pogo and Chip, can be with me while I work. Since I'm single with no kids, they are my immediate family. Whoever said, "It's a dog's life," hasn't seen my two. I wish I had it so easy. On the bottom of my invoices I have a line that reads: "There is no extra charge for dog hair under the paste downs." One of my friends jokes that in the future they will be doing DNA sampling on the dog hair in my books to authenticate them.

I also like the freedom of scheduling my own time. If I want to go to the San Diego Zoo's Wild Animal Park (30 minutes from me) during the middle of the week when the crowds are low, I can. If I want or need to work till 3 a.m., I can do that too.

I also love that I am continuously expanding my horizons. One of my big fears when I left physics was that bookbinding after a few years would not yield challenges to me. I need not have worried. Everyday brings in something new and interesting. It is very satisfying that each book I work on is a little bit better than the last. I like the feeling that I'm improving.

What are your least favorite parts?

Even though it is as important as being able to bind a book well, I don't particularly enjoy the business part of being a bookbinder in private practice. I've done everything I can to keep the paperwork down to a bare minimum.

I also still have a hard time getting used to not knowing that I will have a regular paycheck. Work always seems to come in; it's just the uncertainty that worries me. While in England, I developed my "Plan B." I bought up books that were close to worthless in their current condition, but would be valuable if they were restored, things like first editions of Kipling, Scott and Tolkien. My idea was that if I didn't have work when I got back, I could work on these books and sell them. Fortunately for me, I've never had to use Plan B, so now my bindery and house have several bookshelves filled with beautiful leather and cloth bindings. I just need time to work on them. I've found the ones in the bindery intrigue many of the customers that come.

Another least favorite part of bookbinding for me is trying to dye that leather to get just the right $@#&^% color for restoration work.

Who are your clients?

Basically, my clients can be divided up into three categories:
1. University Special Collections and museums.
2. Book dealers.
3. Book collectors and people who just love a particular book and want to have it restored or rebound.

What kind of relationships do you develop with your clients?

It varies. Some people are only interested in having one particular book worked on, and then I never will see them again. I don't get too many of these. With most of my clients I have long-term relationships. I really like these. It gives me a chance to fully develop my understanding of what they want, and it makes them more open to suggestions that I might have and that they had never thought of. It is also fun to see how their collections grow.

What is your favorite type of work in bookbinding?

I really enjoy rebinding, whether in a period style or modern. I like being able to create something new, that wasn't there before.

I also enjoy making leather drop-back (clamshell) boxes. Over the years, I've worked really hard to improve my design to the point that I'm really proud of them.

What do you feel are your gifts/abilities that make you a good bookbinder?

First, a deep love of working with my hands. I really like making things with my hands, be it a book, a wooden ship model, or practicing slight of hand magic.I also have a deep love of books. In London, every month there are two major book fairs on the same weekend. I went to these every opportunity I could. It was wonderful. I was able to handle so many books, be they simple 18th century leather bindings or Sangorski & Sutcliffe jeweled bindings. I've been interested in the book as an object all my life. I think by handling so many books and examining them that I've gained a real insight into their construction and history. I have a real sixth sense about books. I can usually tell when there is something "fishy" about them, such as when the binding is not contemporary with the book, or when one binding has been "married" to another book. It also makes me pretty good at dating bindings.

What would you like to achieve in bookbinding that you haven't yet achieved?

Lots. My top goal would be able to have the time, money, and skill to make contemporary versions of the great, jeweled bindings that Sangorski & Sutcliffe did around 1900. I was very fortunate to handle their binding of the Keats book shortly after it had been sold at the Chevalia auction. (It is now in the Wormsley Library.) To me, this is the most beautiful binding I have ever seen. I'd like to be able to make modern versions of similar works, with all the skill, craftsmanship, and artistry that this book epitomizes.

Is there anything you would rather be doing than bookbinding?

As a career, no. It would be nice to be independently wealthy so that I could work on my own books and do them the way I want to.

What advice would you give to someone who is considering a career in bookbinding?

The best piece of advice was given to me by Rob Shepherd, who runs Shepherd's Bookbinders and incorporates the old firms of Zaehnsdorf and Sangorski & Sutcliffe. He told me when I was starting out not to be afraid of charging high prices for your work. This makes sense. If you are going to make a living off of bookbinding, you have to charge a decent hourly rate. I look at it this way—I should be making a higher hourly rate than my car mechanic (who is very good). I have a lot more training than he does, and there are a lot fewer of me than there are of him. If you want to make a living out of bookbinding, don't fall into this trap [of charging too little].

I feel that the craft of bookbinding is hurting itself by undervaluing its work. This is usually done by what I call "semiprofessional" bookbinders—ones who have an outside source of income and don't make their sole living off of bookbinding. I usually hear the excuse that no one would pay for the work if they charged a reasonable hourly wage. In my opinion, those individuals should not be taking on work for payment. It is fine if they want to do their own or friends' and families' books for free. It is when you take on professional work and charge too little that the craft suffers. Tini Miura once told me something that is very true. I asked her why her courses at Telluride were so expensive (aside from the fact that you got to work with her). She explained to me that people value them more if the price was higher. She was correct. The general public will value binding and restoration if we ourselves value it and charge a reasonable rate.

The second piece of advice I'd give is to specialize. I am not one of those people who can make their own paper, letterpress print the book, and then bind it. I'm not that talented. Instead, I've specialized and primarily do box-making, traditional method leather bindings, either to a period style or modern, and restoration. I strive in these areas to be the best that I can be and hopefully be someday better than anyone else. Thirdly, I suggest that you handle as many books as you can and really inspect them. Go to book fairs, used and antiquarian bookshops. Handle the books. This will give you a deeper understanding of how books have been bound in the past, what craftsmanship can be accomplished, and where past practices have failed over time. Learn as much of the history of bookbinding as you can. Bookbinding has a fabulous past that spans centuries.

Finally, practice. There is no substitute for doing something over and over again. My father was a physician working in Rehabilitation Medicine at the University of Washington. They did studies there to see how often a patient needed to repeat a new motion until it became automatic. I cannot remember the exact number but it was something like 10,000 or 100,000 times before the motion became second nature. The craft of bookbinding is a very demanding skill. You need to practice over and over again until your work is at a professional level.

For more information on Frank Lehmann, and to see examples of his bindings, go to www.lehmannbindery.com.

Tim Ely:
A Magical Realm

Colfax, Washington
October 2005

Imagine taking a fantasy trip through space and landing on another planet where communication occurs through written symbols and visual form. You walk along paths, following geometric shapes and intuitive suggestions. This magical realm leads you to unexpected self-discovery. This is where my mind took me as I entered into one of Timothy Ely's books, *Mullings*. Pens connect to paper, creating a mysterious realm one can fall into, much like Alice's Wonderland, except instead of written words leading you into someone else's adventures, symbols lead the imagination into one's own inner mind.

Bookbinder Bill Minter and I visit Tim in his home that he shares with his wife, Ann, in Colfax, Washington. We arrive at their enchanted old home with red gabled roof, graphite color stone, and weathered wood. It is surrounded by wildly tamed gardens and storybook trellises.

We step inside to a house full of antique furniture, a magnificent grand piano, an assortment of guitars, and full bookshelves throughout. Tim leads us to a farm kitchen that has been opened up and updated to include a central island and big commercial stainless steel stoves and ovens.

Tim has already started cooking dinner using locally grown herbs and vegetables, a creative experience he enjoys. We talk of creativity, of the quality of sour paste (many benefits according to Tim), of book arts in America, of being self-employed. A cat observes us from the top of the refrigerator.

The next day, after a breakfast of local eggs, we walk up to the attic, which has been transformed into Tim's studio. The walls lining the stairs are lined with bookshelves, filled with books related to bookbinding. He reads all books on this subject that have been published, some numerous times. We are welcomed into a space of vaulted ceilings and generous light. The gabled roof provides charming little nooks in the space: one nook houses a bookshelf filled with his journals behind a comfortable red chair and lamp; one serves as a cozy office. Submarines and other handmade mobiles hang playfully from the ceiling. Equipment and supplies are organized neatly in beautiful antique cabinets and drawers. Tim's artwork graces exposed walls. An exercise bike stands in front of one window.

After touring the area, we look at Tim's work. He shows us some of his intriguing journals, and the book in progress called *Mullings*. The pages include cribriform, his system of writing that vaguely resembles Chinese characters, a discovery that grew out of Tim experimenting with writing backwards in order to keep his hand from smearing the fresh ink (Tim is left handed).

Ultra-creative, and brilliant, Tim affirms that creative expressions are irrepressible and valuable. He celebrates the creativity in Grandmother's crocheted potholders, in stirring soup, in cleaning pots and pans, in doing what you love. It is his belief that we all are creative. I am inspired.

Would you give me a summary of your background and what led you to bookbinding?

As a child, I did not pay attention in school. I was referred to as "difficult to handle." I was not boisterous or rowdy; I was over there doing other things. I remember being sent to the office once, and the note to the principal said, "Tim has too much imagination." I wish I had saved my fifth or sixth grade report card. My grades were terrible; I was bored. The teacher's comments were, "Spends far too much time drawing space objects." I began to note that I had extraordinary peripheral vision, and I could sense when my nemesis, Miss Ingals, absolutely humorless, would approach. If I would be making drawings, I would fold them and put them into the book so it looked as though I was doing English and she would go away. And so I got intrigued with the idea of concealment.

My father had a friend who was an executive at a local paper mill. He literally filled the trunk of his car with 8.5" x 11" bond paper samples for me that they were going to discard. My mother was appalled because it was just feeding my habit. It filled the linen closet so she didn't have any place for the sheets. I had thousands of pieces of paper. I immediately thought that I could fold these in half and make small books. I had my own stapler, so I would staple them through the fold. I loved the small scale. In the summers, I would staple papers together and make little books. I would take a favorite character and insert myself into it. For one summer I was Iron Man; for another summer I was somebody else. I made comic books and gave them to my friends. I made blank ones for my friends; they would draw on them and give them back to me. By the end of that year in the fifth grade, we had five finished comic books.

When I got into art school, no one was interested in books. It was about painting large flat wall works. I was used to working small, and everyone was saying, "No, you need to work large." A decent, logical reason was never offered, it was just, "That's what we do; we work big now; this is modern art." I was making little paintings. It seemed correct to put them in a box somehow. I figured out a way to build a little box. I had no idea books could be put into presentation boxes. I just made a box, like a cereal box. And then obviously, it had to be painted. And then it needed some kind of code on it to tell what it was because I was going to make a second one, and I didn't want to get them mixed up. I was approaching this thing without knowing there was this whole world of bookbinding and portfolio-making out there.

I finally started working in store-bought blank books. The paper was terrible; they didn't last very long. By the time I finished drawing in one, it would begin to degrade. In 1970, I was in a biology class, and I had an edged pen. I work left-handed—if I wrote conventionally, I tended to drag my hand through the ink a little bit and it was hard to read. So I began to write backwards, and this cribriform script [Tim's own cryptic code] was born.

I didn't get into bookbinding to be a bookbinder, but once I started getting into it, I felt attracted to all the processes. It took a while, maybe a year, to realize I didn't want to be a conservator or a restorer. Just before I moved to New York in 1983, I was with my dad on the side of the mountain, fishing. The fish weren't biting, so I hiked up to the top of a hill and found this great rock to sit on. I was thinking about this move to New York and what I wanted to do when I was there. I realized that what I wanted to make were books. I didn't want to bind books for other people, though I probably would occasionally do it. It was just that it wasn't the direction I wanted to go. I wanted to make books on speculation so I could explore this medium, so I could dig around, find out what was in the molehill. I keep running into people that hand me little nuggets of extraordinary information, and each gets grafted onto the next one. I owe great debts to a lot of people for the things they have handed me. They have made my life, in a way, possible.

I think the other aspect, I feel in retrospect, is that it is fortunate that as a very little kid things fell in front of me or were put in front of me and I could sift through what was interesting and discard what wasn't. So the hurdles I had to get over were things like getting in trouble for drawing all the time.

Did you have jobs other than bookbinding?

I worked in my dad's hardware store from the time I was 12 until I was 26; this taught me how to work. I also had a job for three and a half months after graduate school where I designed ads for the yellow pages. It was the worst possible thing I could do for a whole bunch of reasons. But the primary one was that I had to be there at 8:00 a.m. and draw until 4:00 p.m. It seemed a really peculiar thing to me.

One of the conversations I had with my dad was about me making a living as an artist or as a bookbinder. He said, "You need to look at the big ticket item." I didn't know quite what that meant. He said, "A farmer is going to come in here, and he needs a handful of parts to put a piece back on his machinery. He doesn't know quite what it is he is looking for, and he didn't bring the part, so there is going to be a lot of standing around and looking, and saying, maybe this one, maybe this one. After 15 to 30 minutes, we have sold him a handful of things for maybe a dollar. The same farmer may walk through the western gear section and think, "Wow, I could sure use a new pair of boots," and in another 15 minutes you sell him a $100 pair of cowboy boots. My dad's advice was, "Don't make blank books; don't try to make 100 things a week and divvy them out to craft shops or consignment shops and wait for the small change to trickle into your hands; make one book that costs $1,000." You make one sale. It takes 15 minutes to talk someone into spending $1,000; it takes 15 minutes to talk them into spending $25. So I learned to see that my economic connection to the world is a punctuated disequilibrium, where I might not get a check for two or three months, then all of a sudden, like last month, I get three checks. It's falling out of the sky. I was trying to communicate to a graduate student recently that having a job is only one way to pay your mortgage or pay your rent. So I look at this windfall notion: for 30 some years, I've gone from windfall to windfall. It's a really nice metaphor because prior to steel cutting tools in this neck of the woods, the natives here would wait for the wind to blow down a bunch of cedar. And then they would go through it, and they would find ten or twenty trees that were down, and they could whittle off the roots and take off the branches and take the lodgepoles back to camp. They didn't have to cut the trees to the ground. It was all about letting nature knock them down. I go from windfall to windfall. It changes ones' mental axis away from, "Oh, I have no job; how am I going to do this?" That is simply societal-consensus-reality thinking.

There are an astonishing number of people in the craft industry alone (that doesn't even include people working in paper and books). The craft industry is a 14-billion-dollar-a-year business—people living out wherever, making stuff, and not even including the galleries; this is just the crafts people! A very interesting magazine called the *Crafts Report,* which you can pick up at Barnes & Noble, published a survey a couple years ago on this; that is where we got this 14 billion dollar number. I'm sure it is much higher now because the number of practitioners going into the craft is getting higher than the ones leaving. I am no longer alarmed when someone says, "I am going to move to the middle of nowhere, set up a private practice, and do bookbinding for people." In the '70's I would have thought, "Oh, that's going to be very difficult." But it's no more difficult than getting up every day and driving to the telephone company, or driving over to the college and talking to boneheaded teenagers about why they should be really interested in what I have to say about Matisse.

What would you say to someone who wants to be a bookbinder? You were largely self-taught. I don't hear you say that is a bad thing.

I think it's the greatest thing in the world. I think we are all our best teachers. But you have to read the books, and you have to try it and work at it. I went to England pretty well prepared to study with [bookbinders] Daphne Beaumont-Wright and David Sellers. I had been reading carefully. Daphne was astonished that I knew that when you make a made-endpaper, you put the paste on the piece closest to the book so the draw pulls toward the book. That is elementary physics. I only had to do it wrong once to get it right the second time. She said, "You really know a lot about this." Yes, but there was still the invisible stuff that you only get by watching others very closely or having a teacher at your elbow. In Arthur Johnson's book, he talks about paring your leather down to turn-in thickness, but he doesn't tell you what turn-in thickness is. He could have actually measured that and said, pare it to .009 inches. It would have been solved. So I asked Daphne, "What is turn-in thickness?" And she said, "Pare a piece of leather down to where you think it should be." I did, and she folded it down and it sprang back, so I kept going, and when she folded it over and rubbed it down and it stayed there, that was turn-in thickness. I was high for half an hour!

My old mentor and very good friend, Peter Fortune, told me that he thought art school was okay for me, but that I just had to let the materials teach. Your materials are your best teacher. You are your best innovative teacher—you taste it, and you feel it, and find out what it does, and you find what works for you. You discover your favorite tools. I could probably do all my work with the tools that I could hold in one hand, even though I have a vast collection; I could probably do it all with that little box of tools, provided the materials don't alter radically over time. I'll probably work the rest of my career with a really limited interesting range of stuff.

[We move into the studio and are looking at the hand-drawn pages in one of Tim's handbound books where the entire text is his illustrations and cribriform.]

I like the books to be designed like pieces of music, and sometimes I will deliberately look at the peaks and nodes of a certain piece and follow that. Primarily, the cover starts as the big intro, then you get to the endpaper that is a quietude but needs to be interesting and linked to the outside somehow. Then it gets really soft and you kind of catch your breath and then you move to the title page which should connect to the content of the book, should stage it; these are the credits so the movie is now opening; the music is slightly less swollen and vibrant, and then, bam! you are hit right in the head.

[I look at the pages of his book as he takes me through this process, my emotions swelling.]

I love watching other people look at these books. Now I get the opportunity to watch the whole book action move differently. I see all this weird stuff that I don't see unless someone else is looking at it.

Do you know how many hours this took?

I really don't. I spent 18 months on that book. From the notes in my sketchbooks I can roughly tell, but I find that my thoughts start to intrude on the work if I know exactly how long it takes—thoughts like, "I might avoid doing this today because it is going to take too long."

But I have timers all over the shop. I turn on the Kwikprint, and I set the timer for ten minutes or I might forget I've turned it on when I go do something else. I need to only let it stay on for ten minutes, and it is hot enough. For cooking it's exactly the same thing. I have this stopwatch function—I set up to do something, to sew an endband or something, not to be fast but to see how long it took. I use timers. If I am going to write someone an email and I can't do it in five minutes, I'll send it as is. So I have gradually eroded the I-can't-do-that-because-it-takes-too-long business. Timers are great.

Some day these sketchbooks will be worth a lot.

This is my retirement fund. This is my alternative to socking money into the stock market or something. I'm closing in on volume 60 of the sketchbooks. And then there is all the other stuff, the models, the drawings, the stuff in the drawers—there is a huge archive here. I need to find a donor who has a million dollars so when I am finally unable to lift my head anymore they can come and get this stuff. [Looking at another book Tim is working on]

This book is called *Mullings,* and it has 80 spreads. Like mulling something over, or like mulling spice—a metaphor for a whole bunch of intrusive ideas that are my primary theme. As you get through the book, you start getting into some space-time connections. I'm still drawing this book. What I find is that after people have looked at it, they are exhausted. They don't want to look at anything else. Rich Spelker has a term for these things. He calls them lucid dream targets. You look at them before you go to sleep; they are a sort of generator for your dreams. I like that idea. I love things that are mysterious…like this reminds me of a map of a Mayan treasure temple; this reminds me of a crop circle.

I would never sell this.

I made this primarily for myself.

You have an admirable combination of intellect and intuition.

Thank you! You have it too. Absolutely. I think everybody does. I think every impulse, from walking across the room to choosing which shoes you are going to wear today, at the tiniest level, is a creative act. We have spent so long compartmentalizing creativity, like if you are standing at the easel painting, it's considered a creative act, but frying an egg is not. I keep trying to make the picture bigger and bigger and bigger. When I dust my lamp, it becomes creative.

But I feel that where a lot of people get derailed is from hearing the old speech that tells us that most of our lives are not creative or that we are not creative people. But the little old ladies up the hill who are knitting are doing intensely creative work. They say, "Oh no, I'm just making socks," and they demean it and put it in a place where it can be held as an unimportant thing that they do; and I see it as massively important.

The reason I love the quilts that Ann and her mother make is because it's all about piecing together small, discreet bits to make this huge whole. And that's what we're doing in bookbinding. And then pieces from that lead to other things, like paper submarines hanging from the ceiling of my studio made out of scraps of binder's board. If it wasn't for bookbinding, I wouldn't have a diving sea copter. I find lots of cross-pollination between disciplines, always expanding the realm of creativity. You can learn a lot about adhesives and sticking things together from asking your dentist, and I have. And there are lots of crossovers from the kitchen to bookbinding—egg glare and starches to name just two.

Creativity is the thing that propels life. If it wasn't for the creative generative process, life would not be as vital as it is or as relentless. In paving over a space where life wants to be, a plant will work its way through; it will come through the cracks. Creativity does the same thing. Paintings were made in concentration camps; paintings were made in the killing fields of Cambodia. People tattooed each other. The

Tim Ely's studio.

creative impulse is really, really hard to suppress. It's like fungus—you clean one area, and it's growing somewhere else. I'm really interested in that creative, generative process for all people. You are a creative, living being, and you can do anything you want to do.

What is your favorite part of bookbinding?

As you know, bookbinding is a critical component of my work, but is not all of it. It requires the synergy of painting, drawing, and other fabrication techniques as well as a lot of referencing to arcane source material. People often wonder why I put my work into books rather than hang it on the wall in frames. I do this because a book is interactive on a multi-sensorial level and requires a viewer to operate it. And the viewer's experience is on the same scale as mine as the maker of it.

It also flows out of my love of libraries, which I believe represent millions of points of potential, where museums on the other hand represent points in art history, the past. Libraries hold the future. I like to make books to express the swirl of point potential that exemplifies what a library is to me. In a library, things are operational. In a museum, things are decommissioned and in stasis. You go into a library, even our small county library here, and at all hours it's teeming with people seeking information that then promotes action. You go into a museum, often open the same hours, and it's only teeming when they have food.

The fact that I put my work into books requires an overall design, and so you could say that the binding is where it all comes together as a coherent whole. I love this part. Without this, my work would just be a collection of random paintings sandwiched between two boards.

But my favorite part of my process is probably not strictly the binding. There is that point between where you've idealized the whole thing in your head—you've idealized the chunk that is the inspiration, that moment when you pull a sheet of paper out and start.

I love that part because I know I am going from this ineffable, invisible shimmer to putting a mark on this piece of paper. When it begins, it's really amazing and everything else is just challenge and testing and tasting and getting it all to work, and at some point you put down that last endpaper and you say, "This is okay, this is really okay." Or just, "Okay, we'll get it in the next one."

And that little moment starts again with the next book. I once asked Phillip Smith how he handled coming to the end of a really big project. For me it is kind of a letdown. He starts projects with overlap. That is also a very efficient way to work. I've got a pile of books started, so I always have something to draw on. If something is drying or in the press, there is always something to do, something that can be taken to the next level.

But it can be like having 50 cats and they all want food right now. As soon as you put a little food out for one, they are all going to just swarm. You can get really fragmented. That will happen for a while, and this flat file will get covered with projects. I can't tell what I'm doing anymore, so I clean up, I put them back into drawers, I pull out one that is further along than the rest, and I finish it.

Or a phone call comes from somebody: "When is that book going to be finished?" So maybe I move on to one piece for a few days until it's up where it can stand. Projects are stowed all over the place, and nothing is ever really at rest. It's always in movement. Nothing sits still. Change is the only constant.

What would be your advice to someone who is considering a career in bookbinding?

I almost hate to say anything because no one listens anyway, which is one piece of advice I have: don't listen to anybody. Do your own research and your own thinking. If bookbinding moves you, then determine whether your interest is archeological, anthropological, preservational, or directed at something expressive. Research what's happening in those fields and see where you fit in.

Most important, think for yourself, based on good research. There are paths to follow that others have forged, but you can also forge your own path if you are smart about it and engage others in the process. No one taught the first bookbinder, and the first Thanksgiving was ad hoc. Now both are largely just habit, and habits lead to boredom, or can lead to enlightenment. Be inspired by others, and be aware of when you are aping them as opposed to being inspired. Acknowledge your sources.

People like to say they can't learn from books, but learn from books. You have to get over that belief because, though few are perfect, books are miracles of focus and intention toward truth and balance. At the same time, don't take anything as gospel and write down your own ideas and techniques. Build a library of resources.

Also, practice, practice, practice. Make twenty of something before you even ask anyone for advice or input. Keep work journals or sketchbooks, and make those books that you take your notes in! If something works, know why it works; your ability to pass on this information requires that you know this. If something doesn't work—and be critical of your work—figure out why. And be generous; you get so much more back.

Join organizations and get to know others in the same field. Look around, and deeply, at what others are doing. Ask questions.

Keep your tools clean, use good light, don't buy anything you can make, buy a lava lamp, and get a smart cat.

Make a choice and either forget everything I have suggested, utilize all of it, or select that which is relevant. Finally, do what you do to think clearly—sit still or go for a long walk and think about this question. Bookbinding is very easy and very hard; that essence is present in everything that is worthwhile. Name it and it is both graspable and elusive. If you sense a tug forward into the universe of information transfer and the form of that interest is the hand-bound book, then embrace it fully. Anything less than a total commitment is only that— there is nothing wrong with it, but there is nothing much right with it either. And the best of luck to you.

For more information on Tim Ely, and to see examples of his work, go to http://www.timothyely.com.

Monique Lallier:
Gracious and Elegant

Summerfield, North Carolina
March 2006

"May I have your attention?" I first was introduced to Monique Lallier as she stood on a chair at the first Guild of Book Workers Standards of Excellence conference I attended. As the organizer of the annual conference, she was trying to get our attention to make an announcement. She was gracious, stunning, well-dressed, and speaking in her French-Canadian accent.

Monique is married to Don Etherington, perhaps the most well known bookbinder in the USA, originally from England. Their storybook romance took place in Finland. Swiss master bookbinder Hugo Peller had been asked by one of his students, a prominent woman in Finland, to invite an exclusive group of bookbinders from around the world to a conference at her home in Finland. It was there on March 4, 1987, that Hugo introduced Don and Monique. A magnetic attraction brought them together in marriage soon after and has kept them together ever since.

I arrive at their Greensboro, NC home during rose season. The rose garden in the front of their large attractive home, a gift from Don to Monique, is abloom with an abundance of color. Tasteful art is plentiful throughout their house. Inside the front door sits a large standing press that once belonged to Edith Diehl, a welcome to their world of bookbinding. To the left is a room that is their shared studio. The space is large enough that they each have a separate space to work, equipment they share, and a small desk. Hugo Peller's polypress, now belonging to Monique, is a treasured piece of equipment. The upstairs library, packed with books, is Don's home office.

It seems Monique has always been a teacher, first teaching sewing and fashion design. She tells me that she was teaching typewriting, while studying to become a geography teacher, when she read about Simone Roy, who was moving to Montreal where she would open a bookbinding studio. Monique was intrigued. As she continued teaching typewriting, she took bookbinding classes from Simone for three years. Monique continued her studies in Paris and in Switzerland with Hugo Peller, with whom she developed a lasting friendship until he died in Finland on March 4th, the very month, day, and place where he introduced Don and Monique.

Monique is one of the most esteemed design bookbinders in the USA, winning numerous prizes throughout the world for her design bindings. She holds the position as the director of the American Academy of Bookbinding, with locations in Telluride, Colorado, and Ann Arbor, Michigan. Her teaching style is tough yet gentle, firm yet warm, serious yet compassionate, as she focuses on traditional French style bindings. Her students will attest that she is a stickler about detail and precision as she commits herself to providing the opportunity for individuals to learn fine bookbinding in America.

When were you first exposed to bookbinding?

When I was young, 10-12 years old, there was a neighbor who was doing bookbinding in his basement. I remember going to visit him and was amazed by what he was doing. I thought how nice it would be to have a library with all those hand-bound books. I still don't have that library.

We had a library at my home where I grew up, but not hand-bound books as I am doing them now. This neighbor did some books for my parents but not too many. I just remember we had a few books in leather that a neighbor made. Maybe they were repaired books. My parents never shared why they had them bound. That was my first encounter.

But I've always loved books. My father was in the publishing business. My parents loved to read. They were always reading. In those days, we had a TV, but we didn't watch it all the time. Reading was a large part of life, even with my children. I remember going on vacation at the beach, and the first suitcase that was ready to go was the one full of books.

As a child did you have any aspirations of what you wanted to become?

When I was a child [in Montreal], I really didn't know what I wanted to do. I registered to be a nurse. I finally went into fashion design.

I started teaching when I first had my children. My mother was an organizer of all sorts of things. There was an activity center at the church, and she was in charge of that. She said, "Why don't you teach sewing there two afternoons each week?" She was taking care of my children, and I was teaching two afternoons. That is how I started teaching. I liked it a lot. I thought I wanted to become a teacher.

I decided to go back to the University to study education with a major in geography. During the last year, one of my teachers who was the director of a high school asked if I had a typewriting diploma. I had one, as I had taken, for fun, a class in typewriting at the boarding school when I was in college. We had choices of evening classes. So I was hired as a typewriter teacher, and I would already be employed in the school when an opening would come in geography. I had started, in 1970, to take classes in bookbinding. Of course, when the opening in geography came, I knew that bookbinding was what I wanted to do, so I declined the offering, at the great dismay of my director. He understood, two years later, when I asked for a one-year leave of absence, knowing that I would not come back.

In 1970, I read an article in the paper about Simone B. Roy who was coming back from Paris. Others found her the same way. She received lots of publicity when she had an opening exhibiting her bindings. She had studied bookbinding, and she was opening a studio in Montreal. "Oh my gosh," I thought, "I would like to do that." I called her, and she had an opening in the class the next afternoon. If I wanted to, I could start the class. Since I was teaching from 7:30 to 12:30, I had my afternoons free. In the classes I attended in Montreal, it was mostly local people. Classes were once a week. There were five students in the class. Most of the others are still bookbinding in Montreal. We learned design, fine, French-style bindings. Most of the women who attended the classes didn't plan to be professionals. It was more social.

So I started studying with Simone. She really formed the generations of bookbinders of my time in Montreal who then opened studios and schools later on. All my friends in Montreal still have their studios and students. That was a productive time of bookbinding, of fine binding—French-style, and fine binding with design. She didn't know any of the new techniques that we see now. Nor did we learn conservation.

I continued to teach and go to school for three years. One day she said, "I don't think you need to come back here. You need to just go and do bookbinding." I was kind of upset because I thought, "Why is she saying that?" She called me the next week and asked me to go to work with her. So I went to work with her, and I started to teach with her. I was going there every afternoon after I finished teaching at the high school.

In 1976, I started to teach bookbinding with Simone. For three years I was her student, then I worked with her for three years. It was very exciting. I always wanted to know more. I would go back home and practice what I learned. I was thrilled. I thought I would be an eternal student. That is why I love Standards [of Excellence, the annual bookbinding conference]. If you really watch the presenter, you learn something. I like a classroom atmosphere where everyone is working on a project. I love the interaction of the people. Even as a teacher now I learn. When I have advanced students, they come up with new ideas. They really go beyond what I teach.

In 1978 I left Simone and opened my own studio with Nicole Billard, also one of her students. By that time it was too crowded in Simone's studio. In those days, we were not asked to do conservation or repairs. It was mostly new bindings. There was a market for it.

When you were in Montreal, you were very close to whatever went on in France. France was a very strong place for bookbinding. So I went to Paris to study gold-tooling with Roger Arnoult for two years in a row, six weeks each time. In Montreal we would receive all the [bookbinding-related] information and catalogs, and we would participate in [bookbinding] exhibitions in France. We were all reading Art et Metiers du Livre. There was Les Amis de la Relieure d'Art that was starting and AIR neuf, another small group in Paris. We were all members of that. I became a member of the Guild of Book Workers I believe in 1976 or 1978.

In 1982, I went to Switzerland. I studied French-style binding in Ascona with Edwin Heim. I also studied for a month in Solothurn with Hugo Peller. Hugo (with Simone) was probably my most influential

Monique Lallier's studio.

teacher. Edwin was also, but in a lesser way. I was with Hugo more often—two years in a row. I also learned from all my students. I like to be in a class with other students. With Hugo there was no space for more than two or three students.

Later I went to NY to the botanical gardens where Hedi Kyle was teaching a workshop.

So you were working at your studio with your partner and you would do design bindings?

Yes, Nicole and I were teaching four days a week. Sometimes we would have three classes a day—morning, afternoon, evening. Each of us had two evening classes a week. There was a lot of interest and a lot of students who stayed. I'm still friends with them. I have a friend that came in 1976, the first year that I started to teach, and she is still doing bookbinding. She is very good.

I think there is something about bookbinding that is therapeutic, even if they don't do it for a living. It changes their life in a way.

It is not like painting where you need to be really good to put your painting on your wall. With bookbinding you can do a very simple binding, and if your technique is good and the craftsmanship is good, you can have a very nice simple binding. They are still good, and you can fill your library and have a lifetime of work.

So you raised your family while you were doing this.

Before I had this studio, I made a room at home into a studio. I had a board cutter, a job backer, a guillotine, and a table. I was lucky to find good equipment pretty early. I was doing bookbinding all the time. I loved it. I knew the first day I walked into Simone's studio; I knew that that was what I wanted to do. I liked everything—the leather, the old tools, everything about bookbinding. I loved working with my hands.

So it has taken you along the path to where you are today. And you met Don.

Yes, it has really changed my life in a sense. I was not in a happy marriage, and I think bookbinding is how I was able to stay for the children for the last 15 years of that marriage. I was busy and working. When I was home, I was working in my studio. Of course the children were there, and there were activities. But I had the studio.

And then in 1987, I was invited by Hugo Peller to go to Finland to a conference. The Grotenfelt family is a very prominent family in Finland. They own a lot of land. Antonia Grotenfelt always followed her husband during her career. When he retired he said, "Now I am going to follow you. You do what you want." She had started bookbinding and had gone to Ascona to study with Hugo when he was there. So she started to go all over the world to workshops that she was interested in, and he was going with her. One day she told Hugo, "I would like to invite people to Wehmais to give back to bookbinding what I have gotten from it." She asked Hugo to invite 15 people. They thought 10 would come, but everyone came. The deal was, you pay your way to Finland and then when you arrive, they take care of you. All the people who were coming from overseas could come earlier to adjust to jet lag. I arrived on a Tuesday; Don [Etherington] arrived on a Wednesday. The people from Europe arrived on a Saturday.

The conference began on Sunday and lasted until the next Sunday. Everyone had to do something—a workshop or a presentation of their work, or something special about bookbinding where they lived. We had a program. In the morning we were working from 8:30-12:30 everyday. At 1 p.m. was lunch, and then we would go around the countryside. We were in the middle of the country. There were no other houses in sight, just fields and snow and woods. There were trails in the forest, and we would ski. And then we would come back and have another session around 4 until 6 or 6:30.

After that we would change clothes and have dinner at 7. It was sort of semi-formal. The Grotenfelts were older, aristocratic people. It was their way of living. That was great. I was chosen from Canada, Don Etherington from the U.S., Tini Miura from Japan, Sün Evrard from France, Yaap de Kempenowr from Holland, another woman from Holland, Peter Frölich from Germany, another Peter from Austria; and another Peter from Switzerland was a friend of Hugo, and Ramon Gomez Herrera from Spain.

There were 8 languages spoken. The language of the conference was English. When I was invited, I decided I better practice my English. I started classes in January, learning English. Then when I went there and met Don, I had to speed up learning English. I knew I would be moving to Austin. Ten days after we met he asked me to marry him—in a Russian restaurant in Helsinki. We were together every day, taking a lot of walks and talking a lot. I was interviewing him for the Journal of the ARQ (Association des Relieurs du Quebec) of Quebec. We were always looking for things to write about for the journals, so I said I would interview people there. It turned out to be just Don that I interviewed, but I wrote about the conference. It was published in Montreal and then translated and published in the CBBAG [Canadian bookbinding organization journal] in Toronto. Then the Guild of Book Workers published it in one of their journals. At the end of the article in the CBBAG they said, "Monique now lives in the US with Don Etherington." Don and I were married by the time they published it there. We married and moved to Austin in 1987.We have been married 20 years.

What has been your favorite job?
There are two books that I really like, and I will never sell. The first one I did after I came back from Paris, where I learned gold-tooling. I thought I needed to do something important. So I did one binding on a 17th century book about bookbinding. I did a 17th century design, more simple, more restrained in design. When I finished that, I thought I needed to do an 18th century book, with a lot of tooling. I'm really pleased with the 18th century book—I'll show it to you. Then I have

another one, a book that was written just for me, hand-written by a friend of mine who is a poet in Quebec. It is a binding of all boxcalf. It's a very slick, very simple binding with some telephone wires of different colors on the front cover. One of my recent ones I like is the *Phoenix* that was in the last Guild of Book Workers exhibition.

What about clients—how do you get them?

In Montreal we had good customers, collectors who kept coming back. In the states it is more difficult to develop a relationship. Most of my customers I haven't met. They find me on my website, and they ask me to do something. I rarely meet them. Some I do know though. It is very different than Montreal. You have collectors there and they like to personally choose the leather and the end papers. I still make a lot of my own marbled papers, Asco-color papers [learned from Hugo Peller].

What advice would you give to someone who is interested in becoming a bookbinder?

They need to go to a regular class where they work every week, or go to a place like the American Academy of Bookbinding for two or three weeks where they are assigned work for the year. You need to start with a good teacher. It is more difficult to undo bad habits than to start with good ones. I now see many people that start with all these simple techniques. In a sense it will bring more people to bookbinding, and maybe to fine binding. For many people, they think that is what bookbinding is, but they need to explore more. After they feel comfortable doing a binding and working with leather, they need to have as many different teachers as they can. And they need to work regularly. They shouldn't let two or three months go by without doing anything. They lose the details of developing their own techniques. But if they are passionate about it, it is not difficult.

I have Hugo's polypress here, the one I worked on when studying with him. Hugo and I were writing to each other two or three times a year. We were going to visit in May. He wrote back that he was happy and that he was going to Finland. He died there of a heart attack on March 4th, the date he introduced Don and I.

What is your favorite thing about being a bookbinder?

The diversity. Each binding is a new endeavor, a new challenge. I don't have a style that people will recognize in my bindings. People like

Phillips Smith or Ivor Robinson have a precise style that you recognize from their bindings. I read the book and reflect on the spirit of the book. It is the inspiration from the book that makes each book different. And it forces me to do more that what I have done before.

How do you develop the design?

When I read the book, images come up in my head. The atmosphere of the book, in general, helps me start the process. I look at illustrations though I try not to be too influenced by them, just inspired. I take notes when I read. I feel the color, or write down words that struck me as inspirational or helped me understand the book. Sometimes it is more difficult, and I don't come up with things. Then it is a struggle, but you do it; you come up with the best you can even if it doesn't inspire you.

What is your least favorite part of bookbinding?

Sanding. I do it by hand to have better control, but it is a pain!

Is there anything you would like to achieve in bookbinding that you haven't yet achieved? Can you think of a project that you would love to do?

I would like to write a book about bookbinding. I started to work on this but put it aside for a while. It will be a technical book with very good illustrations, a reference book that will especially help people who take my classes. They can read when they are away from class and comprehend what to do when the teacher is not there to answer questions. If students don't have good notes, they can get a little lost. The book will help as a reference to refresh their memories so they can do the work at home.

What gifts or abilities do you have that make you a good bookbinder?

I think it is patience and paying attention to detail. I think these are the main qualities of a good bookbinding—details of the details.

For more information on Monique Lallier, and to see examples of her work, go to www.moniquelallier.com.

Jan Sobota:
Renaissance Man

Loket, Czech Republic
March 2006 & October 2007

Passionate Renaissance man. Those words come to mind when I think of Jan. They are manifested in his life and in his bindings. He has a big presence—grey hair and beard, crystal blue eyes, and a smile that is both friendly and playful. His hands are beautiful—tanned, smooth skin, with expressive fingers. They are hands that have been working at the craft of bookbinding for over 50 years. And not just binding—as a child Jan created marionettes in his Czechoslovakian hometown. He sculpted the heads and even sewed clothes for them. He is accomplished at drawing, sculpting, calligraphy, and illumination. His most famous bindings incorporate his multiple skills. Jan took design binding to a new level when he created sculpted design bindings that also retained the ability to function excellently as books.

Jan grew up in what became a communist country. When the government was shutting down businesses, it only allowed a few of the very best artists and craftsmen to remain in the arts. Jan was a lucky one who was able to continue studying arts and crafts. His life includes the adventures of a young creative boy, the role of a student of the arts, a stint in the army, and a risky escape from his communist country.

When he escaped Czechoslovakia, he gave up all that he owned. He resided in Switzerland (1982-84) for a short time before moving to the United States. He, his wife Jarmila, and their children lived in the US for 14 years, first in Ohio and then in Dallas, learning English and the ways of the west before returning to their homeland that is now the Czech Republic. During this time, his wife Jarmila, who was a psychology professor in Czechoslovakia, learned bookbinding and painting and has become an award winning design bookbinder who creates her own style of bindings that incorporate her painting and sculpture abilities.

In Dallas, Jan held the position of book and paper conservator at the Bridwell Library at Southern Methodist from 1990 to 1997. He continues to return each year to work on their collections. While in Dallas, he also taught bookbinding in his home studio. I was fortunate to have taken classes from him then, amidst the smells and sizzling sounds of Jarmila's delectable cooking.

One of my favorite things about Jan is that he enjoys life. When I tell him this he laughs and responds, "Why not?" He prefers the life of a self-employed person. It offers him freedom to do the projects he wants to do. Despite a life of hard work, loss and risk, he is one of the most creative people I know—creative in life as he sings in his sultry, husky voice, as he laughs and jokes, as he enjoys family and friends, as he actively shares his political opinions, as he joins with fellow artists to create art of all types—most famously in what I consider some of the world's most innovative and clever design bindings. Renaissance man.

How did you get started in bookbinding?

From a young age books surrounded me. I loved to read them. I would enter other worlds and fantasies through books. It started with my father. He was a passionate book collector with many books at home. They were all over our little house. Finally my father converted our barn into a library, which he completely filled up with about 20,000 books. He particularly liked children's books.

When a book needed to be repaired or rebound, my father would take it to his friend, Karel Silinger. Mr. Silinger was a designer bookbinder in the nearby city of Pilsner. I would often go with my father to see Mr. Silinger. During one visit when I was 14 years old (six months before getting out of primary school), Mr. Silinger asked me if I liked what he was doing. He could see my interest in his work. I said yes.

To my pleasure, he invited me to be his apprentice and learn bookbinding. I was thrilled. Mr. Silinger's studio was in the center of a community that appreciated art and attracted many interesting people, including writers, journalists, painters, architects, actors, musicians, and other artists. Many interesting discussions were always taking place in his studio. That is how I began my career in designer bookbinding in 1954.

Starting in 1948, the communists started nationalizing private business enterprises. At first, they were taking over factories and big businesses. Then in 1953, they confiscated smaller businesses. Many books became prohibited and were pulled off library bookshelves and out of bookstores. Everything became property of the state. The people who owned small businesses could still work there, but they were not supposed to have any authority.

Fortunately, there were a few exceptional people in the government who were able to foresee that this would be very bad for craftsmen. They made special business arrangements, allowing outstanding applied-art-craftsmen, including designer bookbinders, to keep their studios. The ones who passed examinations were given permission to keep their workshops, have co-workers, and one or two apprentices. But to be paid, they had to have each bookbinding job approved through the government. That was how the crafts survived.

Not many people working in bookbinding and artistic bookbinding had passed the screenings. Mr. Silinger was one of few who were allowed to work and keep their studios.

I was commuting between the School for Applied Arts in Prague and Mr. Silinger' workshop in Pilsen. At that time I was able to learn all kinds of arts in the school, but I was really interested only in bookbinding. But all I learned about art became very valuable to me later.

I was lucky because I was Mr. Silinger's last student. My apprentice program was not bookbinding, but artistic bookbinding. But he felt that I needed all kinds of bookbinding training, not just artistic skills. There were government regulations to make only design bindings in his workshop. But because he wanted to teach me everything, he was accepting all kind of bookbinding jobs. He said, "Not every time in your life will you have enough commissions for design bindings or other artistic work. You must know everything to be able to always make a good living."

The School in Prague I attended was a three-year program. Mr. Silinger was in Pilsen. I would spend one week in Prague, one week in Pilsen. Toward the end, I spent a half-year in Prague with Professor Emil Pertak in his studio, instead of at Mr. Silinger's place. After finishing school, I worked with Professor Pertak for an additional six months. Then, at 18, I was obliged to serve in the army for two years.

When I came back from the army, Mr. Silinger was very old. His son, Svatopluk, had been working with him, but he quit bookbinding when his father died. Svatopluk never completed the examination for the mastership. He was not interested enough to do something about it. If he had, he could have continued working as a bookbinder and I also would have been able to work there.

Instead, the communists confiscated the Silinger's family business. Svatopluk was a good craftsman, but he never liked to work overtime, nor create bindings for exhibitions or possible examination or for enjoyment. I have created a lot of bindings just for my pleasure, not at all certain about when, or if, I will sell them. Those of us who are passionate about bookbinding, like this, have been succeeding at the end. We have been doing what we like, and we have been able to take our bookbinding art and craft farther.

There wasn't a possibility for me to find a job in Prague at that time. I got an offer to go to Hodonin to work with Ladislav Kolarik in his studio, but I didn't want to go to Moravia. I was in Slovakia when I was in the army, and I had had enough of being so far from home. I wanted to be back home in the Pilsen area where I had all my friends. So I started to work in Pilsen in a cooperative named Druzstvo Styl. There I specialized in leather bindings and taught students in the last two or three months of their apprenticeship.

After one year, I went to Carlsbad, where I was hired as head of the bindery at another cooperative. I worked there for six years, but I did not like this place very much. I had to direct 16 employees, mostly women, who often had relationship problems, and I had to be the arbitrator.

In 1969, I passed the Craft and Artistic Examination at Ministry of Culture. I was awarded the title, "Master of Applied Art in the Field of Bookbinding." Finally, I was able to start on my own. I had already been working on my own during the time before that exam, but only on so called "small laws." It meant that I had to be employed somewhere. I was allowed to do my own commissions at my studio only after work. In communist Czechoslovakia, no doctors, lawyers, or others were able to work for themselves. Everyone had to work for Government Company. Artists were the only people who were allowed to do it.

When I saw how good it was for Mr. Silinger working for himself, I knew I also wanted to work for myself. That was motivating for me. I saw how he stopped work at about 12 o'clock, could go home and come back to work at 6 in the evening and work to midnight—nobody was telling him he couldn't do that. That appealed to me. It had taken me 17 years to be able to accomplish this plan. After I completed the examination, I could (officially) work on my own, without obligation to be employed.

At one time, you mentioned an exhibition in which you participated that led you to the decision to leave Czechoslovakia. Will you tell me about that?

It was an international exhibition, "Book as Art Objects in an Interior," which I organized in the museum in Francisbad. The museum director was my friend and told me I could organize it there.

Shortly after that I had a problem with the secret police. At 8 a.m. one morning they rang the doorbell and asked me to go with them. I had been with them many times. They always asked me questions because they thought of me as an enemy of communists. But this time it was the opposite.

They said, "We have been watching you for many years and were always thinking you were our enemy, but we know you are not because in all of the letters you wrote and in everything you did, you were interested only in books. We know that no political things were there. From this year on, you will be able to go wherever you would like to go at anytime."

Usually we were only able to ask the Czech Secret Police, once a year, in January, if we wanted to visit some Western-capitalist country. They always said no. But this time they said, "Whenever you decide to go, you will be able to go. But to do that, you must do something for us. We know you have a lot of friends who have escaped and who are in other countries. You will visit them, and you will see which ones are not doing very well." I realized they were going to try to turn those people into spies.

I said I wouldn't do this. And they said, "Then you will not be allowed to do your books anymore." They would take away my license to be an artistic bookbinder.

So you wanted to leave. How did you escape?

I was already friends with Jarmila. She got permission to go to

Switzerland for four days with two of her three children, Paula and Jan. Jan had some problems with hearing, and the machine that would help him was broken and could not be repaired, so the doctor gave a recommendation that they go to Switzerland for help. Jarmila was given permission for two children to go, but one had to stay home— they insured her return this way. I was trying to get permission to go too, but I couldn't.

One morning shortly after that, somebody rang the doorbell again. It was a man with a small suitcase. He said he was from the customs office, and he wanted to see my passport to see if something was in there. He showed me some credentials. I gave him my passport and he took it and left. I called the customs office and talked to a man whose son I knew. I said, "Somebody came to my house and stole my passport. He showed me some credentials, and I believe he is from your office. He opened his briefcase, put it in there, and left." He said, "Sorry Jan, we got orders to take your passport."

I had an expired card for getting into Yugoslavia. Yugoslavia was somewhere between the West and East, and it required a different type of paperwork to enter. You had to have someone in the bank give you a piece of paper to change money to go to Yugoslavia. My paperwork wasn't good; it was old. But I changed all the dates on the document and went to the director of the bank, a father of another friend. He gave me what I needed, and I was able to go to Yugoslavia.

From Yugoslavia I had to escape over the border between Italy and Yugoslavia. My son Radek (17 years old at that time) and I were trying to find a way to cross the border to Italy. We chose a popular tourist's area with a beach and a bay. We were thinking about swimming through the water to Italy. However, we had to change our plans.

One evening while we were looking for a good place to cross, we were accidentally witnesses to an ugly scene. Two young boys from Czechoslovakia were trying to escape by swimming through that exact place which Radek and I wanted to use for our own illegal crossing. They were not lucky though. Yugoslavian border guards noticed and headed after them with their boats. One boy was shot to death. They seized the second one. He was sent back to communist Czechoslovakia as a criminal. Yugoslavian border guards had motion detection devices at the surface of the water. They knew if something was moving. I hadn't known that.

How could we cross the border? We couldn't dare to swim. Neither could we scrape through the borderline bushes because they were too thick to pass through quietly. Nevertheless, one evening, we got lucky. On the Italian side, not far away, was a small house with a group of young people playing very loud music. We said, "Today or never." We went through the thick bushes, right past the tower. It took us 45 minutes in the dark. If they had heard us, they would have put lights on us. We had crossed the border to Italy.

After getting into Italy, I asked my Czech emigrant friends who were living in Switzerland to come get us. But we didn't have permission to enter Switzerland. In Switzerland the officers asked me how I got through the Yugoslavian border. I said I made the stop, but they didn't check the car (they didn't stop Swiss cars). I lied, and I got away with it.

After two years in Switzerland, where I had the chance to demonstrate my expertise in bookbinding for Basler Papiermuhle, a museum of paper and printing, Jarmila and I got married. We wanted to move to the US, however, the Swiss authorities were difficult. They didn't want to give me permission to go to America. And they really didn't want to give permission for Michael (Jarmila's child that had to be left in Czechoslovakia) to come to Switzerland. That was a big problem. From Switzerland we couldn't get to America. There were only three immigration camps in all of Europe: Austria, Italy, and Germany. I asked the Swiss to let me go to Germany to the immigration office where I could get permission to go to the US. The Swiss wouldn't let me go to Germany. I had to get into Germany illegally. After I got the papers from the American Embassy in Frankfurt, the Swiss let us go.

So you had to escape to Germany as well.

Funny. [Laughing]

Michael had been staying with his Grandfather in Czechoslovakia, but his Grandfather died. The Czechs finally wanted to let him go to Switzerland, but the Swiss wouldn't let him come. When we got to America, the Americans immediately started working to get Michael to us. The Swiss were not so nice.

Then you got to Ohio. Were you able to go there because they offered you a job?

Yes, I wouldn't have been able to go there if I didn't have a job. The director of the library at Case Reserve University in Cleveland somehow found out about us. Philip Smith had written an article about how we wanted to go to America. The article was also published in a journal for conservation. The director read it. He got our phone number in Switzerland. One day I was at home working and someone called me, talking in the English language, trying to explain something to me. I somehow realized that he was offering me a job, but I didn't know what he was talking about. I knew it was important. After talking for a half-hour I got his phone number, and the next day we had an American friend in Switzerland call him from our house. He told us what this man was talking about.

Did you know much English?

I only knew, "Okay, Baby." I remembered that statement from American soldiers, when they came to my village at the end of World War II in 1945.

It is such a different world where you come from. Getting training 50 years ago in the US was difficult, though now it is easier. What is different about being an independent bookbinder in the Czech Republic or Europe than being in the US?

I don't think it is so different. Many people are able to make a living doing this. They may teach, do conservation and restoration—doing many things helps make a living easier. There are only a few people doing just fine or designer bookbinding. Here in America, how many can live doing just bookbinding without adding teaching or conservation or restoration? In Europe, we have more people doing designer bookbinding, but they also must take in everything. There are not many artistic bookbinders that don't take other work.

For example the young Stuart Brockman [who had presented a workshop at the Craft Guild of Dallas], without going out and showing his work and giving workshops and demonstrations and lectures, wouldn't be able to make it either. Philip Smith was one that really never did anything else. But some years he had a hard time with money. Trevor Jones was teaching too. Many people make use of all possibilities, including teaching and conservation. Today, there are about 42 bookbinders in the Czech Republic that sometimes do artistic books. I persuaded them to do this; they would normally not try design bindings otherwise.

In the Czech Republic, the good bookbinders I know had fathers who were also binders. I have known almost everyone who has been a design bookbinder. The fathers would send their sons (after their apprenticeship ended) to art schools and hoped that they would become better bookbinders. But it is not simple. The bookbinding profession must be in a person's heart for him or her to ever be good.

What about someone who wants to be a bookbinder here in the US?
Let's say they have had a few classes and think they might want to make it
a career. What advice would you have for them?

I think you need to be absolutely passionate about this craft, otherwise it will be hard to succeed. You must put your full soul in it and become deeply involved. Without being deeply involved, you can't really be successful. You must be dedicated deeply in your heart.

Where would you suggest someone take classes? From you?

I wouldn't suggest that because I have too much work to do. If they are dedicated enough, they will find a way. They must find out what they would like to do, see who is doing it best, and ask that person to take them as a student.

You have immense artistic abilities. You are like a Renaissance man—you
have the artistic ability, you have craftsmanship ability, you can engineer
things, you have all those things going for you.

I wouldn't have been able to get permission to work from the Guild of Artists in Czechoslovakia if I was not an artist. I had to prove I was an artist to get permission to work. Also, the life in former Czechoslovakia was not as easy as life in the States. There were shortages of everything. People had to make up for this disadvantage. I had to make my own colored paper, my own metal clasps, and my own tools. I had to be a "Renaissance man" when I wanted to create design bindings with all the components which I wanted.

When you were a child, were you an artist?

Oh, I was able to draw what I saw in a book when I was five—I was able to draw simple pictures. At eight I was able to illustrate books; at 15 I created artifacts that some people thought an experienced craftsman did. I used to make marionettes and hand puppets for a theatre in my little village. I made the papier-mâché heads. I sewed the dresses for the marionettes on a sewing machine. I made clay heads. There was a ceramic factory nine kilometers from us. Our neighbor (my friend's father), used to work in the factory's pottery kiln department in that factory. He would take my clay heads there, and he brought me back fine ceramics. I would also design, paint, and create scenes and decorations for that theatre.

What do you like most about being a bookbinder, today?

I think for me, today, I like best that I can choose which book to bind and how to bind it. I don't need to accept all commissions. In the past, a few times I did bindings the way people asked me to do them. They said the binding must look like that and that. I did that and that, and they were the most horrible bindings I ever did. I did that twice and then said, "Never more!" If somebody wants a binding from me, he must give me freedom. A customer can say, "I prefer a color or something," but he or she must accept that I do bindings my way.

You have earned that right.

If I were to be desperate for money, then I would do what people want. Today, at my age, fortunately I am not as desperate. Of course, like everybody else, I like to be paid for my own work.

In the Czech Republic, we have binders who almost never sell any of their bindings because they make their living differently. They are good bookbinders, but they don't like to sell their design bindings because they make them in their free time, after work. I feel differently. If I hadn't sold the books, I made (and I have made so many in my life), I wouldn't want to do more bindings. I would have my bindings all around me, so why would I do more? I prefer to have only a few at home.

There is a lot of freedom in having your own business as an independent bookbinder. You can choose your hours; you can choose your jobs.

If you are independent, you always work more than if you worked for somebody who tells you what to do. But it is your choice. You can say, "Today, I am not going to do it," and go outside.

I hear people who are in business for themselves say they wouldn't have it any other way, but they struggle a lot, worrying about not having enough money and benefits.

Benefits are always part of the problem. If you don't have enough work or your work is not good enough, then you don't have money for paying for benefits, or you have a lower pension. Everything goes together. Sometimes it was hard, but I must say that all my life, although I was never rich, I made a good living for me and for my family.

What other kinds of things go on in your life other than bookbinding?

From time to time I go to the pub to drink beer and sing songs with friends. Also, there is a group of us who gather to perform various artistic activities. This event is called "Loket's Exteriors." I am one of the organizers. For about ten days each year, participating artists gather together, work together, learn together, and have lots of fun doing art. There are different kinds of artists in our group. Not all are from the Czech Republic—some are from Canada, some are from Spain, some come from Switzerland. Loket's Exteriors' organizers have been inviting many artists from many countries to attend.

That is really stimulating to be with other kinds of artists.

Yes, you always get new ideas because you do something different. Every year we have a theme—wood, glass, photography, artist's books. One year graphics was the theme, another year it was drawing, sometimes painting or photography. Once, we made art items using our own glass. We built our glass oven and did the work in nature. I created a few books with glass decorations. It was really good. After this, we made wood sculptures as a theme. I made (with big help from my friends) a wooden gate for our house, in the form of a medieval book. Last year we celebrated the 10-year anniversary of Loket's Exteriors. We made retrospective artist books in leather bindings. Next year will be something else. We have mostly been working outdoors, staying at the Loket's farm facilities. We started this when I returned to the Czech Republic.

One thing I know about you is that you love to have fun.

Of course!

What was your favorite project?

There are a few of them. When I started bookbinding, I liked paper bindings. Later I liked leather bindings. I also enjoyed making handmade or decorative papers. Then I started to do box bindings; for a long time I did those. Then I did sculptural bindings, which came from the box bindings. My book sculpture, Country Survey (it became known as the "Fish-Pike Sculpture"), is the biggest project I have ever done. I think that was my most mentioned work and probably the most famous book I did. My customer, the owner of this "Fish-Pike Sculpture," said that it was the Mona Lisa of sculptural bindings. But I didn't work the longest time on that one.

So the fish was the Mona Lisa. What was the book you worked on the longest?

It is one on which I worked for 16 years. It is the most expensive book I did. It belongs to our friends in North Carolina. It was interesting—I collected various items found in books—nonsense things like dried flowers, money, insects, feathers, and handwritten papers. People tend to store many things in books that have emotional value to them. Also, there are often items of nature that accidentally become trapped in books. I had been collecting those items during my 16 years of restoration and conservation work.

Then I made an artist's book using my interesting collection, collected through time. The title I used for this artist's book was *The Old Book*. I nested those "book-restoration-found-items" inside the pages that I made.

First I made paper, using abaca, which is a little bit transparent; then I put some of those flat objects face down over it. The second layer is cotton pulp, onto which objects were again laid face up, and then covered with one more layer of abaca. After pressing and drying, the items that were placed between the layers looked like they were growing through the paper.

The motto for *The Old Book* was Jaroslav Seifert's (Czech poet, Nobel Prize winner for Literature in 1968) poem by the same title. I wrote (using calligraphy) the poem in three languages: Czech, German, and English. It took a long time to prepare that book. I wrote the Czech in Gothic style, the German (translation by Jaroslav Schiling) in 18th century style, and the English (translation by Karel Brusak) in Art Noveau style.

I illuminated the title with gold. The pages also include collages made of old prints, which I found in past years, facsimiles and illuminations from books that I restored, and my own illustrations. The book is bound in a historical style with wooden boards. On the top board is a balsa wood relief of Jaroslav Seifert's face.

During the New Horizons conference, with all of these famous binders watching me, I put on the relief wooden board leather covers

Jan and Jarmila's house gate.

(previously decorated) as part of my presentation. Some said that no one has ever worked on such a valuable book as part of a demonstration in front of so many people. But it was fun. The last steps, which I finished later, were to attach metal corners, and do the doublures, which included parchment illuminated with the initial "H," symbolizing Heaven on the front and Hell on the back.

That really was a whole book created by you.
Yes, that has been my most complicated artist book.

How do clients find you?
I don't do anything. I'm not hunting. Somehow they come. Some of my clients are our students and friends as well.

Is there anything more you would like to share?

I was hoping I would have more time to do my design bindings when I retired. I've been working on my new style of binding, with no shoulder hinge, that I find simpler. Bindings with shoulder hinges always break. Four years after I came back to the Czech Republic, I played with the three-boards binding. Today I have solved all the problems with the structure, and I can now do anything I like with it. That was holding me back from doing something bigger again. I wanted to finish it to be sure it would always work. Today many people are using it. Some people have won prizes using the structure.

You are a binder that has a signature. People think of sculptural binding when they hear your name.

When I don't do a sculptural binding in a competition, they are disappointed. Many people didn't know that I came up with a new structure, which was more important to me at the time. Even bookbinders don't notice the new structure because it is not visible in the binding. Innovation is not just in design but in structure too. People didn't realize it was done a different way. It's funny. For example, my double or triple board bindings are made differently—finished doublures (on binders' board) are attached to the book block first; top boards and cover are attached in the end. Skilled and careful bookbinders should be able to see this.

So now you and Jarmila have returned to the Czech Republic though you continue to travel to the US regularly.

My wife, Jarmila, and I have our hearts in two countries today. The Czech Republic, country of our birth, and the USA, a country that helped us in time of need. We are happy that we are back in our homeland today, but we are visiting the States every year. The reason is not only that our two daughters and their families are living there, but also, we have many customers in the USA.

We have used our experience from our bookbinding life in the USA in our country. After returning to the Czech Republic, in 1987, we, along with our friend Jana Pribikova, founded the Association of Czech Bookbinders. In 2001, with the help of the town hall in Loket and sponsoring donors, we created the Museum of Bookbinding, the only one of its kind in the world. During my more then fifty and Jarmila's more then twenty years of bookbinding life, we have developed many students and many friends who have participated in the Museum's project by donating their design bookbindings.

We have managed to buy and renovate a small house in the beautiful medieval town of Loket. Although the house is in the middle of the town, it is situated behind a passage, on a small, quiet square with only three houses. It is more convenient for us then our original, rented house, which stands exactly in the middle of Loket's main square. Our son, Radek, and his family are living and working there now, ensuring that the Sobota's Book Arts Gallery continues.

For more information on Jan Sobota, and to see examples of his work, go to www.jsobota.cz.

Priscilla Spitler:
Hands On Bookbinding

Smithville, Texas
April 2006

Hands On Bookbinding—a fitting name in so many ways for Priscilla Spitler's bookbinding business. During a time when she questioned her career situation and was still badly shaken by a devastating auto accident, a friend suggested that she visit a "hands-on-healer." Through the sessions with the healer, Priscilla uncovered her direction.

Priscilla stands tall, with classic chiseled cheekbones and hazel colored eyes, framed by glasses that pierce into those she looks at. She uses her fingers to comb back her long, thick, honey highlighted hair.

I arrive at her bookbinding studio located in a small strip shopping center in Smithville, TX. Sweet scents from the donut shop next door drift in. A sitting area in the front also serves as her office—computer, printer, and phone. We move through a room with a work table in the center, cluttered with papers, surrounded by high stacks of labeled boxes and bins—"wheels," "wings," "tails," "figures," "trucks." Priscilla's husband, Don, a pilot and antique and junk collector, stores items here as well as in several rooms in their house—things he has collected since childhood. He sells items online and in a co-op antique shop in downtown Smithville. He dreams of opening an aviation museum where he can sell and display his collection.

We continue to the back of the shop where there is a bathroom and a kitchen. Walking toward the front, on the other side of the space, we see Priscilla's bookbinding equipment—job backer, board shear, book presses, Kensol stamping machine, guillotine, tools and supplies—all arranged for optimal efficiency for her limited edition binding jobs. Walls display colorful posters of bookbinding and printing events, pictures of exquisite bindings, favorite photographs. Her hands point to each one affectionately as she tells stories about them.

Priscilla's hands have touched many lives. She has put together exhibits for the Guild of Book Workers and Lone Star Chapter (national and regional bookbinding organizations in America). Her bindings, now some of them award-winners, show her signature look that incorporates her handmade paste papers, bold colors and designs. She also teaches classes all over America. "I feel like I am trying to pass on the torch. It really pleases me to inspire someone to learn to do design binding and fine binding."

It was on the way home from a regional meeting in Dallas with her bookbinding friend that the fateful car accident occurred on I-35, when a drunk driver smashed into her car, forcing it to ride along the center median before it swung off the side of the road and wrapped around a tree. Her friend who injured her hand in the accident is convinced that they lived because Priscilla never took her hands off the steering wheel. She was the one who urged Priscilla, uncertain about her life at that time, to go to a hands-on-healer. "She moved her hands over me and all this stuff started coming up about my life. Within two months, I made the decision that it was time to start my own business." Hands On Bookbinding. Soon after, she married Don, a musician, pilot, and antique dealer. For both, in their 40's, it was a first marriage. They settled in rural Texas, outside Austin. Since this interview they have relocated and are now the owners of a building in Truth or Consequences, NM that will be Don's air museum, Priscilla's bindery, and their home.

How did you become interested in bookbinding?

All my life I've been artistic. My mother was a painter, and my father was an amateur photographer, so I've always felt comfortable drawing and working with art. My sister who is 8 years older than me introduced me to textiles. During high school, I used to do printed fabrics and card-woven belts. I made handbags and clothing and even got commissions for hippie weddings doing embroidery appliqué, so I really thought I was going to go into textiles when I graduated from high school in 1972 in Southern California. I ended up going to the California College of Arts and Crafts (CCAC) in Oakland as what I figured was going to be a textile major. But fortunately the art school had a requirement that was part of their basic studies program, and all incoming students had to do a wide range of classes to expose them to other mediums. I discovered that I loved to draw, and I went into printmaking. I actually had dreams and aspirations of becoming a master printer, a lithographer. That is what I majored in.

During the last year-and-a-half at CCAC, I studied with Betsy Davids, a letterpress printer, well known in the field, who has her own private press, the Rebis Press. I had taken a course that combined lithography with letterpress, text, and image. I was intrigued by the handmade book. Betsy was printing limited editions at her own studio. So I helped setting type and sorting type—I was a printer's devil.

She had an NEA grant to print a book written and illustrated by Johanna Drucker. There was so much work done in printing and illustrating it well. When it came to binding, they did an appropriate structure for the book. The book, *As No Storm or The Any Port Party,* was about a motley crew of people who got stranded on a boat out at sea. It was limp bound in sailcloth and sort of side stitched.

Afterward I thought, "You put all this work in producing the text, but where can you learn to do proper binding?" There seemed to be a lot of printers but not a whole lot of binders, so I was really curious at that point. My parents were living in New Mexico at that time when I graduated in '75. I followed them to Albuquerque after my college years. By then I was more intrigued by binding, but I didn't know where to learn to do it.

What do you do with a degree in art, especially with a degree in printmaking? My first job out of college was working in a commercial print shop in Albuquerque. I was the only woman in the print shop trained to work on an AB Dick offset press. They also did silk-screening. We were silk-screening mirrors, like bar mirrors and things like that. That was my first experience in a commercial shop, and I didn't think very much of it, to tell you the truth. I was doing printing, but it was commercial stuff. It was interesting technologically, but I didn't like what we were printing, so that didn't last.

I had a boyfriend in Southern New Mexico. I was always commuting there. So I ended up in Old Mesilla, outside Las Cruces. There weren't a lot of jobs there. There was a wonderful bookstore on the plaza that sold books on the Southwest. The people that owned it grew up on the

Navajo reservation; they were traders. I was just a clerk. At that point I thought, "What am I going to do?" I had worked a year-and-a-half after college. I could go get my masters in lithography at University of New Mexico. Or maybe this bookselling thing was a good way to go.

I got that book called, *What Color is your Parachute?* I give my nieces and nephews a copy when they graduate. It helped me go through this process of figuring where my strengths and weaknesses are. I put together this little resume with very little work experience and started marching around to booksellers in Santa Fe and Albuquerque, trying to find a clerk job, and they started offering me assistant management positions. In no time I was hired in Santa Fe to work in an independent bookstore. I was 23 years old. In three months, I was managing the bookstore and doing the buying. So that is how I ended up in Santa Fe. At the bookstore I met all these people who are my close friends today. I managed the bookstore for two to three years. But I was just dying to get back to working with my hands. That is when I started going to the print shop at the Palace of the Governors museum, just to smell the ink and be around the old equipment.

There I met a Japanese-American woman named Mina Yamashita, a graphic artist, who had gone to Pratt Institute. She had taken a bookbinding class with Laura Young—it was required of Pratt students. They had to learn to do their own portfolios and presentations. She was the first person who gave me a lesson in bookbinding in Santa Fe. I was hooked. That was 1977. I started thinking that maybe I should go this route. I loved bookselling, I loved book printing, and the bookbinding made a lot of sense.

I was still working at the bookstore when I took my first trip to Europe. I went to the Victoria and Albert Museum; it was like an epiphany. I saw an exhibit of design bindings by Edgar Mansfield and William Matthews, contemporary bindings on fine letterpress books. I said, "That is what I want to do." I saw a leather onlay, and I thought, "This pulls all my interests together." Because I used to do textile onlay work with fabric, I could see it translating to leather. I said, "This is it. This is what I want to do. I want to learn to do design binding, and I want to learn to do it right. Now where do I go?"

I came back to Santa Fe, and I started searching around. Where can I study it here in the States? In the late '70's, there weren't places to study unless you had an opportunity to be European-trained. There weren't any schools here. If you went into library settings you might learn binding skills. I was probably among the last wave of a group of Americans that went to Europe to study, like Laura Wait, Frank Mowery, Peter Verheyen, Paula Gourley—the whole group that went to Europe to study and then came back. I wanted to go to London. That would be a cool place to live. I chose London, too, because of the language.

I had a friend in London who was helping me find a place to study. The Camberwell program is where I wanted to go, but they had closed the bookbinding aspect of it. The only school there was the London College of Printing (LCP). I had seen the Arthur Johnson book on binding when I was bookselling. I thought I wanted to study with Arthur Johnson at the LCP. I was originally accepted to go there in 1979. That was when Maggie Thatcher was in office. I couldn't pull it together financially because I had to prove I had enough living expenses before I got into the country. The work situation was really bad in England; they didn't want you taking jobs away. So, as a student I had to prove that I had financial support and even had to have a place to live when I got there. I couldn't pull it together the first year.

But by the second year I sold everything I owned to get to England—books, furniture. Friends even had parties where they pinned dollar bills on my dress to get me to London. I got there the second year. The overseas tuition had tripled under Maggie Thatcher. I was the only foreigner in the course. I was paying around $4,000 tuition whereas all of the other students were paying $300-600. That is how I ended up picking bookbinding. Things kind of fell into place.

The year I was in London, 1980-81, I was doing the certificate course at the London College of Printing. Alfred J. Brazier was my main tutor. My finishing instructor was John Mitchell. Alfred Brazier was a delight. He was only about five feet two inches tall. We worked hard—from nine to five, Monday through Friday, we were at the bench. There were ten students. When I started out in this course, I had no idea what I was getting into. I wanted to make beautiful books, but I didn't know what was involved.

The first day of class all we did was fold paper! We folded down sections, in quartos, octavos, and we folded and folded. I thought, "I sold everything I owned to fold paper!" I really had some second thoughts. It was hard for me. I thought I was running a race for the first three months. I was one of the slower ones (there were about three of us who were really slow); I was trying to keep up. I was one of the mature students, 26 was mature; they were 18, 19 years old. They were zipping along. I broke down in tears trying to lace the keys on the sewing frame one day as I was sitting there fiddling with the sewing keys. But I gained speed in the end. Once I got it, I really did.

In my situation in England, because of my degree in art, I felt like I had an advantage over the other students. I had a sense of color and design and composition that they didn't teach at LCP. I know the French [bookbinding] schools teach design and color to the students. We had History of Gold Finishing. They taught us about keeping books and costing out. They had a fellow teach us science—testing paper. They tried to expose us to other things, but they really didn't teach us about color and design so some of the students struggled with that. Our assessor, we found out later in the year, was Bernard Middleton. In England, when you go for those programs, they rank you. You finish first, second, third, etc. It's very serious, and it can make a difference if you can get a job in England.

At the end of the course, we had to do a little paper and we had an exhibition. We had to put on display everything we did during the year. We could display it however we wanted to, and all the prospective employers would come and look at the work. That is where a lot of these young people got jobs in the binderies. At the end of the year, each one of us—I remember this vividly—was called in one-by-one, and we had a private interview with Bernard Middleton. I didn't really know who he was at the time. We were sitting in this room waiting, and you could hear the clock ticking. One-by-one we went in. I wasn't concerned. I was going back to the States. I learned more than I ever expected to learn. I wasn't worried about the outcome. At the end of the course, I was told that I finished third, after starting out so slow!

When I had my little interview with Bernard Middleton—you know Bernard is very soft spoken—he asked, "What are you going to do when you go back to the States?" One of the things he stressed was to stay informed and not to be isolated, to keep up with what was going on, find the community. That is why I joined the Guild of Book Workers, so I could keep in touch.

I came back to Santa Fe in July of 1981. I started taking freelance work from booksellers downtown, sort of struggling along, trying to figure out what I was going to do with this new skill. I was often going to the museum to visit Pam Smith, who ran the print shop. She was thrilled that I had bookbinding skills; also my friend Paula Hocks was excited. Paula wanted me to collaborate with her artist Xerox books.

Pam created a position for me at the museum, so within six to seven months, I was working at the Press of the Palace of the Governors. It was a working exhibit of old presses, historic to the state of New Mexico. It was like Williamsburg. People could come in and see us at work, whether Pam was printing or I was binding. She would produce limited edition books that pertained to New Mexico history or culture that were hand printed, and because of my printing background, I was able to help her set type. I really learned a lot from her. Pam Smith came out to New Mexico in the early 1970's and basically created this whole working exhibit. We became a great team. We felt isolated in Santa Fe and wanted to bring some well-known book people to us.

Mina Yamashita, the woman that gave me my first bookbinding lesson, gave Pam the idea to have a book arts fair. By the time I came on board, she had already gotten a grant for it. It was an educational grant so we had to orient it toward children. For five years, we had busloads of kids come in and we demonstrated for three days in the courtyard of the palace. I was in charge of getting the demonstrators together. We had everything from casting type to lithography demonstrations, letterpress printing, map-making, calligraphy, illumination, bookbinding, on and on. It was really great. In conjunction with that, we would bring in a guest speaker. We had a theme each year. For five years, we got bigger and bigger grants.

I had a little studio downtown during the time I worked with Pam, and in my studio I did portfolio boxes for photographers. There was a whole community of photographers in Santa Fe, and also artists. I remember when I was studying in London I said, "You need to teach me how to make clamshell boxes (they called them Solander boxes)." So they kind of reluctantly showed me how to do these boxes. I was making all this money doing boxes for these photographers while I was also working for Pam at the print shop.

You know how they talk about the bust and boom in Texas? The oil bust also affected us in New Mexico, and our funding for the book arts festival dried up. So, Pam and I took off on a six-week leave for a book arts tour east. Our object was to see other printing exhibits, work like ours, and also to visit other notables in the book arts. This was

1985, and we traveled through the Midwest, up to the East Coast and back through the South. We knew about W. Thomas Taylor, the Austin, Texas bookseller, who also commissioned design bindings. I was real eager to meet him. All along the way I kept hearing about this other guy named Craig Jensen, also down in Austin. I started seeing examples of his work, how beautiful his editions were—the finesse! In my mind I was seeing him in this huge bindery. We finally got to Austin in October 1985. That was the first time I had been there.

As I said, I really wanted to go see Tom Taylor because he commissioned design bindings, and that is what I ultimately wanted to do. So we went downtown [to see him]. He had a fine rare book business on an upper floor, with beautiful light; you could go in and look at the books. He was about to leave for a flight to some book show in California, but he said, "You are welcome to go in and look at books."

So here was this beautiful room with all these books and all this pre-Columbian art around it. On a round table there was one pre-Columbian piece of art in the middle of a pile of books. I picked up this one book, *Stone Beloved,* which I think that Craig had bound. It was in this slipcase that was rather snug, and so I was trying to get this book out of the slipcase when I knocked over the pre-Columbian figure, and it came crashing down and it broke.

I was mortified. Pam just looked at me: "Oh, Priscilla, I'm so sorry." I went running into Tom's office: "I'm afraid something terrible has happened." He came running out, and he was so great, he said, "Oh, well, I should have never put it there." He picked it up: "It was my grandmother's favorite. I'm glad you did it and not me." I asked, "Can I pay to have it repaired?" and he said, "No, it was just a copy, but a good one. Don't even think about it." And that was that. I thought, "Boy, I made a really good impression on Tom Taylor." I left there so depressed. We had been on the road for six weeks.

The people in Austin were so great. They threw a party for us. I just wanted to go home. I was so depressed. When I got back to Santa Fe, I said to myself, "What can I do? I have to do something." Tom Taylor was so gracious. So I got this first edition book on pre-Columbian art that was illustrated by Miguel Covarrubias. I thought, "I am going to do a design binding on this pre-Columbian book and give it to Tom Taylor."

So you went from working in Santa Fe to what?

I worked in Santa Fe with Pam until 1986 when I took a little detour through Tucson, Arizona. Actually I got swept up by a Hollywood film editor. I was on my way with him to Australia when it all blew up. I got as far as the West Coast and said, "I'm not going." I came back. I had given up my job in Santa Fe and my studio. When I left Santa Fe in 1986, I had sort of burned my bridges there. I had even made arrangements to work with Australian binders while this man I was involved with would be working on a Peter Weir picture. When I came back, devastated, my mother said to me, "You don't have to go back to Santa Fe," and I said, "You're right. I'm going to go to Tucson." Some of my Santa Fe friends had lived on a ranch outside of the city where all these artists lived. They had bought an old dude ranch back in the late 60's and communally owned it. There were all of these houses on the land, and they allotted the houses depending on how much they each had been able to put into buying this property. There was one center area with studios and gallery space, and a little guesthouse where I was the "guest" for three months.

I had put the [pre-Columbian] book aside months before, when I was distracted by the Hollywood film guy and I was wined and dined. I decided, "I am going to bind this book for Tom Taylor." I didn't have radio, TV, or phone at the ranch. It was my first design binding since my student years, and I had most recently been doing editions. I had problems at every step—paring the leather, working on a French chevre skin that didn't tool well with that coating on it. I decided to do a Mayan design in relief, and I was trying to sculpt leather and blind tool around it with gouges. I did elaborate paste papers. I struggled at every point. I had a terrible time paring, I had a terrible time tooling, and then I would resolve it. It was like I was working out this failed relationship on this poor book. It was just me and this book.

Then I heard about the program at the Harry Ransom Center in Austin. You had to submit a binding. I had finished my binding, so I thought, "It's not good enough, but maybe they will see that I have potential."

So in 1987, I was accepted to do the two-month program of study with James Brockman. It was called "The First Institute of Fine Binding and Conservation," Don Etherington's dream. I got to study for two months with Jim Brockman. I was like a sponge to water. All those problems I had on that book, he had all the answers to. I couldn't have been more ready. The actual fine binding technique I use now is really Jim Brockman's—cushioning of the board, lacing of the board, structure and technique that honed my skills. I kept such detailed notes. That was the direction I needed. It was such an incredible summer in Austin.

Afterwards, I didn't know what I was going to do. I had worked at a little bookstore in Tucson while I was doing private work for one collector in Tucson, but I was struggling financially. I had come to do this two-month program and literally, I didn't know what I was going to do next.

Well, Craig Jensen offered me a job, and I stayed in Austin. That is how I ended up in Texas. The funny thing was that it was this action where I broke that pre-Columbian statue that prompted me to get the book and to bind the book that eventually brought me back to Austin. How about that! I never thought the book was good enough to show Tom Taylor. Two or three years after I was in Austin, I called him up one day. I had a group of design bindings by that time and I said, "Can I show you my books?" He said, "Yes, bring them on down." I was really nervous about this. I showed him my bindings, and I just threw in the one of the pre-Columbian art and you know he said, "Of all the books, this is the one I want, the pre-Columbian art book." I think breaking that pre-Columbian sculpture, even though it was a copy from the 30's or whatever, was the catalyst that brought me back to Austin.

Craig had come to Austin when Don Etherington set up the lab [at HRC]. Craig had done his internship at Library of Congress, and Don brought Craig to Austin to work as the head book conservator. He got tired of institutional work and started his own bindery called Jensen Bindery. On that trip, the famous trip Pam and I made, I finally met Craig. I thought he would be working in this fabulous bindery and yet he was working in this little space in his garage, just a tiny little space. After Craig moved Jensen Bindery to a commercial building, I worked with him one year doing edition work for Tom Taylor and some others. He was always struggling. He is such an innovator and problem solver and master craftsman. I think about having the opportunity I had to work with Jim Brockman and then Craig—they were both amazing, really diverse.

I worked at the Jensen Bindery and then BookLab [when he joined with two library bindery partners]. Although I had previous training in bookbinding, I really learned Craig's "house style." If you go into binderies often, you will find there is a certain style. I trained the crew at BookLab in the BookLab style, which was Craig Jensen's style in the editions we did. I was able to take over more of the edition work.

Next to doing fine binding, I chose to do edition work for my bread and butter. I think when you go into binding you have to make a choice. If you are going to try to make a living at it, you may aspire to do artists books; you may aspire to do design bindings; but if you really want to make a living at it, it's either repair work, conservation, or in my case, I chose to do edition work, which comes from my experience in printing. One of the things I loved the most about lithography in the print studios was the collaborative spirit, the aspect of working with other people; edition binding is an extension of that. What I really like about edition binding is being part of this collaboration, being the finishing, the housing of the object that many people are involved in. So realistically I felt like that is what I had to do for a living if I was going to make it in bookbinding.

During the eight years that I was at BookLab, I had the opportunity to see some of the finest small press work from all over the country coming into BookLab—everything from individual small presses, to university presses, to big places like the Limited Editions Club of NY that had large volume editions, and I had the chance to work with Craig Jensen and Gary Frost who really taught me about structure, really understanding structure. I think of my years at BookLab like a journeyman period when you go through an apprenticeship program, a real hands-on experience. I had my hands in thousands of books. The fact that Craig was always willing to take on the unusual meant we were always challenged to take on new structures, new materials. I really feel like I honed my skills during those years. I also had to train people to work with a crew in terms of planning.

The thing I like about bookbinding, and edition work in particular, is that, especially when you have a team working with you, you get the job done very quickly. BookLab fell between a commercial and hand bindery. We were doing really fine handwork, but we were speeding it up by using glue machines, hydraulic presses, and other equipment that made the process go faster. Yet we didn't compromise the product. The thing I loved about it was there was a beginning and an end. There was so much satisfaction seeing a job started, in process, and finished. I get great satisfaction from that, even in my own studio here. I work by myself, but I occasionally have somebody working with me. When the job is done, I have accomplished something. A lot of times people say to me, "How can you stand doing this tedious work over and over again?" Well, you play this game in edition work. You start seeing one pile get smaller and the finished pile get bigger; it is this numbers game and I just find it very Zen sometimes. When I was working on the DeGolyer binding for the fourth competition, as usual I was trying to squeeze it in between other jobs, and it was an odd deadline of December 31st, but for me it worked out well because all my pre-Christmas jobs were done, and I had two weeks to really blitz—come in here and work day and night. By the time I was through with that binding, for better or for worse, I couldn't wait to get back to the edition work. Being obsessed with one binding for a length of time can drive you a little crazy. Edition binding brings me down to earth and is very centering. If I am bouncing off the walls, all I have to do is come to the bench and start doing some multiple operations, and then I focus. It is very calming for me; I really enjoy that.

The years I was with Craig, the interesting thing was, though I aspired to do fine binding, I would be real picky about every little detail. After I started doing production work and gaining more confidence in the fine binding, I started relaxing about a lot of things and letting things happen that I wouldn't have done in the earlier, less experienced days. I may not be the best binder, but I enjoy what I do, and I try to work within these confines, but I also will allow things to happen and follow a direction. The book has a kind of soul. That makes me happy. I will go off and obsess about tooling and spots here and there, but get over it after a while. When I finished the DeGolyer binding, I couldn't stand it; I took pictures of it. It was of a text that Laura Wait had done, and I didn't even show her the pictures for two months. I looked at it yesterday and thought, "It's not so bad." You kind of have to distance yourself. Sometimes in my work I feel like the edition work balances out the fine binding work. As I get older I would like to do more of that, but I do have to make a living. Thank goodness I can do box work and edition work. It comes to me in little Smithville.

What happened at BookLab that made you come to Smithville?
I worked there eight years, and I saw the company grow from about

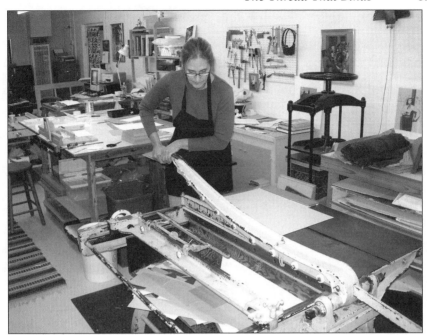

Priscilla Spitler working in her studio.

six people to almost thirty, and of course with a large group like that, you start getting into personality conflicts. It's a big job managing that many people. In the early days, we used to pride ourselves on being a little bit different, an interesting gathering of people. There were a lot of artists and musicians on staff. And after a while, it became a problem because there were too many egos. I knew that I had a job there that was highly regarded. Some of the other staff did library work when they wanted to do edition work, which was considered precious.

Some other things were happening in my life. I met Don. He had his own antique store. He worked on weekends, and my only time off was weekends and that was always a conflict. When I worked at BookLab, we were up there at seven o'clock in the morning, and I would be working late. At one point I was teaching classes in the evening. I put in long hours down there. It was kind of hard to have a personal relationship, especially with someone who worked on the weekends. So it was a little bit of a conflict. But also, I just felt like I had put my time in and that there were others that could be trained that needed to move up within the company.

I had an automobile accident, coming back from Dallas after the Dallas Guild meeting, and that was kind of a catalyst; that was October of '94. A couple months after that, my friend Mary Margaret sent me to a hands-on healer; she was into this new age stuff. Mary Margaret was the passenger in the car when we were hit by this drunk driver at ten o'clock (at night) on Interstate-35 coming down from Dallas. She was always convinced that because I drove through whatever we were going through—it was a very violent impact, and riding on the center median and being swung off the side of the road and wrapped around a tree—that we survived because I never took my hands off the wheel, sort of negotiated what I could do though I didn't know what was happening.

She wanted me to go to this hands-on healer to deal with the shock. I started going to this hands-on healer who moved her hands over me, and all this stuff started coming up about my life and financial stuff and work stuff, and within two months, I made a decision that it was time for me to leave [BookLab] and start my own business.

During the time I was at BookLab, I had started teaching bookbinding at the Laguna Gloria Art Museum which is now the Austin Museum of Art. I never thought I would like teaching. I thought I didn't have the patience for it, but to my surprise I really liked it. For eleven years, I taught little weekend workshops at Laguna Gloria. That opened up a whole world for me. I started really enjoying seeing other people get excited about learning bookbinding. I was being invited to teach bookbinding classes around the country by other chapters of the Guild and other regions and other book centers, and I couldn't because I had a full-time job with a lot of responsibility.

I started feeling that my life was getting larger than BookLab. There were demands that I personally felt like I couldn't do anymore with that full-time schedule. I had bought my house, and I had remodeled the little garage to be a bindery. I decided, "Now is the time to set up and teach more classes." And I thought, "I can still do a little bit of binding on my own and teach classes."

When I came back from Christmas of 1994, I gave Craig notice. He was real disappointed. But I gave a three-month notice, so I trained someone over that period to take over my responsibilities, and we parted on really good terms. Even after I started setting up my classes—and I had a whole schedule of evening and daytime classes on my own—Craig started making referrals to me of jobs that they couldn't take on. Either they were too small or required too much of a workload. I started getting small jobs and edition work, on my own, and things sort of fell into place. It was a good transition for me.

Within that year, Don and I got engaged. I had a year to get used to that idea and to get used to working for myself, so it wasn't this radical thing where I got married and I quit my job. I was on my own, and then I married in the fall of 1996 and moved my whole bindery to Buda for a year-and-a-half before we moved out here. It was the right time for both of us, a mature bride and groom. We had never married, either one of us, and we shocked both of our families. It made sense for me to go to Buda since he had the shop on Main Street in Buda, TX and my work came to me.

Meanwhile, Craig was calling me back to work on certain projects, like for Vincent FitzGerald in New York, this wonderful fine art publisher who does incredible books. He would call me in to help sew or work on some of those books or occasionally call me in to train new employees to do box-making, so I was sort of doing contract work for BookLab even after I left. That was really great.

In the meantime, we could see what was happening to Buda with all the growth down Interstate-35, and we didn't like what we were seeing. We decided we wanted to move to a small community within an hour of Austin, where his family is. We started investigating little communities with little airports so Don could bring his plane over. We fell in love with Smithville. It had the antiques community for Don; it had the little airport; we were within an hour of Austin. It's a funny little town. We subscribed to the paper for a year-and-a-half and got to know everything going on. We burned all our bridges and bought a house. And we said, "Oh, we hope we like it."

What are your favorite parts of being a bookbinder?

Well, I mentioned edition work, seeing a project through from the beginning of the process to completion. But I also enjoy the technical challenges, trying to create something beautiful but also being challenged by the structure. I like that. Sometimes it drives me crazy, but it keeps it interesting. You always think, "I can do better the next time." I don't get bored with it. I get bored maybe with a job that goes on too long. Like when I was working on the Richard Gere deluxe edition of photographs. That was one job that Craig turned over to me because they had too much work, believe it or not. And they wanted it in too short a period of time. It was 500 coffee-table-sized books of Tibet by Richard Gere—500 machine sewn books with 500 slipcases. I cased every single one of them in my small standing press myself. When I got to 250, I wished the job was over. It took me four months in my little studio. I had a team—I had subcontracted and basically pieced out parts of the job to my old BookLab buddies. But that was the swan song of large editions for me. I said no more. I'm leaving it at 250; that would be a big job for me, 250 to 300. Now most of the editions I do tend to be around 50. The Jim Dine box and book edition was 37 books, but it had a lot of complicated tippings and stuff. I can't think of a book I did that was 100 copies in a while. Fifty seems to be a good number—50 or 60. I love the little 25 book jobs.

To finish the story of when I started my business and moved out to Smithville, I was just sort of cruising along, and to my shock and everybody else's, Craig calls me up and says, "You got a minute? We are closing BookLab." I was shocked. They had had one of the best years ever. But the partners were in disagreement about which direction they wanted to go, and they decided to dissolve the partnership. Lo and behold, he says, "I've got some pretty good jobs that I would like you to take over," and so I inherited a lot of the clients from Craig. One big one was Vincent FitzGerald. Vincent called me and said, "Well, I guess they are closing BookLab. I would like you to do my next job." It was like the deluxe of private press work. Others would have liked to have it. I haven't done a book for him lately, but he comes around when he is ready. I have these repeat clients, and new ones and referrals. I don't advertise and never go out looking for work. I just sit here and get e-mails. Of course it helps to have a website. I get inquiries all the time. But a lot of my clients have come from one happy client referring me to another—printmakers, small press people, photographers.

When you go through a job with a client, there is an exchange of education that takes place; then after that you get this relationship going. Part of it is educating them. Then it gets easier for them and also for me.

It seems like in your whole life, one thing led to another and it naturally laid itself out before you. I am in awe that you have gotten rid of everything at least a couple times in your life and put your life on the line.

Seeing my picture on the wall in the history museum in Santa Fe last year when I went back to the "Lasting Impressions" exhibit was a big highlight—seeing all the old printers that I knew (it was old home week). It's been a real journey, this whole book thing.

When I look back to age 26 I think, "How in the world, whatever possessed me to go into bookbinding?" It is an odd thing. To me it was something different, the technical challenge. It was a craft, and I was still craft oriented. Who knows? Sometimes I think it was past life stuff that drew me to this. I don't know. But I caught the wave; I got into it at the right time.

It was really great for a lot of us that started at that time because when the book arts movement started, we were given the opportunity to teach workshops. Now I am in a phase where I feel like I am doing a lot more teaching, like the fine binding workshop that I did last year. That was the first time I brought it to that level. I feel like I am trying to pass on the torch, so to speak, and the technique. It really pleases me to inspire someone to learn to do design binding and fine binding, to get them excited about it. It has always been a struggle financially for me. It's not like the door is opened wide and I am out to make millions off of this. I have been able to make a living, and when I want to take off I can, but a lot of what drives me is I have to pay the bills.

It's been tough for me over the years, learning how to bid accurately on jobs and paying myself a decent wage in the end. I'm still figuring it out. I had an employee who would really get after me about my bids, and she ingrained in me that you have to stick to this hourly rate and how you establish this hourly rate. It took me the longest time to really believe it. It is one thing saying it, but to say I am worth it, that is a hard thing. And I still underbid things all the time. In my profession, if you underbid it, you are stuck with it. It's not like conservation work where you can give an estimate; you bid a job, you have to stick with that job. Each time, I am careful with my bids. I've even bid in the inspection and wrapping. That is another operation. You have to remember that is part of the job. I bid a job and then I'm working at it and I think, gee it would be really nice if I did this, and you start adding these little refinements that you didn't account for. You have got to watch that. You've got to stick with it.

I was real busy when I first moved here [to Smithville] and BookLab closed. Things were booming! I had the Richard Gere job; that was a big job. Then 9/11 hit—the economy was already taking a turn before that.

2002 really slowed down; 2003 almost came to a grinding halt. It ebbs and flows; it's a fickle thing. But I've learned that with the classes I have scheduled—and I'm getting a whole crop of students from Houston now—the teaching gig keeps it constant. I can plan my classes and keep a constant cash flow. I will only be able to do production for ten years or less; it is demanding. The deadlines, the stress. I have to be here seven days a week to get a job done because they may have planned a book signing or opening—get here early, go home, fix dinner, come back, be here until ten.

The bookbinder is always the last person in the deal. It can be delayed here or there; it shows up and I have to make up the time. I foresee another eight to ten years more of production work and then hopefully I can teach and do my own work, whatever that may be. I also have some publishing, some manuals I want to work on, like my fine-binding manual I put together for the class last year. I want that to be published. Pam Smith is helping me edit. It is evolving, adding more pictures. It is English-based. It is a working manual on fine binding, step-by-step. I'm hoping to do more of that sort of thing in the future.

Will you do more of the fine binding workshops like you did last summer?

I'm not ready for it yet. It was intense. It was great, but it was a lot of work for me. I had two of them. I had one in the studio over the summer for my Austin and San Antonio students. They came in, and we did it over seven Sundays during the summer, just to see if a fine binding could be done in seven sessions. We are talking about going from sewing to covering—full-leather, cushioning the boards, paring the leather, sewing the headbands, and covering, but not any of the decorating. And they did it!

So from all the handouts that I prepared for that seven-session trial over that summer, I pulled together the weeklong intensive. The students stayed in the cabins at the state park nearby, and I rented the old hall and moved equipment out there. Craig was an assistant and Olivia Primanis was an assistant. It was great! We had 13 students; several pulled in from out of state—Virginia, Alabama, Illinois. It worked out really well and was fun. Then they all wanted me to teach them to do decorative work, and so last summer I had the first group of locals from Austin and San Antonio. This past February I had another one with the out-of-state folks from the intensive. Karen Hanmer, Anna

Embree—about seven people in all—flew in and stayed in a hotel and that was really fun; we did it over three days. They brought their books to decorate, and we had a blast. It was really neat, and I really enjoyed that because everybody's design was really different. First I had them working on little sample cards to try different techniques, and then we talked about the design and they made their little maquettes. So they knew how they wanted to execute their designs from the techniques that they learned. And then we focused the next two days on doing the design. I really do like to teach.

Was any one teacher most influential to you?

Well I would say Jim Brockman, because the fine binding that I do today was really cemented by the structure and the techniques that he taught. He might look at some of the things I do now and say "what?" because I have since added a little input from Craig here and there, but I didn't do any fine binding at BookLab, so I have stuck pretty much to what I learned from him, with my basic English training. And Craig—I would consider Craig Jensen to be a great influence on my career and everything.

Is there an ideal commission you would like to have some day?

I don't know about ideal. I keep going for the DeGolyer prize. I don't know if I'll ever get it, but I think it would be nice to have that. I keep winning all sorts of little prizes. I keep trying. It would be nice to get one of those mysterious MacArthur Foundation awards. I once tried to get on their website to nominate Gary Frost for one of those genius awards, but they wouldn't take nominations.

What would you tell someone who wants to be a bookbinder who dreams of making his/her living as a bookbinder?

I get that a lot—emails and such from housewives whose sons or children have left home and who would really like to do bookbinding and maybe make a living. My advice is usually to invite them to take a workshop with me and see if they like it because having the idea that they would like it and the reality of cutting and measuring and doing it is another thing. But if someone is interested in learning to do it I try to question them and ask them, "In what direction do you want to go with this? Do you want to do repair work, or stationery work or artist books?" I try and direct them as best I can as to where to go and where to take workshops, and as to whether I can teach them things.

I generally encourage them to join the Guild or look into other sources and to do the research and get out and join the local book arts group and get out and meet people. I've always been sort of a networker and am good at connecting people with other people. I have been helpful with getting people jobs. I could have been a career counselor or job placement person. Craig used to call me: "Do you have any students that would be good at working at BookLab?" They used to call me from BookLab after I left, because Craig knew I was already training them in the style we used, so a lot of my students would go on to get jobs there.

To somebody who wants to make a living at it, first of all I would say you have to love it to pursue it. Take one thing at a time and don't try to do it all at once. Specialize in one aspect; try and decide if you're planning to sell the product; then go out and do research. Is there really a demand? How much is out there already? Look at the prices.

For more information on Priscilla Spitler, and to see examples of her work, go to http://priscilla.bookways.com.

Craig Jensen:
*The Road Back to "Two Guys
in a Garage"*

San Marcos, Texas
April 2006

The elusive Craig Jensen. A couple of times, many years ago, I visited BookLab, a bindery in Austin run and co-owned by Craig, where the Lone Star Chapter of the Guild of Book Workers occasionally held meetings. There I met bookbinders Priscilla Spitler and Gary Frost, and even esteemed publisher W. Thomas Taylor, but I never met Craig. I thought of him as this unseen mystery man. In the summer of 2005, after BookLab had closed, I finally met him in Iowa at a book arts event organized to remember and honor master bookbinder William Anthony. Craig is very friendly with a warm smile that reflects a hint of humor. A long grey braid falls down his back; his eyes are blue as sky. He agreed to be interviewed, so I traveled to his home/bindery in the unincorporated countryside outside of San Marcos, TX, just south of Austin. A long lane leads to his contemporary home, beautifully landscaped with native plants, and with a swimming pool on one side. A vintage 1942 Gibson guitar leans against a wall in the dining room where we sit. Craig used to play long ago, and he still fantasizes about being in a band. He seems to have passed on his musical talents—his son builds guitars; his daughter plays double bass.

It seems that bookbinding chose Craig more than he chose it. After two years of missionary work in Asia, he enrolled as a student at Brigham Young University. An Asian Studies major, he became interested in BYU's extensive collection of books on papermaking and studied all the Dard

Hunter books on the subject. The curator of Special Collections noticed Craig's interest in papermaking. Bookbinding wasn't on his mind when the curator encouraged him to apply for the job of book conservator at BYU. He was offered and accepted the job, and the library agreed to pay him to travel to various places to work and learn with master bookbinders. Craig eventually interned at the Library of Congress in Washington, DC, where he met Don Etherington.

He returned to BYU and developed their book conservation program, working there for five years. He then took a job as book conservator at the University of Texas Humanities Research Center, where Don Etherington was then head of the conservation center.

Craig excelled at bookbinding. His ability to develop and execute solutions for complex binding projects made him well respected in the field. Leaving institutional life, he started Jensen Bindery (euphemistically called "two guys in a garage") with good friend, Gary McLerran, in a cramped garage. Four years later, with the support of two financial partners, he started BookLab, Inc. in Austin.

As the business continued to grow and change, BookLab consumed his life. After ten years he was ready to get out. Following the closing of the company, he continued an association with one of the partners doing software consulting. He hadn't been working at the bench, and with the exception of a few colleagues, he had not been in contact with the world of bookbinders. "I lost myself..." With his wife's blessing, Craig took off on a road trip to find direction. He traveled rural roads, camped, played music, visited old friends, spent time in solitude. He returned home still uncertain about what he wanted to do. After considering various book conservation jobs around the country, he relocated to San Marcos and set up BookLab II in his home with the help of Sabina Daly. A few years later, after Sabina moved on to other ventures, Craig re-established contact with Gary McLarren, and "two guys in a garage" were reunited. About 22 years after their original start, he came full circle. Craig has folded himself into the bookbinding community again with his fun-loving nature, his excellence at bookbinding, his sharp mind, and his innovative ideas.

How did you become a bookbinder? What led you to bookbinding?

College meltdown. I didn't know what I was doing in school. I was at Brigham Young University in the early '70's as an Asian studies major.

I didn't know what I was going to do with that. There wasn't much you could do with it back then. I was always looking for something to distract myself with. I stumbled onto an article by Catherine and Howard Clark in a craft encyclopedia on papermaking, and I thought, "Well, that will be fun to do." So I researched papermaking. There were some bibliography titles with the Clarks' article, which led me to a large number of Dard Hunter and Henry Morris books in BYU's Special Collections. These books were completely handmade and were an eye opener. BYU had a big press collection, but nobody had ever looked at them or used them. I was actually the first person to look at many of those books.

I eventually made a paper mold. I went to a sheet-metal shop and had them make me a vat. I bought pulp and started making paper. In the course of my dabbling in papermaking for 6-7 months, one day the curator, Chad Flake, said to me, "We have this position for a book conservator. Why don't you apply for it? I think you'd be really good at it." That didn't interest me at first, because I didn't even know what it was. But he kept bugging me to consider the job. At some point when I has feeling particularly despondent about college and what I was doing there, I thought, what the heck, I'll apply for it. The position had been open for a year. They hired me. I had no experience; I didn't know what I was doing. They said, "We'll send you anywhere you need to go to study and learn. We'll pay for it, and you'll have a salary."

There were only a handful of book conservators then. There was no such position as preservation administrator. The Columbia Preservation and Conservation Studies program didn't even start until 1980. BYU hired me because they thought my interest in papermaking was close enough, and I had a pulse. I think Chad went to A. Dean Larsen, who eventually became my boss, and said, "There is this kid here who might be able to do this." Who knows? Their hiring me didn't have anything to do with what I might have demonstrated except a knack for craft and handwork. I was spending hours up there pouring over an almost complete collection of Dard Hunter books. Chad said, "Come here and let me show you something else in the vault." There were all these Grabhorn Press books and a complete run of Bird and Bull Press books. I started looking at the bindings and thinking, "These are beautiful." But it still hadn't clicked yet.

When I got into the book world, there was no school to go to in the US. There were places to go in Europe and in England, like where Priscilla Spitler, Peter Verheyen, and Frank Mowery went. But there was nowhere to go and study in the states. It was strictly if someone would take you in. So I went to Capricornus School of Bookbinding in Berkeley and studied with Anne and Theo Kahle for three months. I worked with Paul Folger at the Mormon Church Historians Office in Salt Lake and later at the University of Utah. I went to many one-week and two-week workshops wherever I could get them. In between workshops, I worked fulltime and continued my undergraduate studies.

The second year of my employment, they sent me to Library of Congress. Dean Larsen met Fraser Poole of the Library of Congress at an ALA [American Library Association] meeting and said, "We've got this young guy who we've hired to be our book conservator, but he needs some training and experience." Fraser said he'd take me if I stayed for one year. So I went to Library of Congress as an intern for a year in the employ of BYU. That is where I met Don Etherington.

Are you a supporter of workshop training?

I am if it is like it was back then, where people take you in and really teach you something. But if it is a weekend warrior workshop, no. It was when someone would let me come and stay with them, and I would work there, that I learned. When I worked with Paul Folger, I commuted every day to Salt Lake City and worked with him full-time in the shop.

Then of course, there was the year at Library of Congress. During that year Tom Albro, the head of book conservation, would oversee my work during the day. Also, many evenings, Tom would also let me work at his home bindery doing private work. It was an intense year of training.

After I returned to Utah, I continued working at Brigham Young until September of 1981, when I moved to Texas.

It sounds like you fell into bookbinding because someone offered you a position. Is there anything in your past that would have suggested that you would be interested in bookbinding?

That is interesting. I actually made a book right after high school. I made an accordion book. I found it a number of years ago, and I still have it. It was all stuck together with tape, but it was an accordion book in a slipcase. When I was in grade school and made reports, I always labored over those things and spent a lot of time on them; I never just stuck them in a three ring binder. So maybe that is a connection.

Did you have an art background?

I've always dabbled in art. I never majored in art. The thing about this story is that I was raised as a Mormon, and that is why I was at BYU. Two of the years that I would have been in college I was on a Mormon mission to Hong Kong, which is why I was majoring in Asian studies; I had all that language training because I had lived in Hong Kong for two years while everyone else was going to college. I attended one semester of college in Southern California before my mission. I attended BYU for about a year-and-a-half as a student, and then I got the job as conservator; then I finished maybe another three quarters of a year. If I had stayed in school, I would have been a senior. The field really pulled me away from it. The last class I took while I was working was organic chemistry. I couldn't see any reason to take more unrelated classes at that point in my career. I was so busy working: I got to design and build a lab; I was hiring people; I had a staff; I was building the program.

It was unique. I'm still very proud of the program there. After I left the Mormon Church, it became very difficult to be there. You can be a non-Mormon and work there, but you really can't be an ex-Mormon. I had evolved intellectually, and spiritually, if you will, to where I didn't fit in anymore. So when I decided to leave, I had to recruit my replacement, because otherwise they would have been in the same boat they were in five years before, when they hired me.

I had built the program up from a Scotch-tape repair station to a serious, well-developed conservation program with a rare book conservation lab and a repair unit. I think we had 12 people working there then. I recruited and helped convince Robert Espinosa to take the job. He was at Library of Congress, and we had become friends through AIC [American Institute for Conservation]. As a non-Mormon, Robert did not face the same issues that I had as an ex-Mormon.

In the meantime, Don Etherington had heard I was tired of Utah and wanted to do something different. He asked me if I was interested in coming to University of Texas. My wife, Ann, and I came out and interviewed and fell in love with Austin. Don hired me as the head of the book conservation section. I worked there for a little over three years, but I burned out on institutional life. Shortly after I left Utah in 1984, I started Jensen Bindery and did a few small editions, but mostly book conservation and box making and a fair amount of on-site consulting, condition surveys, and things like that. I soon hired Gary McLerran, who had been working at the Humanities Research Center (HRC); we referred to ourselves, tongue in cheek, as "two guys in a garage."

Around that time I met Gabriel Rummonds at the HRC. He had sold a complete collection of Plain Wrapper Press books to Decherd Turner. Gabriel called me up one day and said, "I have this book I'm working on, and we're starting the book arts program at the University of Alabama. Would you come down and consult with me on the book, the program, and the lab?" So I said, "Sure, I'll come down and check it out." In the course of working out some structural issues on the book, I became quite interested in doing the edition myself. I asked, "Who is going to do the binding?" He said, "Well, I don't know. I don't really have any binders I like right now." I said, "Why don't you let me do it?" He said, "Oh, it will be too repetitive; you'll get bored." I said, "No, I think I would really like to bind the edition." He agreed. I wasn't really considering being an edition binder at the time. I thought of myself as a book conservator. But because Gabriel let me do this book, the last Plain Wrapper Press imprint, it immediately put my name on the map as someone who could do high quality edition work. Gabriel is notoriously critical of his binders. He started telling everybody what a good job I did and that I was good to work with.

Suddenly I wasn't a book conservator anymore; I was a limited edition bookbinder. When I met Priscilla Spitler, she had heard about me from my doing the book for Gabriel. She and Pam Smith were doing a road tour, and they came through Austin. Here we were in this little 200-square-foot garage, me and Gary McLerran. They were shocked. That is the reader's digest version of how I got into bookbinding.

So after Jensen Bindery, you started BookLab with two others?

Paul Parisi and Jim Larsen, who own Acme Bookbinding and Bridgeport Bindery (I didn't know all the details at the time), were contemplating merging their two companies. They thought that they would start a separate company to see how they worked together. A mutual friend of theirs had recommended me as a person to perhaps head up that company. Paul Parisi called me and asked if I was interested in going to work for them. Jensen Bindery was about 4 years old at that time, at the end of '87. Paul asked me to come see him in Boston.

I think I was on my way to New York to teach a summer workshop at the Columbia Preservation and Conservation Studies program. The workshop covered things that I thought conservators should know about running a business, even if they were in an institutional setting—how to be productive, how to move things through the shop, how to account for your time, and stuff like that. At BYU, if I wanted new equipment or any kind of growth for the program, I had to show them that I increased my productivity over the previous year. They had a metric that they imposed on me to show growth in production, both in repair and conservation treatments. That was the reason I taught that workshop about the business of conservation at Columbia.

I said to Paul that I was not interested in a job, but I might be interested in a partnership. Our business needed some money at the time. We had grown quite a bit, and we needed some cash to expand. It was hard to get money from banks for what we were doing.

By the time I hooked up with Jim and Paul and formed the partnership we called BookLab in 1988, Jensen Bindery had almost completely abandoned library work. We were doing almost all limited editions. The only things we did for libraries were production runs of boxes. We had gotten completely out of the conservation side of things. In 1988, BookLab began to take a fresh look at library services. That was when we got into preservation photocopying. Gary Frost came shortly after and was the fourth partner. We also did what we called "collection maintenance repair"—a book repair treatment between rare book conservation and library binding.

Did you burn out?

Oh, did I ever burn out! At the end, the partnership wasn't working either. We were competitors more than we were partners. We were competing at the end, and it was an unfair advantage for them, because they had much stronger, bigger companies and access to capital that BookLab didn't have. And because of the partnership arrangement, I couldn't go out for capital myself without having board approval. My hands were tied behind my back for expanding BookLab, which I really wanted to do, particularly in the digital realm. The combination of having a dysfunctional partnership and burning out caused me to approach the partners. I told them I was either going to resign or shut BookLab down and asked them what their preference was. They said, "Shut it down." The last three months of '98, we sold everything.

Did you have a separate place to work when BookLab closed?

When BookLab closed, I didn't do anything. I just holed up at home and tried to regroup mentally. In the meantime Paul Parisi, one of the former partners, offered me a job in Boston. I didn't want to move, so I telecommuted from Austin. He picked up most of BookLab's imaging business and the facsimile business. I went to work for him. I set up half of the front room in our house as an office. I had a scanner there and a couple of computers. I designed and maintained Acme's website. I started working with some of the imaging software and hardware companies to ensure that their systems worked for book production as opposed to office systems. I got really involved in that for about three years as a consultant for Acme with one particular software company. I went to Boston periodically and worked with the imaging staff, setting up their workflow and installing equipment.

Then I burned out again. I think Paul burned out on me too. He wanted me to move to Boston. We seriously looked at it. Ann and I went out there and house shopped, but when I told him what he would need to pay me in order to make a lateral move from the Austin to Boston cost of living, he said that wasn't going to work, so I resigned. That was about a year before we moved to San Marcos.

I didn't do anything for a while and probably had the kind of grieving period I should have had in '98 when we closed BookLab. I really felt like I lost my soul in all these transactions; I'd lost what I was good at. I had almost completely detached myself from the field. I hadn't gone to any professional meetings in a long time, so I hadn't seen anybody except the people I knew in the area. I hadn't made anything. I had been living in this sort of virtual world for three years where everything was electronic; I wasn't making anything physical. Plus I was stuck in the house all the time, so I was really nuts.

With my wife's blessing and approval, I took off on a road trip and drove around the Southwest for about two months, camping and sight seeing. My son was at a guitar-making school in Phoenix at the time, so I drove out there. Then I wove myself back, trying to stay off the interstates. I hung out with some friends along the way. I visited Pam

Craig Jensen's Booklab II bindery.

Smith, who was in a similar transitional stage of her career.

When I got back, I still hadn't figured out what I wanted to do, but I started to look at conservation jobs around the country. In the meantime, Ann had sold her business and was considering a job working for her former business partner at Texas State University here in San Marcos. I encouraged her to take the job with the idea that I'd set up like I did way back in '84 in the garage and go back to a little one person shop. I started calling around. It seemed like there was some work out there, some interest, so that is what I did.

BookLab was one of a kind, wasn't it? It had cool people working there.

Yes, there are a lot of creative people who live in Austin because it's a cool place. We employed a number of musicians and visual artists, interesting people in their own right, never mind what we were doing during the day. They just wanted a good day job, something to pay the bills, but that wasn't demeaning or that wouldn't suck the life out of them. BookLab filled that bill for many of them.

What is BookLab II doing?

Now I am doing limited editions, and lots of box making, and some of the repair type stuff for libraries that Gary Frost and I worked on in the early days of BookLab. I'm not doing treatment work, like rare book conservation. I really don't enjoy that.

I did for a while, but it is tedious and slow. It requires the kind of focus that doesn't come naturally to me, and it's hard to make money at it. People don't appreciate the kind of time that goes into it. So I've pretty much turned that work away and focused on work that is more production oriented or that interests me.

So libraries will send things to you?

Yes. I have my website so people can go there and see what I offer. My love is edition binding, and I love to work with the people that make those books. That is the biggest draw for me. And I like making boxes. One would think that is the most boring of all, but the thing about boxes is that I can almost make them in my sleep. So it's easy to take a bunch of boxes and push them through and get some cash flow off of it. Hardly anyone makes them as neat or as nice as I make them, so I get satisfaction from that. There is hardly any risk at all associated with it. I don't have to handle anything valuable, because the client sends me the measurements. It's a real nice thing to underpin the business with, a foundation to work off of.

People have made boxes for a very long time, but BookLab evolved its own style and construction methodology. BookLab made many thousands of boxes over the years, either for editions or single boxes for institutions. We learned a lot about how to make them. Our goal at BookLab was always to have something that looked and felt like a handmade object, though we weren't hung up by doing everything by hand or by some traditional way that was passed down to us. We didn't see anything wrong with automating where we could if we never compromised the quality. So we developed a lot of production techniques that really squeezed the time down. So instead of taking 2 hours to make a box, it might only take 40 minutes, or so, to make it. Getting from that two hours down to 40 minutes is that the kind of challenge I like. I enjoy working out those kinds of systems and solving those kinds of problems. At BookLab there was always something I could focus my attention on and something I could streamline and smooth out, some assembly sequence that needed greasing or needed something done to it. That was a constant stimulation.

There is a possibility that I'm going to take a partner in the next few months. My friend Gary McLerran may move back here. The original "two guys in a garage" may be back together again. I would like sometime in the future to completely remodel our 1,000-square-foot garage—put skylights in, vault the ceiling, and make it into the perfect studio. That is my ambition for BookLab II: a couple of guys working out of 1,000 square feet as opposed to the upwards of 35 people working out of 10,000 square feet like we had at BookLab. I don't have visions of the original BookLab happening again. I don't know if I have it in me anymore. Plus, I want to be making things. When you get to that size, you spend most of your time managing.

What are some of your favorite parts of being a bookbinder and some of your least favorite?

I told you some of my favorites. I really like trying to figure out how to put things together. I like challenging projects. I like difficult books; books that other people don't want to do as editions. Challenging projects, beautiful books.

I also like projects where people invite me to get involved on the design side. I don't have to have that, but it is a treat to be involved in the design. Early on, I was influenced by Gabriel Rummonds when he said, "I don't want a bookbinder telling me how to design my books." That is why he had problems with a lot of bookbinders. They were really skilled American binders (when he started using state-side people), but until he met me, without fail, they were telling him, "Oh, you don't want to do that, you should do it this way," or, "You don't want that material, you want this material," or, "This color would look better." He didn't want them to do that. He designed his books all the way through; he designed every aspect of the book. He taught me that I was the service provider.

Since then I have always couched my advice to the customer in terms of structural issues or mechanical issues. I might say, "I really love what you are doing here, however for these reasons there might be a problem. Your book may not work very well if I do what you said to do. Here's why." Early on I got focused on structural stuff, the engineering side of it, and we got a lot of weird projects that garnered recognition because other people weren't up to the challenge. The Whitney Museum's *My Pretty Pony* project, a Stephen King, Barbara Krueger collaboration, is a very large book, 17 lbs, with a stainless steel cover that has a clock in it. The first binder just couldn't get his head around the production of it. Our solution was elegant and it is a highly sought-after book.

What about your least favorite part of bookbinding?

I've eliminated a lot of them. We talked about single-item treatment. A lot of the finicky treatment work, I just don't do that any more. I got really tired of it, even when they were wonderful, beautiful books. I have a lot of friends who do treatment work and it works for them, but I burned out early on it.

I like to enlighten clients, but I don't like to educate them on rudimentary stuff, because you have to explain why they can't get what they want for $15 a book. Let's say a medium-size offset company is doing a limited edition for a designer. They are used to going to a place like Custom Bookbinding, a great little trade shop in Austin. About fourteen people work there, just a small little shop. But everything is priced under maybe $15 a book. They have a couple of in-line perfect binders and an old Smyth machine, so they still do sewn books, but they use cheap materials and labor. A potential BookLab II client may have done projects with a shop like that in the past, and then for whatever reason, they come to me. I have to try and explain to them why it is $40 a book instead of $10 or whatever. That is a problem, especially when clients are unwilling to disclose their price point up front.

I think it is key to do what you like to do.

If I hadn't done that book for Gabriel, I probably would still be doing rare book conservation right now, and I would probably be as into it as some of my good friends are. But I got diverted into limited edition work, and that changed my whole outlook on books.

I think back on the BookLab days. Toward the end, I really got tired of dealing with employee problems, which kept me away from doing the things that I love to do. I miss a lot of those people; it was the problems of running a business wore me down.

Which is why you are now in private practice.

The other reason is I just don't know what else to do.

Is there any particular job you have done that is one you are most proud of?

Yes. The Ellesmere Chaucer facsimile was far and away the greatest thing we ever did. I don't have a copy in the BookLab library, which is kind of sad. The super deluxe edition, as it was called, was bound in the same style that Tony Cains specified and did on the original. It is an early 15th century style binding. We did 50 books like that.

I can say with some confidence that, at that time, BookLab was the only company that ever did an edition of authentic medieval bindings. There are lots of facsimile books out there that have wooden boards, but they are not completely authentic in all of their details. Ours was genuine from top to bottom, even the thread and cord. We twisted all the cable that we sewed the book on. We did everything.

It took over a year to do the whole project—50 super deluxe; 100 of what they called deluxe, which was a quarter leather with bare oak board sides, also authentic in all its details; and then there were 100 in what they called the quired edition (folded and gathered unbound sheets) that were in leather-covered boxes with rounded wood spines. That was probably the greatest thing we ever did.

Is there an ideal commission that you would like?

An ideal commission would be an edition of up to around 150 with no constraints on the budget. I'm not talking about the Chaucer thing. It doesn't have to be that elaborate, but a nicely done book, modest sized edition, where they are more concerned about the end product than how much it is going to cost. That is the perfect thing for me. The details can be whatever, I don't care, anything.

For $70 to several hundred dollars a copy in the production costs, we can do all kinds of wonderful things. We can do wonderful things for less than that, but that is kind of pulling out the stops and going for it and doing something really nice; having boxes for it, and going the whole 9 yards. It can be $40 a book and still be really nice. But it seems when you get more into that higher price range, projects start to get interesting and exciting and we can push the envelope and do things we haven't done before. Usually, when people are willing to spend that kind of money, they let me get involved more intimately in the design of it. I am not trying to influence the color scheme or even the way it will look to the layperson, but the details underneath the hood, so they are all genuine, the real thing, and we aren't cutting corners or abbreviating things.

As an independent binder working here at your home, do you have a routine?

I spin my wheels a lot of the time. That is why I am interested in getting the partnership with Gary McLerran going. It will make me more motivated, keep me going. Multiplying by two is going to produce more than double what I am getting times one now.

Do you like working in partnership?

I first started BookLab II with Sabina Daly, who was a great partner. But in that first year or so, there wasn't enough work to support two people, so Sabina moved on. Since then I've been working alone. When I'm by myself, I'm easily distracted and I lose focus. Gary is a person I worked with for two years. I know what his work habits are like; I know him very well, so I am pretty sure it is going to solve the problem. Because there will be only two people, we will be working side-by-side, but there will be a lot of tag-team work; you can really streamline things when you have two people. With one, it is absolutely sequential with everything you do.

We are at that time in our life that we want to slow things down a little bit and neither one of us are so well off that we can just kick back and not do anything. We have to work, but we don't want to work like we are 30, because we're not! It seems like an ideal way to wind down. We've considered calling the partnership "two guys in a garage" but do business as BookLab II. BookLab is such a valuable name. The name is worth a lot because of what the people who worked at BookLab and I did during the 10 years of its existence.

What are your other interests? Is there anything else you would rather be doing?

I am really into music. I play guitar. I used to play a lot when I first met my wife. I was in a folk rock band playing fingerpicking type stuff. If I had been playing all these years, I'd probably be a picker by now, a blue-grasser. This is the pipe-dream side of the things—I always think it would be cool to get in a band and do open mikes and play around.

Every once in a while, I dream of doing all my own stuff where everything I do is mine, including the insides of the books. That is the sort of thing I hold out for somewhere down the road. I've often thought that someday I might have my own press and print my own books. I've done a little bit of design for other people; I've printed a few books with other people. I don't know if I'm really that much of an artist because I've never really tried.

It seems like you've been able to succeed in everything you've tried.

It's a funny field, you know. If you persist and keep at it, you'll have some modest amount of success. You'll find your little niche.

That leads me to my last question. What would be your advice for someone who decides they want to be a bookbinder? Let's say they are just starting out.

They have to love it because it's hard, real hard. It's not the kind of work you get rich doing. I would dispel that idea. I'd have done a lot better monetarily if I'd just stayed in institutional work as a book conservator or preservation administrator.

What I would tell a newcomer to the field, and I've actually had the opportunity to do this a couple times, is try and find the equivalent of what I found when I started out: people who will let you come and work at the bench with them. It means you may have to be prepared to work for free for a while.

I don't recommend workshops unless they are long intensive workshops. Even those I don't think are very beneficial unless you have already had a fair amount of experience. You go and you finesse your craft and your skill level, and you are learning another person's methods and techniques that you can then apply or adapt for your own use. But if you are inexperienced, you don't come away with much; you may think you learned something, but you often come away more confused than when you went in. There are a lot of people out there now who have hung out their shingle, doing their work as professionals, and that is all the experience they have ever had, a handful of short workshops. My advice would be to try and find someone to take you in on an extended basis, a modern version of an apprenticeship. Other than that, I'd say, "Persist!"

That is why I am interviewing private practice binders, because there is not a lot of money in it. I want to know what keeps them in it.

I'm in it because I love the work. I love the challenge, and I love the people I get to work with, both colleagues and clients. There's also a certain amount of satisfaction that comes from being recognized for the quality of my work.

For more information about Craig Jensen and to see examples of his work, go to http://www.bookways.com.

Scott Kellar:
Keeping Traditional Bookbinding Alive

Chicago, Illinois
October 2006

To visit Scott Kellar means that I get to visit my Chicago hometown. I arrive in the northwest side of Chicago in an old, established, well-to-do part of town. Small businesses and stores sprinkle the streets. It is chilly outside on this October day. I park on the street and walk into an office building that includes a travel agency and a computer technology business—not the place I expect to find a bindery. Dressed in jeans and a golf shirt, Scott Kellar meets me at the door and welcomes me in. He is somewhat reserved, and I find myself talking too much, trying to fill in the quiet spaces. He is warm but serious.

His bindery is spacious with high ceilings. Piles of books are stacked on top of metal paper drawers and on worktables that line the walls. It appears that he has plenty of work. Bookbinding equipment is arranged throughout the space—board shear, Kensol and Kwikprint embossing equipment, standing presses, backing presses, guillotine, paper-drying racks. Tools lay scattered on the work areas. On the walls are book-related posters, family pictures, a large fabric print of a Celtic knot through which light filters from the window behind.

Rolls of bookcloth stand vertically, creating a wall that encloses his office. He sits at an old wooden desk in front of a shelf unit loaded with books, mostly about bookbinding. I sit on a metal folding chair next to it. He answers my questions with short but thoughtful answers.

Most of Scott's work involves conservation and restoration. But there is an artist inside him. His design bindings are handsome, well designed, and well executed. He won "best design binding" for a book he submitted to the exhibition/competition, One Book, Many Interpretations, at the Chicago Public Library. We both had attended the opening of the exhibit and awards ceremony at the library preview night. Scott would like to take art classes to learn more about color and design and have time to do more design bindings. With a family that includes two young children, and a wife who stays home to care for them, his spare time is limited. His work is done with great care and judgment in order to maintain a reputation that will bring in an income.

As a young man, Scott learned bookbinding from a book and became a hobby binder. He enjoyed it so much that when a job became available at Monastery Hill Bindery in Chicago, he took it. Although he learned a lot there, he tired of repetitive work and wanted to develop skills in conservation. He kept his eye on opportunities at the Newberry Library and was eventually hired. He credits most of what he learned there to his mentor, Barclay Ogden. After working at the Newberry, Scott went into private practice for five years before taking a job as Collections Conservator at Northwestern University Library. Seven years later, in 1994, he yearned for his own business again and began Scott K. Kellar Bookbinding and Conservation at this location. He feels fortunate to have had great people work for him through the years, and credits them with helping his business succeed.

Scott is an advocate of quality fine bookbinding in America. He helps to keep it alive by teaching bookbinding classes and participating in design binding exhibitions. His design bindings attest to his abilities as a craftsman who can execute a design of simple beauty and intricate detail.

[I traveled to Chicago to attend the opening and awards presentation of One Book, Many Interpretations, an exhibit of design bindings at the Chicago Public Library. Scott and I were both awarded prizes for our bindings.]

It was fun to prepare for this interview. I don't usually sit down and wonder, what is it, exactly, that I do? So I had to collect my thoughts— not that there were any surprises, but it was helpful for me to pull some thoughts together.

I was very encouraged with this exhibit [One Book Many

Interpretations, Chicago Public Library 2006] that you and I were both in. It is nice that we were both recognized [with Best Binding awards] for our work. My colleague, Lesa Dowd, the conservator and design binder at Chicago Public Library, was instrumental in organizing this exhibit.

In what way were you encouraged?

I was encouraged because it was exemplary of what design binding can be and still is for the book world. We were using literature as our medium and it was primarily design bindings with a few artist books sprinkled through. This whole artist book versus design binding phenomenon I think is of very high interest. We are seeing an incredible transformation of the book art organizations and the bookbinding field, especially in this country. I think it raises a lot of questions like, what is the future, if any, of design binding? And what is the future of artist books?

They both have a future, don't you think?

I think they do. But in this particular country there is a change that is a little bit alarming to me because we don't have a lot of people grounded in traditional bookbinding skills. I see a decline in design binding exhibit work in this country, which I think is a result of this. I see a rather fragile base, possibly decaying, that is a concern. A lot of people may not care! But this exhibit demonstrates to me that there is still an interest and an energy in design binding. There was a preponderance of design binding and a smaller quantity of artist books versus what we are seeing in other exhibits.

Getting back to an example of my concern, the Helen Warren DeGolyer competition had a rather small number of books entered this year. That is discouraging because it is all about design binding. There were prizes to win and yet still not much response.

Another example of my concern is that there is less than a handful of people doing design binding in a place the size of Chicago.

It doesn't pay the bills.

No, by itself it doesn't and probably never will except for a few very rare people. There is a relatively large group of book artists and book conservators. They are intermixed, and some people do both. This whole thing has been of interest to me. When literature is chosen as the base, however, I'm seeing the design binding skills come out. When it is completely open, there seems to be a greater amount of artist books coming out. More and more exhibits are of the latter type. What does this say about the place of literature in our modern culture?

What would you say is the defining difference between artist books and design binding?

I will greatly simplify my definitions in order to focus on the 'defining' difference.

Design binding is focused on the intellectual and imaginative content (thoughts, stories, ideas, illustrations) of the printed text. The result is reflective of the book, body and soul. It wants to be read.

Artist books are object/image based, usually adapting book-like characteristics, much more of a sculptural or three-dimensional art form. The result is reflective of the book artist.

There are many other interesting differences and similarities that are significant and have been the subject of countless book art forum discussions.

How did you start in binding? What brought you into bookbinding? And where did you grow up and live?

I was born in Missouri and raised in Seattle, Washington. We moved back to Missouri when I was nine. As far as how it relates to my bookbinding, my parents encouraged me to read. My television watching was limited for which I will be eternally grateful. I think that this had something to do with my interest now in books. I've always liked to work with my hands but I don't know if I can point to anything specifically in my childhood where I was more craft-oriented than anyone else. I got involved in bookbinding after college. A friend of mine saw a bookbinding manual advertised in the Whole Earth Catalog back in the early '70's. He said it might be a nice hobby. At the time I was just doing a nondescript job; I think I was 18 and working at a warehouse or something. So I got this manual, *Basic Bookbinding,* by Arthur Lewis, and I tried to figure out how to bind books from it. That was my first contact with bookbinding. I loved it. It was never completely off my mind from then on.

How did you get materials?

Yellow pages, finding companies under the listing of "bookbinding." Going out there and saying, "I'm trying to learn hand bookbinding out of this manual. Do you have any tools or glue?" Just finding ways and improvising equipment. I remember melting down gelatin animal glue and trying to get that stuff on the spine of a book. The manual didn't say you had to add water to it!

You started bookbinding through a manual. How long did you do that? Did you keep persevering on your own?

This went on for a number of months. Then I wondered if I could get a job at this. I started beating the bushes in Chicago and finally interviewed with John Dean who was the bindery supervisor at the Newberry Library at that time. A friend of mine had walked into the Newberry and noticed that there was a bindery. He said, "Hey, you say that you are interested in this binding thing?" So I went over there, not having any connection with the world of bookbinding or book conservation.

Having no beginning level positions open, John suggested that I develop my skills in a production environment because I think that is how he got started. I can't remember where he is now, though he has made significant contributions to the field of library conservation internationally. He was an accomplished English binder that was hired and brought over by Paul Banks (who was the chief conservator at the time) to run the conservation bindery. He mentioned Monastery Hill Bindery. It was a kind of low-scale production custom bindery, which still included significant manual work. I got a job and worked there for two years. It happened that Richard Baker, a colleague, was also hired at that time. We kept each other company as we both had the same ideals of hand bookbinding with high quality.

I loved the inspiring things that the Arts and Crafts Movement embodied, also the nascent field of book conservation. We both worked there for two years, and we both quit within two weeks of each other, independently of each other's knowledge.

We worked under Josef Zuffant, who was a master binder: both an accomplished finisher and forwarder. He had been there since the '20's. We were trained to do a lot of different things—case-making, casing in, rounding and backing, leatherwork, hot stamping. Encyclopedia Britannica had a contract with them so if there was a client that wanted a leather-bound set, we would bind it using huge hand-operated standing presses to case them in. It was great experience with repetitive tasks to train muscle memory. For that I am grateful.

Did you know when you were doing it that that was what you really wanted to do?

Yes, I knew where I wanted to go. The ideal of hand bookbinding was what I still wanted to do, and this was close enough to it for the moment. We were forwarding books, rounding and backing, paring leather, developing hand skills. It was a start. I even liked it to a degree, even though it could be a bit boring and repetitive with a factory environment. We punched in and out for our half-hour lunch breaks. It was not to be forever! But Josef Zuffant had a lot to teach. He had been doing the fine bookwork for 50 years by the time we got there. Even though they didn't use all of his skills appropriately, he had a lot to teach. Unfortunately, he also had some mental issues.

At that point what led you away? Did you want to try a different direction?

At that time I got a job at the Newberry Library. I had been waiting for an opening there. I was constantly checking with them because that is where I really wanted to go. The Newberry was a cutting-edge library conservation center. Paul Banks, Gary Frost, Sherelyn Ogden, and Barclay Ogden were all there. Barclay became my mentor when I finally did get a job in the conservation bindery. At that time, they bound all their own periodicals and did enclosure making and miscellaneous repair work. They had the conservation bindery and also a conservation lab, in the basement, where Paul Banks and Gary Frost worked. There were seven or eight people in the bindery doing production-type work with a conservation emphasis. Barclay Ogden was a very enlightened mentor for me. He knew that I was eager to learn as much as I could. I became assistant supervisor and embarked on a reading program under his leadership. I went through a lot of good basic literature as preparation for moving in the direction of book conservation.

What kind of basic literature did he want you to read?

The Newberry had developed a great research collection about books. I read literature on the history of bookbinding, papermaking, printing, rare book bibliography, etc. I also read everything pertaining to the physical materials used in bookmaking, from its infancy to the modern time. Also, currently available information on the art and science of book conservation. It began to open up a whole new world for me. I saw a lot of things come together from what I studied. That is what we did in the reading program.

Was he the most influential person in your bookbinding career?

Yes, in book conservation particularly. More the history and conservation of book materials and, to a great degree, structure. He was fascinated with structure. He had a very inquisitive mind. We would try all kinds of things to better bind and conserve the books—different kinds of endsheets, etc. I designed an adhesive fan-binding machine that we constructed out of materials from the local hardware store. We pursued adhesive-binding for periodicals instead of oversewing. He was very encouraging in my pursuit of becoming a bookbinder and book conservator.

My life as a design binder, however, was influenced by others. The great binders from the Arts & Crafts Movement on are probably the most influential. Kerstin Tini Miura, a design binder who continues to produce beautiful work, was the most influential living binder in this area. Classes, methods, and techniques that I acquired under her have been invaluable.

How long did you work at the Newberry?

I believe it was seven years. I was also developing more traditional bookbinding skills at that time through various workshops. I also took classes with Bill Minter.

And then at the end of those seven years, did you go off on your own?

Yes, I did. But before that, I was able to spend some time in the lab with Paul Banks and Gary Frost and do some work with rare material. The whole department was encouraging. A lot of people went through there as interns back then that are now department heads. From there, I went on my own for the first time. It was called Scriptorium Bookbinding. I've been in private practice twice. Barclay Ogden had left for bigger and better things. He was, and I believe continues to be, the preservation officer at Berkeley. Things ground to a halt as far as my interests at the Newberry. I had been there a long time and was no longer content in my position. I went off and started my own business in bookbinding, book conservation, and box-making. I had my studio briefly on Montrose Avenue, then for five years on Damen Avenue. That worked out pretty well for me in the 1980's. I had one assistant and a couple part-time helpers. I also taught bookbinding one night a week at the studio.

After five years, I took the job as Collections Conservator at

Northwestern University Library in Evanston and developed their conservation lab, treatment manuals, and policies. It must have been 1986-94. I seem to have worked in seven or eight-year increments! That was a very valuable experience for me and generally interesting and useful in developing management skills. However, after a certain point, I had developed the conservation program to a point that it didn't really require any more creativity. I was at a maintenance point and not using my craft skills very much because I had so many administration responsibilities.

Not being able to work at the bench because of administrative duties seems to go with the territory, doesn't it?

It's an old story, yes. If you want a decent job with decent pay, they will put you in a place where you are not going to be working on the bench. It is universal. They may even lie and tell you that you will, but you won't! Institutions require extensive administrative responsibilities of anyone in a professional position. Apparently it's a law of the universe.

After eight years, I was getting uncomfortable with where I was at and where I was going, and where I wasn't going, with my own skills and interests. I considered going private again, which I finally did with my current studio, Scott K. Kellar Bookbinding and Conservation. I left Northwestern and began again in 1994 at this location in Chicago.

You can go in whatever direction you want.

Yes, there is a certain freedom, and there is also plenty of work. Doing work of the highest quality and being respected for my craft and aesthetic skills is very important to me.

[We talked about how Scott finds people to work with him.]

Julie Naggs had previously worked with Bill Minter. He moved to Pennsylvania, so I asked her to work with me. She worked for me for eight or nine years. Julie Naggs is an expert bookbinder, learned very quickly, and has a fine sense of aesthetics. She married, started her own shop, and then had a child. She has a nice studio and carries on the tradition, doing more design type work than I do—presentation cases, albums, portfolios, new stuff for corporations and individuals. After she left, Laura Berenger moved into the city from the East Coast. She has been an incredible person to work with too—talented and dedicated. She has since had one baby and works three days a week.

I have two other great part-time people doing things that I need to get done. Ideally, I would like to work again with a full-time assistant.

What do you like most about being an independent bookbinder?

I love the independence of setting my own priorities and hours. Business and organizational work takes time, but 60% to 70% of my time is spent at the bench.

How many hours do you work each week?

I teach class Monday nights here except in the summer months. I teach the advanced bookbinding class at Columbia College in the spring on Thursday nights. So I teach two classes a week at those times. I work 40-50 hours a week, maybe 60 hours in the spring. I don't kill myself, and I don't want to be a workaholic—I have a family. I have two children. Sofie is about to turn four. Caelen is two-and-a-half. I love my family. My wife, Christy, also an artist, is very supportive of my craft.

Is there a certain type of bookbinding that you are partial to?

I guess I like any job that I can do well. I like restoration work. I like to successfully complete a challenging job. I like it to come out right. All along the way I'm not often sure, and I have to work through it and make a lot of decisions—let it sit overnight, and come back to it, and then see that it's done and it's right. That's really satisfying.

That doesn't mean you like an easy job. You say you like it to come out right, but I hear that you like the challenge.

To take something that has been torn apart and treated poorly and getting it back together, restoring something old so it is still functional and looks similar to the original, I get pleasure out of that. Conservation, restoration—those are the two areas, basically. I enjoy the restoration more than making a nice leather album because of the sense of accomplishing a special challenge, bringing something of quality that is old and deteriorated back to close to the original state. With design binding, it is different and isn't part of my job. I do occasional commissions, but mostly I do exhibit work for my own purposes. I get a slightly different satisfaction from that. It is also a challenging job, and I like bringing it to a successful conclusion. It includes design of course.

I think you have a good design sense. Did you have an art background?

No formal background.

It's a very clean, nice design sense.

Thank you. It is a struggle for me to come up with a design. I can spend as much time on the design as executing the entire book.

How do you come up with a design? Do you read the book and let it simmer?

Yes, then start sketching. I feel the lack of experience in drawing. I wish I could draw better, and I wish I could visualize better—look at my idea, make changes or else discard it. Often I will proceed and proceed and proceed, then toss it in the wastebasket!

What about the things you really dislike about your job?

Oh, there is plenty of that. Dealing with annoying clients, but as long as I have plenty of work, I deal with them as briefly as possible. But sometimes I have continuing clients that are a little annoying that I have to deal with. There is a lot of boring work in conservation— everybody knows that—so I get material from archives or institutions that is as boring as dirt, but it is bread and butter work. If there is a large quantity of it, you can multiply your profit, and it can be an important part of the income. That is not particularly pleasant, but it is not horrid. I enjoy coming to work. I hate making mistakes. I hate coming up with a solution that turns out not to be the right solution.

Do you find that you are successful in your pricing?

Yes, pretty successful. I don't go about it terribly scientifically, but I have a basic sense of what I want to charge people. I want my work to be high quality. I want that to be the first thing that people know about me. Then I will charge accordingly—charge well for my work, but make sure it is the best possible work that they can get. Anything else someone else can take.

Do you generally refer them to someone else?

Those people are usually not really interested in this anyway. They just didn't know it. Some say, "Well, I can buy a new copy for less than that." I say, "Do it!"

A lot of my work, over two-thirds, is from continuing clients. They know what they're getting; they know what I can do for them.

You have to educate your new clients. Do you charge for your bids?

I don't if they bring it here. If I have to go there, which I rarely do, I'll charge for that.

Scott Kellar's bindery.

If they bring the work here, can you bid the job on the spot?

If it is a single item or a few things, I do it on the spot as much as possible. If an institution brings me several boxes of stuff, they are usually continuing clients, so they aren't going to say, "Oh forget it!" after I've spent several hours going over it. I will send them the estimate with a description of all the things I would do. Then they can come back and comment, and finally we settle and generally go ahead with it. But I don't charge separately for those estimates even though they take a long time. It's sort of included in the whole job.

What about turn-around time? Are you able to tell them when it is going to be ready and stick to it?

I used to [be able to]. I'm starting to drag a little bit. I'm doing work that I received in May. I'm telling people four months. I occasionally do rush work. It has been four months or as long as five months for regular work. It has been amazingly consistent, three-and-a-half to four months for a long time, and I have no idea why. We just do the work and it keeps coming in. I don't ask for it. We have 40 or 50 jobs sitting here waiting.

Do you advertise?

I don't advertise. It's mostly word of mouth. I have a website. Until this year I had a listing in the yellow pages, but somehow that got dropped. I've had this website, *www.scottkkellar.com,* for a couple years now. Mostly, if people call me, they have been referred to me. I'll chat with them, and I'll tell them to check out the website to get more information. I use it that way.

Do you have someone who takes care of your website?

Yes, I have a web mistress who is actually a book artist who designed my website because she is into graphic design as well. Her brother has a webhosting business so she connected me. It is nice to have.

If they are looking for me, they will find me, so I do get a little bit of business that way, but not much. There are some ways to tweak your website to get it to pop up. I have a colleague who has a web guy who gets his website to pop up before Don Etherington's website.

Have you had any famous clients?

Probably the most famous client is Oprah. I've done a few things for her. You know she always promotes reading. One Christmas she was giving away blank journals to her friends, so I made 125 of these for her. There is a small inscription in front. And then we made a photo album, a gift from Stedman, of her African visit. Not too many other famous clients. I've done a couple things for movie producers, like for *The Lake House* with Sandra Bullock, which is kind of celebrity-like.

Who are most of your clients—institutions, individuals?

It is really a combination of institutions, individuals, collectors, and book dealers. We get a quantity from institutions when they do come over.

Do people ever bring you an old book and ask you if conserving it will lower its value?

I get that question a lot. I say if it is properly conserved, it will increase the cost in most cases. There are a very, very small number of book artifacts that you don't want to touch for any reason whatsoever. The book dealers usually know that themselves. There was a book by Mark Twain, *Punch,* first edition, which he had used to annotate to make the second edition. I made a box for it. It was pretty unreadable, but it was in that category. If I ever run across something and a red flag comes up I say, "I really want to research this and make sure that it is okay to touch it." By and large, things are better off if they are functional. We are such a niche profession. Reputation is what people should look for when getting work done.

What relationships do you develop with your clients?

The longer you have a relationship, the easier it is to work with them. Some want to go over all the details; some just want you to take care of it. Some are more likable than others; they become friends. You get a fair number of eccentric people because of what are we doing—something that is unusual.

What are your gifts and abilities that make you a good bookbinder in your perception?

I think I have hand skills and dexterity, which is not uncommon, although not everybody has it. Experience, being in it as long as I've done it, being able to use that experience to solve problems and recognize problems, remember solutions, combine them to come up with new ones. Always keeping an ear to the ground about what other people are doing, new things being used, new ideas. I think that I have an aesthetic sense as well.

Do you think things like the Guild of Book Workers Standards are useful?

The Standards seminars are great. The bookbinders listservs are occasionally useful; being around other people who are intensely involved in what you are doing is nice, though I feel somewhat isolated. Having a really good assistant is very useful because you can bounce things off each other and all of a sudden come up with new things. I think teaching is a gift too. I think I can do it. My students keep coming back. But I've seen really good teachers, and I don't think that I'm in that category.

I tend to be a question-answerer, or if I spot a problem, I'll say something. But to take somebody and push them and mold them, I don't even know if I can even do that in one night a week. But we have a good time. It's kind of a social thing too.

What would you like to achieve in bookbinding that you haven't yet achieved?

I would like to do more design binding, get better at it. That to me is like building a portfolio. I wish I had more free time! Making a living and pursuing artistic goals are two full-time jobs. I think we all struggle with that, unless we are being subsidized.

Is there anything you would rather do than bind books?
No.

If you won the lottery, would you still bind books?
Yes, as I mentioned before, I'd do more design binding. I don't know if I could handle it full-time. I possibly could. Who knows? I will work on it for a weekend, and it sits there all week long. There is the unconscious process going on where you are not thinking about it directly, but by the time you get there again it is fresher; it has sort of simmered, and you can move ahead a little easier. I think if I had to work for eight hours a day on design binding, it would drive me crazy.

What would be your advice to someone who is considering a career in bookbinding?
As far as hand bookbinding in this country goes, there is the AHAA School (American Academy of Bookbinding) and North Bennet Street Craft School. A few universities have useful programs. Otherwise, apprentice with an experienced binder. I think determination, commitment and patience, and often mobility, will be required of anyone, especially in this country. It is possible for one to get a lot out of smaller training opportunities with the best teachers if you work hard. There is certainly a great need for new talent.

Is there anything else you want to share?
I think it would be fun to self-publish a children's book—collaborate, write, illustrate, and bind a book with somebody—do the whole book. That is something I hope to do some day.

For more information on Scott Kellar, and to see examples of his work, go to http://www.scottkkellar.com.

Sol Rebora:
Creating Design Bookbindings in Buenos Aires

Buenos Aires, Argentina
(interviewed in Dallas, Texas)
October 2006

"I have been trying to reach you for so long!" I heard the Argentinean accent of Sol Rebora's voice on the phone. There were two weeks left of Sol's month-long fellowship at the Southern Methodist University's Bridwell Library where she studied the Bridwell's collection of historic bindings and worked on a binding for the library. We were at opposite ends of the SMU campus the entire month, neither of us aware of our close proximity. We had met briefly a year before when she visited the campus during the month that master binder Jan Sobota worked in the library's conservation lab. She had shown me her well-executed design binding with its delicate-looking onlays that playfully opened to reveal surprises underneath. Her youth, fresh designs and enthusiasm impressed me.

We meet for a brisk, outdoor lunch on campus. She stands out among the typical golden-haired, conservative-looking SMU students. Her long dark hair curls and cascades down the back of her petite frame. Her dark eyes engage easily. A friendly smile highlights a long face that extends to a prominent chin. A long flaxen scarf circles her neck several times before artistically draping over her shoulder. She looks creative and exotic. In her lovely Argentinean accent she tells me about her fellowship opportunity at SMU, her binding experience, her life in Buenos Aires. Her energy is infectious. I want to interview her for my collection. She is only going to be here for another ten days. She is interested in teaching decorating techniques to local bookbinders. We plan a workshop the following week. She will teach her style of leather inlays and gold-tooling. The class fills. Sol's easy-to-execute technique makes use of small pieces of leather, great for someone on a budget. She is a conscientious teacher—she communicates clearly and is mindful of her students' comprehension of what she is teaching.

Sol's excellence at binding is a result of her persistent and resourceful character. Though she had some training in basic bookbinding as part of her schooling, there were no opportunities for learning fine binding in her hometown of Buenos Aires, and there were no guarantees that bookbinding would provide a living for her there. She was a young adult who had never left Argentina. Her father had passed away. Her mother worked as an artist. Sol was responsible for supporting herself. Despite the challenges, Sol managed to find ways to study bookbinding with some of the world's best bookbinders teaching today. She attended conferences in England and America, introduced herself to bookbinders, has entered and been accepted into prestigious fine binding exhibitions, and has already won numerous international awards.

Through hard work and well-thought out decisions, she transformed herself in less than ten years into a noted independent, self-supporting design binder, breathing energy and youthful life into the field of design binding.

When did you start bookbinding?
I started working with bookbinding when I was 17.

How did you begin?
I went to a secondary school, which was kind of an art-technical school. During six years, I had taken different classes of art such as drawing and composition. From the fourth to sixth year, you could specialize in graphic design, interior design of houses, or fine arts. I chose the fine art specialization. I had bookbinding for three years as one of the classes. I also learned to work with metal, silver and brass, and engraving.

My aunt is an antiquarian bookseller. She needed some bindings for the books she would sell, so she asked me if I would do them. I started to work when I was 17 just to have money for me. That was the way I began working with cloth bindings. At that time, I thought I would be a fashion designer.

My boyfriend at that time wanted to make a trip to study outside the country, so he went to the Italian Consul to get information. He got a pamphlet for me about a Florence institution of book restoration and conservation. That is how I got the idea to work with books as a professional.

When I was 17, I was in the fifth year of secondary school. Through my brother, who was working in a conservation and restoration materials shop, I had the opportunity to work for an artist who needed to put all her work together in a book to show at an art gallery. She went to this shop to buy some material, and she asked him how she could make this book to show her work. My brother thought I could do it. I did it, and she was very happy with it. It was a very precious work for her. She showed it to the curator of the gallery. This man asked her who made the construction of the book, so she told him about me. He asked because he is an editor of books for collectors. He had made an edition of 40 books, and he needed a person to make the 40 boxes for those books. He had a bookbinder, but he died, so he needed to find somebody else. He said nobody wanted to do these boxes; I don't know why. When I met him, he asked me if I could do these boxes. I thought I could do it. It was a great opportunity; I had to try. He wanted them to close in a certain way, very precise, with one millimeter of air between the top and back. So I tried to do this, and I did it. I started to work for this man. He was 80 years old at this time.

I was making funny design bindings at school, not really fine bindings, but I started to show these books to him. He realized I was interested in bookbinding, and he showed me a book with photographs of twentieth-century French bookbinding with all the beautiful designs. I realized I wanted to learn to make fine bindings. At that time, I was thinking of doing conservation and restoration, and going to Florence to study it. He said in Buenos Aires, people were already working with conservation and restoration but there was no one working with design bindings, which I really preferred.

My father was an artist; my mother is an artist too, both painters. I always liked drawing and working with color. Since I was a child, I liked to work with my hands; I liked craft things. Design bookbinding was a perfect combination.

By the time I met this editor, my father had already died, and I needed to work. So the editor asked me, "Do you want to work? Do you need to work?" I said yes, so he started to give me work. He was also the president of Bibliophiles Society of Argentina, so he knew a lot of collectors. He started to recommend me to other collectors. So I started to work with other collectors.

Once I finished secondary school, I studied for two years with a private teacher, a bookbinder in Buenos Aires. I learned to do half and full-leather, French bindings. I set up a place to work at my mother's house. I would do new bindings, mostly for books on the history of Argentina. They were either not yet bound or needed a new binding on an already bound book.

When I decided to be a bookbinder, I didn't really know if I could make a living at it. In Argentina you never know what is going to work. It is difficult to get a job, and the economy is always going up and down. There are lots of people who have great training and abilities, but then can't get a good job. So I thought, "I am going to be a bookbinder. I like it, and if it works, good, and if it doesn't work I'll do something else." When I think about it, it had a big relationship with the fact that my father died, and I needed to build something strong in my life, a good career, something that would support me.

I started to look for scholarships or fellowships or financial help to get out of Argentina, to study in Europe or here in the States, to have good techniques, and get a good quality of bookbinding training so I could have work in my country. I did it! I started to get fellowships and financial help.

First, I tried with institutions, and I didn't get it. But in the middle of trying, I met Ernesto Lowenstein who worked as a partner with the old man that I told you was an editor. Together they had Dos Amigos Press. I started to work for him. He has been absolutely important in my career, and he is still accompanying me in my career. He met Deborah Evetts in New York when he was on a trip trying to organize an exhibition of Dos Amigos' books. Deborah went to Buenos Aires, to give a talk on an exhibition of art in Argentina, invited by Ernesto, where Dos Amigos was located.

During this visit to Buenos Aires she went to my studio because Ernesto asked her to go see my work. He wanted her to tell him whether my work was good or not. She visited me. She asked me how long I had been working on bookbinding, and some other questions. She recommended I go to Canada to study with Betsy Eldridge who had intensive workshops for one week each session. Betsy teaches French, English, and German techniques. I would learn for one month and then go back to Buenos Aires to work.

We started to work on this plan, I think in May. In October of that year, 1998, I would go to Toronto and take classes there. I started to study English. I had been studying French because I wanted to go to Paris, but as this opportunity appeared, I started to learn English. I took four days of classes per week, three hours per day. It was crazy. The plan was to go two weeks in Toronto, one week in NY, and back to Toronto for one week more. Fifteen days before I was to leave for Toronto, I had a problem with my arm. One of the veins had a block, and so I couldn't make the trip. I was in the health center for fifteen nights. I think it was because I was really stressed. It was too much. It was going to be the first time I would take a plane, the first time I was going to be in another country. I was working very hard to get everything ready so I could be away for one month because I already had clients. I was twenty years old, and it was too much.

My first studio, after the place I had in my mother's house, was an atelier for artists in an artist town in Buenos Aires called San Telmo. I rented a place to set up my independent bookbinding studio. I decided to live there so I could stay up working as long as I wanted. In this building of little apartments, I didn't have a private kitchen or washroom. I had to share everything. It was fun; I was 20 years old, and it was a good way to start.

Six month later, I rented a big house together with my mother and a friend, artists both of them, so that everyone had a nice studio and a little more privacy and quietness.

It was at the end of the year that I was supposed to go to Toronto. One or two months after I got out of the hospital, I took a plane to NY. I visited Deborah Evetts and the Morgan Library there. It was great trip. I went to see bookbinding shops and museums, and I met the great city of NY. It opened my mind.

The next year, in October, I went to Toronto and New York and also two days to Montreal. I went to Montreal to meet Louise Genest. She was really nice, and she told me about the competitions in Europe and in the United States. I showed her a portfolio with photographs of my work. She told me lots of things about my work, including how important it was to take good photographs of my bindings. She also told me to send books to the competitions because it is a way to show my work. Maybe a collector would see my work: "If you get into an exhibition through a juror, it makes a reference of your work." I didn't know anything. It was so interesting.

After this trip, Ernesto Lowenstein, who had paid for my trip and courses, and had helped me to organize everything, asked Betsy for a letter referencing my work during the courses; it was a great letter, and he was really happy. Then I went back to Buenos Aires for one month and a half and then left for another month in Toronto, New York, and North Carolina.

The first time I was in Toronto, I took Bookbinding I and II, and then I went to NY to visit Deborah Evetts. With Deborah I didn't really take classes. We talked about design and techniques, she showed me her bindings, but she couldn't technically teach me because she was working at the Morgan Library.

On the second trip to Toronto, I took Bookbinding III and finished learning gold-tooling. I already knew how to do it but I learned a really good way with Betsy Eldridge. Then I went on a one-week trip to North Carolina to learn edge-gilding from Monique Lallier. It was really interesting and fun to learn with her. Then I went back to Buenos Aires, and I started to work with all the things I learned.

After these experiences, I realized I had to learn how to make a design for a binding, especially after a talk with Deborah. She told me I have to think of design on three different planes or surfaces: front cover, back cover, and spine, and they also had to work together. So I started to take classes with my mother. For three years, we did exercises and every design I made, I worked with her to learn about the compositions of a drawing and the colors. I prepared the drawing on white paper, but then I tried different combinations of colors making a collage with papers. I really learned a lot with her. Now I still make the design on a white paper, but then I try different composition of color on the computer; it is really better.

The next year, I went to Monique's atelier for 15 days to learn design bookbinding, the French style. I made two projects with her. We had classes for eight hours a day, and I could stay working longer if I wanted. It was excellent!

I started to send books to exhibitions. The first important competition in which I participated was in Europe; it was Point de Paris.

Sol Rebora's studio.

They made the selection and had the opening exhibition in Belgium. Then they sent the exhibition to Blaizot, one of the most important antiquarian booksellers in Paris. It was great! I was really happy because it was the first time I sent a book to a competition, and I was able to get into it, together with bookbinders like Monique Lallier, Edwin Heim, or Paul Delrue, whom I had read about.

It was 2001, and in Argentina we had a big economic crisis, so I couldn't afford the courses outside the country anymore. I started to work in Buenos Aires with all the information I had from the trips and courses. I kept sending bindings to different competitions. But I didn't know exactly if what I was doing was the way to become a good designer bookbinder, because I was working alone in Buenos Aires. I didn't have any person to ask whether my bindings were good or not. It was like a whole world that I didn't know anything about. "What do you have to do to became a designer bookbinder?" was my question. I didn't know. I found this answer in Ascona, Switzerland when I met with Edwin Heim.

The first time I went to Ascona was in June 2003, for the opening of the exhibition and competition, Innovation Prize, which Centro del bel Libro organized. I had participated in it, and my book got into the exhibition. After a year-and-a-half, I took a plane again to connect with the bookbinding world; I arrived in Ascona. The experience was so rich. I stayed in Ascona for five days. I visited the bookbinding school, which I loved, and I met great people and great bookbinders. I had the opportunity to have a personal meeting with Edwin Heim, who was very kind. He took the time to see two books I had with me, and we spent time talking about design bookbinding. I remember it so well; almost every word he told me was a complete discovery for me.

In the past, I would read the book and think about a design by looking at the illustrations of the book, try to find images from the book. He offered to me a completely different way. I remember he took a white paper and a pencil, and he started to make a list (I still have this paper with me, like a souvenir). Read the book, yes, but think about the paper of the book, the color, the texture, the printing design, its shape and its size, the letters, the colors of the print or the illustrations if it has them, also the smell. Then I think which construction, which material—leather, paper, cloth—and create a design to make it one, bringing together binding and textblock.

Since December of 2003, I have been going to Ascona to take different courses. For two of them Edwin was not the teacher, but I asked to meet with him to show him some books I had made in Buenos Aires and see what he thought about them. I had learned so much from him. He has been really influential to me.

Every time I talked with bookbinders like him, or Sün Evrard (who I met at Society of Bookbinders Conference 2003 where she gave a talk), it's so interesting; I learned so much from people like them. They work so precisely and think about design, and yet in a deep way which gives me a great feeling. This is what I'm interested in.

How do you know how to price your work—per hour, per job?
I try to price it per hour, plus materials. But it is hard. Now I am starting to learn more about it. It is really hard, and I have asked a lot of questions to other bookbinders and booksellers. I try to see what the prices are in my country and what the prices are outside of my country. Now, after I have been working more than ten years, I have a better idea of what my prices should be. Of course if my work improves, the prices will go up too, because I have to ask prices according with that too. It has to be a balance—if I ask too much, I probably won't have

clients; if I ask a price too low, they probably think my work is not good enough.

What is your favorite part of being a bookbinder?

I can't say I have one favorite part, but the feeling of taking a book which is not in good condition or doesn't have a binding, and giving it a nice and beautiful "house" to live longer, and thinking of materials and a design for it, and once it is finished, if I really like the result, I get so happy. I could say that is one of my favorite parts of being a bookbinder. Then it is so great if the client also likes it. When I go to their houses and see other bindings I have made and see how they look on their bookshelves, it is a great feeling too.

I love when I have to think of how to do a very special piece—like somebody asks me to make a box for a couple of books that need to be put together in a precise way, or with special materials that the project requires, I get very enthusiastic. I like to share with my client the feeling of looking for something special, even when it is very simple and precise—precious. It is clear that I love to work with full-leather bindings on very special books, playing with colors and textures, and creating an original design; this is the best for me.

What is your least favorite part of bookbinding?

I don't really like the sewing part and the sanding; it is so boring for me. I have to make a special effort to concentrate, especially on sanding boards, because it looks like an easy part, but if it is not good enough, you can see it through the leather and it can't be fixed.

Is there anything you would rather do as a career?

I would probably like to be a singer. I love it, and I do it as a hobby. I discovered how much I loved it about two years ago. If I took up singing instead of bookbinding, I don't know what I would have been doing during the last ten years. Or if I wasn't bookbinding, perhaps I would do jewelry. I studied it one year after I finished secondary school with the intention of including it in the bindings. I liked it very much, but then I realized that I preferred to use that time for bookbinding.

What would you like to achieve that you haven't achieved yet?

I would like to learn more about non-conventional bookbinding constructions, or non-adhesive construction—play with different materials. Even though I love French construction and I work with it in trying to find or introduce special materials or ways to work with the leather, I would like to really go deeper. I know in a couple of years, I will find the time to spend more hours on those kind of things.

I would like to work more with artist books making the inside also or work together with other artists like painters or photographers and collaborate.

What advice would you give to someone who is interested in pursuing bookbinding as a career?

The first thing I would say is that bookbinding looks like it is not so difficult! But it is; it takes time to learn. First your mind must understand, but then it takes time until your body and your hands understand it. I think bookbinding is as difficult a career as any other one. If you want to be a good professional, the difficult part is that there isn't a university to go through, during five years let say, that tells you what to do and what to read. In bookbinding, you have to build your university. For me it was important to learn about drawing and composition of colors and shapes; it is not only knowing diverse bookbinding techniques. Be patient through it, learn from different teachers, and then take the things you like and find your own way to work with books.

A book is a precious object, and it is important to think about it. Once a client, an antiquarian bookseller, told me, "We shouldn't think we are the owner of a book; we should think we pay a rent for it when we buy it, and then somebody else is going to take care if it after us, so it is important to be careful with what we do with it." I think being a designer bookbinder is a beautiful career, really rich not only for the fact of making a beautiful book, but also because there is a big world around us. There is always something new to learn, to create, competitions, conferences, courses around the world with different teachers with different techniques and ideologies, so I think it is just great. I love it.

For more information on Sol Rebora, and to see examples of her work, go to http://solrebora.com.ar

Catherine Burkhard:
The Bible Lady

Dallas, Texas
January 2007

The Bible Lady. So many bookbinders tire of rebinding and restoring Bibles. But Catherine Burkhard enjoys working on them and has earned the reputation as *The Bible Lady* in the Dallas area where she lives. She finds great joy in making old things new again, and especially in fixing people's cherished Bibles so they can continue using them.

I arrive at Catherine's home/studio, a place I have been to several times when she hosted bookbinding workshops. She answers the door with a smile, short white hair in place, wearing purple, her signature color. She leads me into a cozy living room filled with knick-knacks, symbols of her Lutheran faith, a bottle collection, and many things purple—pillows, afghan, a stuffed animal. The walls are artfully decorated with framed pieces of her attractive calligraphy—scripture, inspirational verses. We sit close so she can hear me. Catherine and I share the same initial bookbinding teacher, Dorothy Westapher, who taught bookbinding in Dallas from 1976 to 1999. Catherine was already a calligrapher, with her children almost grown, when she started taking weekly bookbinding classes from Dorothy at the Craft Guild of Dallas, and then in Dorothy's home. After taking classes from Dorothy for many years, Catherine began teaching bookbinding classes at the Craft Guild of Dallas, and then later in her home where she continues to teach, in addition to doing custom bookbinding jobs.

In her one-story 1950's ranch style home, Catherine has converted the den into a classroom/studio. Through the use of all sizes and styles of storage bins and a custom-made tabletop (leaving no space unused), she has created storage areas and a workspace for six students. Empty bins for student supplies are stacked under the worktable. Tidy, space-efficient storage containers seem to hold every tool I have ever yearned for. Against one wall is a tiny wooden shelf unit that holds a collection of at least 50 miniature books, many of them design bindings. Another shelf holds miniature bookbinding equipment. All wall space is used—either for storage, books, or for attractively framed calligraphy. A TV and rows of CDs and DVDs create an entertainment center on one shelf. The workspace spills into the kitchen, in which she tucks a Kutrimmer, a file, storage drawers of more supplies, and a small round table that doubles as an eating table and extra student workspace.

The kitchen/studio opens to an addition that attaches the house to the garage and includes an outer door that provides an entrance for students and clients. The garage has been converted into a well-stocked warehouse. Tall metal shelves are lined up with just enough room for one to walk between and browse at the stacks of clearly priced items for sale—press boards, rows of mending tape, all types of adhesives, rulers of all kinds, bone clasps, cleaning pads and erasers, knives, bone folders, brushes, soaps, lotions, leathers, decorative papers, Japanese tissues, book cloth—row after row of stuff. I'm in heaven. Paper drawers support another work area near plastic bins that house client books waiting to be worked on. A guillotine, another Kutrimmer, a drill press, a polypress (German press and plough), and another TV are also housed in the garage. Besides the affordable cost of her classes, one of the great perks of taking classes from Catherine is the plethora of bookbinding supplies available that can be purchased at reasonable prices.

In her spare time, Catherine carries out the duties of Secretary of the Guild of Book Workers and newsletter editor of the GBW's regional Lone Star Chapter. She encourages her students to attend the GBW Standard of Excellence annual meetings where a devoted entourage can usually be found surrounding The Bible Lady.

When did you start bookbinding and how did you get interested?

Actually I started formal training in about 1985. But I had already done some binding via the calligraphy world. In fact there was one major workshop where we had to do a manuscript and bind it. And I had done simple bookbinding as a child. My mother taught me to do my book reports. My mother was an artist and had taken art classes at some college here in Dallas. She painted, mostly, but she did many things with her hands. She taught me how to bind my reports and make them fancy, and that way I could get extra credit towards a better grade.

Did you enjoy binding as a child?

Yes, oh yes. It invigorated me to do it, not only because I could get a good grade, but also because I just enjoyed it. I even remember my daddy getting involved because I made one of my book covers out of wood. My dad was a hobby woodworker; he worked with his hands too. Both were very art and craft orientated. I have known all along I wanted to do bookbinding, and with the calligraphy versus book exposure, I knew. I just had to wait until my kids got old enough so that I could go take one of Dorothy Westapher's classes.

So you knew about Dorothy long before you started taking classes from her?

Yes, I wanted to take a year or two before I even started, but my husband felt like it was too expensive. Finally, I said to him, "I'm going to do it."

Were you working as a calligrapher at the time? Did you sell your work?

Yes, and I did commission work at the time.

How long were you a calligrapher?

I did lettering as a child and teenager, but it all formally started in 1978. I took classes here in Dallas. When you are doing calligraphy, you get called on to do invitations, and address envelopes, and that normal stuff. But it wasn't my support. It was extra income for our family, for four children. I worked in the health and life insurance business when the children got older. I became a licensed agent, and I did sales in-house and on the phone. Whereas the agent I worked with did the footwork, I did the paper work and such in-house. We split commissions. I couldn't do that until I got my license. Having my license in life and health insurance, I could help him sell. I did that for several years. Then after starting to bookbind, I was still working in his office. It was part-time. I wasn't there every day of the week. I was there maybe half-days. It was a good arrangement for me.

I'm thinking by this point in time the oldest was going off to college.

I was trying to give them some pocket money. The calligraphy and the insurance work provided the pocket money. And then when I got into the bookbinding, that helped some more.

So you started taking classes from Dorothy Westapher in 1985?

That's what I remember, maybe in the fall of that year. I went once a week when the Craft Guild was at the Kramer location. I remember seeing you. It was right at the time when you, Dorothy, and two others went to Switzerland to study with Hugo Peller. I had no idea how important that was until later. But I remember that when Dorothy came back, we had to learn her new way of casing a book. I was told by others in the class (I don't know whether they were jealous or what) that I was very privileged to learn another way. They were going to have to learn on their own, but as a new student I could learn. And there were others that were learning this new way.

How long did you take classes from Dorothy?

Well, actually 14 years, until she died in 1999.

When did you start teaching?

I was teaching day workshops, even some workshops here in my home studio—accordion folds, little pamphlet books, things that the people were hungry for—mostly my calligraphy friends. They would make an accordion fold card to letter things in. They were mostly my friends, but I do remember going out to Euless, TX to teach in a calligraphy shop called "Script Tees" (they also did t-shirt imprinting), and teaching over here in the neighborhood recreation center. Then I think the real formal teaching started when I began teaching long-term classes at the Craft Guild of Dallas.

What other training did you have?

I studied with Raoul Bollin for six months. I would truck down to Austin one weekend a month. I brought him up here several times for workshops. I feel like I gained a lot from him. Then what we learned at Standards—I am sad to say Dorothy frowned on my learning from anybody else, so I had to keep it a secret. But I remember a couple of workshops that Jan Sobota had at his house that I went to. I tried to take workshops from other places. Then I went out and did an internship at Don Etherington's conservation center in 2002. For about four and a half weeks I had to check in at 7:30 in the morning and check out at 5:30 in the evening, with 30 minutes for lunch. He came around checking on you; of course, I had my supervisor too. But I really learned how they did things and so many things that have helped me to this day. You were also exposed to all the other things that go on in the Center. And now that they have expanded, I've been back to see the expanded shop. I wish I could go back because they are doing even more paper and document preservation and conservation. They had interns often. I understand they usually only came for two or three weeks, so my staying a longer time was good for me. I was paid by the hour. Though it barely paid the room I rented, I got a lot out of it and it was well worth it.

While I was there, I took classes from Monique Lallier. Then I went to Monique's in 2004 and studied two weeks with her, working every day. Cindy Haller and Julie Sullivan were there with me, too, and we could say what we wanted to learn. She could not believe all we wanted to learn. She said, "You aren't going to have time for it. But I'll see." Well, we had time for it. We had to work over the weekend, but she let us come to her house while she went out and played golf. It was all very productive.

I never had any real long-term formal training, except my weekly classes with Dorothy.

When we go to the Standards Seminars and come home, I type up my notes and make diagrams and then put them in a notebook. To this day I go back and pull them out and refer to them.

I've always admired your organizational abilities.

I figure if you are going to pay the money to go and learn these things, you've got to have a way to remember them. Things that I learn I equate to a particular Standards. They are beginning to run together since I've been to so many. And I like to have an organized place in which to work.

Other than bookbinding, you have been a calligrapher and insurance agent. Anything else?

I've had my hands in lots of crafts. When my children were little, I was a seamstress. I did mending and would take in work. With four kids it was a tough go, so I did what I could to bring in a little extra. When we lived in Port Arthur, Texas, I got in with a dance teacher who had me sew costumes. I'll never do that again. It was torture. Once I learned to do that particular costume and did it times 30, I was pretty tired of it. That was short-term. I did a lot of handwork. I sewed a good bit for my children. My mother was also a dressmaker. To this day, those skills have carried over into bookbinding.

What do you like most about being a bookbinder?
    I like being a bookbinder, especially in restoration, because I like to make old things new. I laugh because as a child I always used to make a little playhouse. And the minute it was fixed, I would tear it up and redo it. I liked to keep making it better. My goal is to make things better or more functional. I like restoration work, tedious things, things that give me a challenge. A book will come in here from a client and it looks pitiful, and I am thinking, "I don't think there is anything that can be done with it," but I am challenged that I will figure out a way to do something with it. Generally I do. I like working for myself because I don't like to do hundreds of the same things, I like one-of-a-kind or edition binding, but I don't want to have to be on a production run with short turnaround time and little pay. Also, as an independent person, I feel like I can ask my own prices and base it on my overhead and time involved. No, you don't make a lot of money because you have to be in tune with what the market can bear, but I don't have somebody over me telling me what I have to do about that.
    My least favorite part is mass production. Though I don't mind doing editions of 25 or 30, don't ask me to do 250 as I was recently asked to do. Then bookbinding is not fun. The creativity is there even when you're restoring an old book. Some say creativity is not in restoration but is in design binding. I look at it as creativity being a part of any of this.

Particularly when you say you have to think of ways to put that book back together. That takes creative thinking.
    Exactly. I like to ask for long turnaround time because I will spend quite a lot of time thinking about that project.

Do you charge for that time thinking?
    No.

Are you comfortable with the prices that you charge? You say you don't make a lot of money, but it must be enough that you continue doing it.
    Yes, I am. I do slightly increase every year because the goods go

Catherine Burkhard's studio.

up—paper, binders board, products, so I try to raise my prices gently. I'm fully aware that when somebody calls and asks me to redo their Bible, they say, "I can go buy one cheaper." I say, "That's fine but you are looking at handwork and labor, etc." I usually tell them that they will get a better book if they get it redone than if they go and purchase it because today's books are not put together very well. But nevertheless, as far as getting the money out of it I am comfortable with it. My overhead is low even though I certainly do figure in the amount of square feet of my house that goes into it. There are some things that come in the studio that I feel I can charge more for than something else. I will say that if I have a poor widow lady coming in and she wants a Bible fixed, I may drop it down $25 or so because being a Christian, I feel very wonderful about fixing up someone's Bible so they will use it. I know a lot of bookbinders don't agree, but I feel good about that. Fixing her Bible so she can use it makes me happy. But I am not going to give it to her free. She will pay for my supplies and generally a bit of my time.

People refer to you as "The Bible Lady."

I don't know where that got started. That is indeed what I do a lot of. I like to do them.

I'm sure that a lot of bookbinders will be happy to hear that so they can make referrals.

There is a bookbinder that I met at the Portland Standards. She came to me for help. She said there weren't many classes up there for restoration. We started corresponding. She was paying me to write up helps for her. She would ask me questions. She realized over time that I was capable of doing these big family Bibles and that she didn't like to do them as much, so guess what? People are sending me things now because of her. I'm very appreciative of that.

Are you backlogged?

I'm always backlogged. For general study Bibles, maybe five or six weeks. For the big family Bibles, I ask them to give me anywhere from six months to a year. If they don't care and they just want it fixed, maybe longer. Right now I have quite a lot in-house. I work on several at a time. I have an assistant who comes in. I've worked with three assistants. I have one now that wants to learn the business. I'm delighted to help them. They get a low wage because they are also learning while they are doing. They are not fast. That helps me get done what I call some of the grunt work.

They are somewhat like apprentices?

Yes, that is what they call it. They are learning; they are helping me.

The Bible Lady thing, I just don't know where that got started. But it is true. I would say 80% of my work is Bibles. I'm not talking just study Bibles. I have a Danish Bible back there right now; the paper is totally brittle. You pick it up and it just cracks. I am encapsulating every page with Filmoplast R (tissue that has a heat-sensitive acrylic emulsion) and rebinding it, fan glued. That was all I could do; they wanted it done, and they were willing to pay for it. That is not the only one I'm doing like that. When paper just totally becomes brittle, there is really not anything you can do. They want their Bible, and they want it back as a book that can be used. I'll work on it a little at a time. The trained conservators will go, "Aghh!" But this is to make something functional and useful. It is not something that is going to go on the market and be considered a rare book or anything. On one of those big thick family Bibles I am doing the same thing. It gets expensive. I have already paid something like $600 on just the Filmoplast. The client knows that. I've got about a quarter of the book left to do. When it is all done it will be double fan adhesive bound. That will be the big test. I shunned away from that for a long time. But I got on to that method and learned to do it at Don Etherington's. They were doing it to some books and I was aghast at it being done, but I thought, "If Don Etherington's Conservation Center can do it, I can too."

What is a day like in your life? Do you work every day?

Pretty much. Not every hour of the day every day. I have things that I do at church, not as much as I used to. And then there are my classes. With any other time, I am working in the studio. This coming semester I am teaching four classes—two in the morning and two at night. Sometimes I will add an extra one if I have a lot of beginners, or workshops. But I haven't done the workshops for a long time.

Where do you get students and clients?

I have had a lot of my students for a long time. I don't know where I get them, maybe referrals. The clients are strictly referrals since I've been doing this for so many years. For example, a man came back recently after ten years and wanted another book done. I couldn't remember who he was. It is satisfying to work with people who like what you've done. I am referred by Christian bookstores. I just don't feel I need to advertise. I can't say my website is pulling in business, though I can have people go look at it. I had one of my apprentices do it last year. She kept encouraging me to do it, as I was reluctant about doing it. But it has paid off as far as letting people know what I do, both in calligraphy and in bookbinding. They can take a look at that.

Is there anything about being a bookbinder that you really dislike, anything that gets frustrating?

I do get frustrated when a person calls and describes the book they want fixed and they don't want to pay the price. We are out there to educate people. People think they are going to get this for ten dollars. I give them a description as to what all is involved. Even if they slam down the receiver or say, "No, I'm not interested," I still feel like I've spent a little time educating the public as to what is involved in bookbinding so we can get back to thinking that this is a fine craft that is out there for the public.

That is worthy of payment.

Exactly! If they are willing to go pay an artist for a watercolor that say an artist slapped paint on for two hours, and they are going to pay several hundred dollars for it, where does it stop with bookbinding? Even though I feel like a lot of the clientele balk over the price, I do go in and try to explain a little bit. I just want to briefly describe what is involved: having to buy the leather, pare the leather, mend their pages, etc. It doesn't take very long to describe what is involved in the charge. Some people just think you just slap on a ready-made cover. I tell them, "You don't put a clean band-aid on a dirty wound." I've had people call to ask, "How do you clean off a spine?" I then say I will set up an appointment and for $50 an hour will explain it to them, knowing full well they can't do it when they get home because they don't have the paste or tools. That is what stops that. That is a frustrating thing to me that they are just not willing to pay for the handwork involved.

As far as the least favorite thing, it would be cleaning off the spines, ironing the dog-ears, and mending the tears in all these study Bibles. But I do it. I'm sure I don't get paid for that more than maybe ten cents an hour. It is boring, and I don't like being bored. So sometimes that is what my assistants get to do.

I have a question about whether you develop a relationship with clients. I find it is an intimate act to work on someone's book.

I agree with you totally. I really feel like I have made friends. I may never see them again, and certainly won't in a social way, but I feel like I really have made friends. We talk on the phone, and they come, and we write it up, and then they come pick it up. In that amount of time, you have chatted often. I've even gotten hugs from people because they are so excited about what I've done. I think that is so uplifting. I also feel that being friendly is what will bring that person back or they will pass my name along. It is not put on, just something I do. I love making someone's book functional. It gives me a lot of joy to see that person like their finished book or Bible.

What gifts and abilities lead you to be a good bookbinder?

I mentioned the sewing, working with my hands. Even macramé has helped. It is something I grew up with—my parents and even my grandmother were really craft oriented. I just thought that is how you did things. I've done a lot of crafts over time: oil painting, watercolor, macramé, knitting. I've ruled those things out and always gone back to the calligraphy and bookbinding that I remember doing as a child.

What would you like to achieve in bookbinding that you haven't yet done?

I probably have tried most everything. I would just like to get better with tooling, gilding, and onlays and inlays—those things that people equate with bookbinding. When you do a lot of restoration, you don't get into those things. But I don't know how many years are ahead for me—of course none of us do—and so I ask, "Do I want to spend the time?"

You've got to stay with it, practice it. With the amount of work that comes in here, do I want to take the time? I have the supplies; I have the tools; I have the knowledge. It is the practice I need.

When I was learning onlays and inlays with Monique, I enjoyed how she did it. Hers looked so exquisite on her books. But her way of doing it, the French way, takes so long. I like what I learned that I understand as "the Hugo Peller way." That is simple. I can handle the onlays and inlays pretty well, but it is not going to be a Tini Miura, and it's not going to be a Monique Lallier. But at the same time, why do I have to set that up for myself? Yes, that's a goal, but if I'm never going to do that full-time—I've done only some work—it isn't ever going to sit out there on the same level as theirs, but it will be mine. I don't know if you remember the older lady from Corpus Christi. Her onlays were crude and yet quite interesting. I don't want to do that but yet, what's wrong with it?

Yes, she was out there doing it.

Exactly, and people were paying her for it. She even won something at one of the DeGoyler competitions. Well, I feel I could do better than that, or maybe that is just how her technique looks. I think out of those three (tooling, gilding, onlay/inlays) that the onlays/inlays would be the one I would continue to finesse more. I would like to be better at all three but just don't think I will ever get there.

What would you rather do than bookbinding?

Right now, not anything. My whole world changed when my husband died. I'm very happy with what I've got going right now with my business. I'm very blessed. This is what I would like to do until I can't, and the calligraphy too.

Do you have other hobbies?

Oh yes, I am a stamp collector; I collect bottles; I collect a lot of other things, but the collecting is slowing down. I'm not doing it as much anymore. And genealogy—I have put that on the back burner, I'm sad to say. I have files and files and tons and tons of stuff on the computer. I can just see tons of hours to finish and put that all together so I can see that it will probably never happen, just because I know the number of hours it will take. I go out and look at the number of books waiting on me, and I go in and look at the genealogy waiting, and it's not going to work. Not enough hours in the day. Having a 93-year-old mother makes me think about priorities. I'm not trying to be fatalistic. I'm trying to be practical. What do I want to do while I still have the capabilities of doing them?

Our life is finite. What is most important to us?

My mother used to do the most beautiful handwork—petite point, tatting, tailor-made suits—and now she can't do any of that because of arthritis.

Maybe you can do genealogy later. I think about that too.

I'm glad I'm not the only one. In fact, you are probably the only one I have mentioned that thought to in that scope.

What advice would you give to someone who is interested in pursuing bookbinding as a career?

First of all, if they truly were interested in bookbinding, they would have had to have some exposure to it.

So perhaps they have taken a few classes and are thinking maybe they want to be a bookbinder.

Yes! And that is why I have assistants. They come here to work. I don't mind having clients come here while they are working because they can see how I work with clients. I give them advice all the time as we work: "And this is what you are going to have to think about… and here you are going to have to order x amount of material…here you are going to have to have inventory…you are going to have to have money invested." That is the kind of advice I give for somebody who wants to be a bookbinder. I did that with Julie Sullivan before she branched out. She worked for me years ago. As far as particular advice, I think they have to be exposed to the whole concept of what all is involved.

What about training?

I would tell them to get out and take everything they can that's related to bookbinding. Go to Standards [of Excellence]; go to workshops;

keep track of what you're learning. I think we are talking about people who aren't going to get to go to the Academy of Bookbinding—who can't afford it or don't have the time.

What would you say if they expect to make a living out of this?

I would talk to them about the amount of money you would have to put out for the education, the inventory, what kind of charges you have to do, what kind of equipment you have to have in order to do this and this and this. The money part of it is the bottom line. You can't just set up shop with a needle and thread and a bonefolder; there is bookkeeping involved. My son set up a program on Excel that helps me with accounts and tells me profits and losses. Each account has a number. You have to categorize your expenses into an account and your income into one of those accounts. When I do my report, I just do totals and hand them to my CPA.

One of the things I think is so wonderful about you as a bookbinder is that you have been teaching, becoming one of the bookbinders out there sharing the knowledge, getting more people involved, and keeping the bookbinding world going. I think that's been a really good thing that you've done.

Thank you. But I can't tell you how many times I've thought of giving that part up because of the workloads. There are people that turn me down, not only because of price but also because of time. They want these books done in a week. I told one guy, "If your book was the only one I had to do, I could get your book done in five to seven days, but you would not want me as a bookbinder. If I was sitting here twiddling my thumbs, that would mean people don't want to use me because I can't really do the work. If I've got a lot of work here, then that means that people put their trust in me." I also know I can get this out faster if I didn't have to stop and teach classes. Before classes, I have to put all my stuff up and have class. I can't get much out Tuesdays and Wednesdays, when I have classes. Then Thursday morning I can get it back out and work through the weekend. I do think of not having classes and then I hear the students fuss about such an idea.

There are people who come here just for pleasure, doing it as a hobby. I am aware of that. I love the camaraderie. I look forward to my breaks. But when it is time for the students to come back, I look forward to their returning. Being by myself so much, it's really nice to have them around. I love the fact that they are learning. Even if they are not going to do anything as a professional, at least they are learning the craft. What is sad though, Pamela, who is going to take over around here? People want to do it but not teach. That concerns me.

For more information on Catherine Burkhard, and to see examples of her work, go to http://www.booksandletters.com.

Jim Croft:
Old Ways

Santa, Idaho
(interviewed in Dallas, Texas)
February 2007

Jim Croft smiles easily and laughs often. His beard, though not long, is scruffy and grows down his neck, unpruned and liberated, but it doesn't disguise his strong dimpled jaws. Tommy Hilfiger jeans seem odd on the lean body of this wilderness-man. His t-shirts are souvenirs from bookbinding and papermaking events. Short ashen brown hair is beginning to recede above his temples, though it is usually hidden under a baseball cap or a hand-crocheted skullcap. Thick, brown-stained nails on his scarred hands attest to a life of physical labor. He uses words articulately and with knowledge. I sense a gentleness in him.

With his wife Melody, he arrives in Dallas in a vintage 1952 Chevrolet truck, robin-egg blue, with a hand-fashioned covered wagon on the back, canvas fitted tightly around the framework of hand-formed cedar. Inside the truck are tools, workshop materials, a bed, clothes, a trombone and accordion, a tennis racket, and balls.

Melody is tall and strong with crystal blue eyes and wavy, grey, shoulder-length hair. She is crocheting flax cord into a handbag with an Aztec design when I introduce myself. Her movements and voice are soft, and she speaks sparsely. They have been on the road for six months, teaching the old ways of bookbinding, and Jim has accepted our invitation to teach at The Craft Guild of Dallas.

I had seen Jim at national bookbinding meetings, selling his handmade tools. His booth was always crowded, so I never met him;

I just admired his beautiful handcrafted bone folders—plain-looking tools, like tongue depressors, that bookbinders use for folding and burnishing. But his are sculpted into beautiful and functional shapes.

I call them the wilderness couple. After getting a degree in history, Jim worked as a pantry boy on a ship, earning his seaman papers on a passage that took him to Europe where he quit his job and explored. He refers to himself as an angry young man in those days of civil rights violence and the Vietnam War. Shunning big cities, he acquired a kayak from his brother who was in the army in Germany, and he navigated the Rhine. It was in the small old European towns that he discovered and fell in love with all things old, made with fine craftsmanship, made the old way.

Melody was a free spirit. After graduating from high school, she traveled through Mexico by bus and train, bought a bicycle in Guatemala, and rode into El Salvador and back to Guatemala before selling it and returning to the States four months later. She eventually made her way to Oregon where she played music in coffee houses, becoming known as the "zither lady." Jim played the trombone and sometimes would go into Portland and play at all-night music sessions at a coffee house. That is where he first saw her—playing the zither. After seventeen years together and three children, they wed. For thirty years they have "camped out," as Jim calls it, choosing a self-sustaining life in the remote Idaho countryside. They say they prefer a life lived largely in the outdoors with less need for money. They like that much of what they have is what they crafted. Their water is hand pumped from springs; they use an outhouse, woodstoves for heat and cooking, and solar energy for what little electricity they need. Natural herbs and plants provide home remedies for healing.

Jim works a couple weeks a year reforesting—a job he loves—and he earns enough for necessities, taxes, and auto insurance. The rest of the year he lives his passion, making hand crafted tools and creating books the old way—making paper in the stamp mill he built, creating leather and parchment from the skins hunters leave behind, preparing book boards from the leftovers from trees the lumbermen bring down, and crafting brass clasps from scrap-yard metal, accumulating a valuable collection of hand-crafted medieval-style bindings, ready for a one-man show.

Was there anything in your past that related to bookbinding?

I always loved books and spent a lot of time reading. I especially liked stories about valuing older things. There is a book called *T-Model Tommy* that I read in seventh grade about a guy who started his business with a really old truck. He made a good living with his little old truck, with his determination. And other stories about obsolete things that were replaced by modern things, and people disdained the old things and threw them away and then something happened that made them wish that they had kept the old things. That is a big main theme that I really liked and continue to like.

Good tie-in. Did you work with your hands, doing crafts?

Yes, I did some. I used to go out in the woods and make lean-tos and dig holes. I was into cub scouts and did some crafty things. I didn't get the bookbinding merit badge though. But I did like making things. It wasn't a big part of my life. I liked other things. I didn't really think making things was what I wanted to do when I grew up, but I did enjoy it. And you fall back on some of those things. My family did work with their hands a lot so that may have had an influence, that mindset. Being an American—the pioneer philosophy, the can-do that makes a hero out of the pioneer, being self-reliant.

What led you to bookbinding?

I think because I went to Europe and I saw old quality things. I didn't know the word "sustainability." I didn't really love old stuff that much, although I do remember liking old cars.

I got a degree in history and then went to New York City and got a job on a Swedish passenger ship with American tourists. I knew that if I could get a job on a ship, I could eventually go to Europe, which was my goal. I was the pantry boy—emptying the garbage, peeling garlic, cleaning out the pots and pans. The reason I got the job was because no one else wanted it because it was pretty disgusting.

The first day out I asked where we were going. They said we were going around South America for two months. We circumnavigated South America and went through the Panama Canal. South America wasn't my goal, but it was interesting. I knew that I could go to Europe eventually if I got my seaman papers.

The next trip out we did go to Europe. I got off in Spain. You can give seven days notice and go wherever you want. It was 1970. I made

75 cents an hour and time and a half for over 50 hours a week. I think I worked 70 hours a week. And of course I got room and board.

I worked in the crew kitchen, and they told me, "Don't let the passengers see you." It was because I was so disgusting with the garbage on me. Something about me liked being the low man on the totem pole—sort of this white guilt. I wanted to feel what it was like to have the grungiest job in the whole place. Some part of me actually liked that.

When I got off the ship in Europe, I was totally lost as far as having a goal. I was just going to Europe.

When I was in Europe, I was an angry young man because of Vietnam and civil rights—you know, the '60's. It was still going on in the '70's. So I didn't want to be in any cities in Europe. I stayed out of all the big cities. I went to visit my brother in the army in Germany. He had built a kayak to escape to Sweden, though in the meantime he had gotten kicked out. I took the kayak up the Rhine River. That was a really historic turn-on. If you stay in the small towns and the rural areas, you can't help but see all this old quality stuff that has been around for hundreds of years. It was a whole new way of thinking—something besides white bread. It really turned me around. I didn't know why I was there other than to become more worldly, but what it did was give me an appreciation for old quality things.

When I finally went to a big city, London, I stayed with some people I had met in Spain. I went to the British Museum every day. I saw the Lindisfarne gospel from 800 or so. It was on display. I saw the elegant carpet pages—intricate knot work in color. I said, "That is what I want to do." I remembered my Alden Watson book on bookbinding. At that point, I thought it would be a nice hobby. I was planning to go into anthropology.

Before I left the States I had made friends with these people who had a bookstore in St. Louis. I was looking through the books. There was a book called *Hand Bookbinding* by Alden Watson. I thought, "Oh, that looks like fun." I showed the owner. He gave me that book for Christmas, just before I left. I left in January and toured Europe from March to July. When I got back, that book was waiting for me. First I made my own tools. The last chapter is about making all your own tools to do bookbinding. I did that and started learning from that book in November 1970.

When I got back to the states, I eventually made it to Lawrence, Kansas. I was going to go to graduate school at University of Kansas. The first day I made bread. The second day I started setting up to bookbind. Then I started making blank books and selling them in head shops for three dollars. I did pretty well. I had low overhead, and for some reason there was a need for little books in Lawrence, Kansas. I did that for six or eight months. Then I started doing rebinding and thesis binding.

I hitchhiked to New York City and bought more tools. There I met Elaine Haas at Talas [Bookbinding Supply Company]. She called up [bookbinders] Carolyn Horton and Deborah Evetts at the Pierpont Morgan. They were nice and gave me a tour. They thought it was cute that I was self-taught. I saw what they were doing. They introduced me to the world of conservation and historic binding. I had never really seen that in the US, though I did when I was in London.

The University of Kansas had just opened up a rare book library. I visited there and was turned on to books by Edith Diehl and Douglas Cockerell—new books on bookbinding that I hadn't seen before. I started learning from those. I got a bunch of tools from two retiring bookbinders in Kansas City. They were both named Chester. I got Chester Bullinger's whale bonefolder that he had used for 40 years, and some tools: finishing press, tooling tools, and miscellaneous stuff. He thought it was really funny that I was so enthusiastic. He probably thought, "This kid is going to have a wakeup call when he gets in the real world." His business was itinerant binding and repair of ledger bindings at county seats. The very porous whale bonefolder was totally red because those are usually red leather. It actually had thumb wear from where his thumb had worn a groove into the folder.

In the summer of 1971, I went with a bunch of friends to check out Oregon because it sounded like a cool place to go. After I had done one semester of anthropology, I quit. I thought, "Man, I love bookbinding. It really turns me on a lot more than anthropology. I am going to be a bookbinder, a poor bookbinder. (I could barely see making money at it.) This is what I want to do. This is what makes me happy. I love books. I want to make the ultimate book." I had read books by Edith Diehl and Douglas Cockerell. Lawrence Town was another; I learned a lot from his book, *Bookbinding by Hand.* He is not as well known. I went to Oregon and showed my little books to a guy in downtown Portland. He said he would pay me a hundred bucks if I would move to Oregon and set up my shop in his craft shop. "For $20 a month you set up a booth and people come watch you work and hopefully buy something." So I did. I went home and packed up all my stuff and moved to Oregon. I started working in that little basement. I lived down there even though you weren't supposed to. It wasn't too long until I moved to Eagle Creek, out in the countryside outside of Portland. I found a cabin for $20 a month that was pretty rustic—no electricity, an outhouse; you had to haul your water from a well. I thought that was great. By then I was really getting into hand tools. I had the bookbinding tools, but the only carpentry tools I had were a coping saw and a hammer.

That is how I started my homesteading—with a bookbinding shop, a coping saw, and a hammer. I lived there for four years. I did an edition of 500 books. Some guy in Portland was a big fan of Steve Lind that had the great hit, "Elusive Butterfly." He was publishing a book on his poems and lyrics. He got burned out on binding them and got me to bind them. That bought my '37 Chevrolet truck for $175. It limped around and finally died out there in Eagle Creek. I learned how to fix it and drove it until 1993. I was basically single for those four years. I really got into it, probably the most concentrated time of binding in my life. I cut wood by hand and learned traditional woodworking.

In 1971, when I was still in downtown Portland, I wrote in my diary, "I want to make the whole book from raw materials." Many years later I discovered Dard Hunter and realized that is what he wanted to do also. He of course had already done it. We had had a similar goal at a similar age, but I was saying that 60 years later. I didn't do any papermaking for many years, but I thought it would be cool to make a book from local—local is the key word—local materials, and build the ultimate binding, which in my mind then and now, is the gothic style—large, thick, round spine, wood boards and clasps. I really got hooked on that. Any book that I bound from 1972 on would have raised cords, packed sewing, and though not always wood covers, wooden covers was my real love. I'd even take paperbacks and guard every page and make sections out of them. I did lots of them for hardly any money. If somebody brought me a paperback, I'd say, "I know what to do with that." I'd guard every page, double cord, packed sewing, wooden cover, leather spine (I didn't do clasps until 1985). All I cared about was learning that style, so whatever came to me I would make into that style. The overtones of Cockerell and Diehl were, "There is nothing worth doing except the raised cords." They show other things, but they say the ultimate binding is a raised cord binding, definitely not sawn-in cords. Later on I mellowed out on that. So for many years I was only doing raised cords, packed sewing, wooden covers.

It's funny, when I talk about making those raised cords, packed sewn, wooden boards, my typical charge for those was anywhere from three dollars to twenty dollars. I always had a problem with charging enough. I've rarely made much of a living at binding because I never could charge enough. People were going to want to know what it was going to cost, and I was afraid I would scare them away if I would charge too much, so I always bid way low.

I've heard that before.

Is it a recurring theme?

It is one of those threads that binds.

The three dollars for the full-leather, totally guarded, raised double cords, packed sewing, wooden cover paperback, *Salvador Dali,* by Abrams—that might be an all-time low. Then a guy complained. He wanted me to do another book and I said, "Well, this time I'll have to charge five dollars." He said, "Oh, that's too much, a rip off." He grudgingly paid me five dollars for the second one.

Then I met my wife, Melody, at the Oregon Renaissance Fair (now Country Fair). I'd heard of her. Sometimes I'd go into Portland and play trombone with friends of mine. There were these all-night music sessions at a coffee house in Portland where I played music with friends. They were talking about the Zither Lady. The zither is sort of like an autoharp except you don't press buttons; you play it like a harp. She was playing the zither when I first saw her; I thought that has got to be the Zither Lady. I gave her a book with Bodleian handmade paper and wood covers with Yin Yang inlay.

First Melody and I lived in my place in Eagle Creek, and then we moved to her place in Friend, Oregon. She was on the east side of Mt. Hood. Then we had a kid. We were camping out. We have basically been camping out ever since we met, by American standards. That means without running water, electricity, using an outhouse, doing many things by hand. I didn't have any power tools until 1994. I only wanted to learn the traditional way. I didn't care about learning the quicker ways of doing things. I liked cutting wood by hand; I still like it. Maybe it is good that people keep those things alive. Look at hand bookbinding. It seems so obscure and irrelevant to your average American. It is in the same vein; it takes a certain kind of person to have the patience. And the amount of set-up it takes to establish a bindery in that style is huge. It's not a very easy craft to just jump into. It takes a certain mindset. That is another thread that binds.

I kept making more and more of what I now call Gothic books. I didn't really have a name for them back then—double cord, packed sewing, wooden boards. That is all I cared about. Eventually I started doing other styles and enjoying them.

In 1976, I went to meet Lloyd Reynolds, a famous calligrapher in Portland who popularized italic calligraphy. At that time, he was a leader in the book arts community there. Calligraphy is part of book arts. I met him and showed him some books and some woodworking things I had done. He was nice, though he didn't give me any work. In the afternoon, I went to meet Jack Thompson who had just moved to Portland from Indiana. He knew a lot about conservation and historic binding and materials. He and I became pretty tight friends.

The next year, I moved to Idaho. I always thought we'd be camping, squatting. I had found this cheap land out there that even I could afford—$250 down, $45 a month, for five acres. Jack would come to Idaho and we'd jam on stuff, and then I'd go to Oregon and work with him in Portland. That is when I was introduced to Dard Hunter's book and Bernard Middleton's *Restoration of Leather Bindings* (1978). Middleton's book was my textbook for the work I was doing for Jack. I started learning about rebacking and the world of restoration and conservation. I learned a lot from Jack, and he learned from me. I had bound hundreds of books by the time I met Jack, but I hadn't taken many classes at that point. I went to San Francisco twice by then and visited Capricornus and the Aardvarck Bindery. Bob Futernick at Aardvark Bindery is now the conservator at the San Francisco Art Museum. He helped me out a lot. When you do it on your own and try to learn it from books, and then you talk to someone who knows something, you've got some really good questions to ask. You see their bindery and you learn a lot in a short amount of time. I showed them my books and asked pertinent questions. When you try something time after time after time, you've got some good questions to ask.

Jack and I kept up the friendship. I'd continue to do my gothic-style books and book repair at home. In those years I was doing a lot of tree planting for income—reforestation in the national forest in Idaho and sometimes in Oregon. We, along with my core group of neighbors, had a little co-op in tree planting. I'd make pretty good money. My main money was coming from tree planting, but I'd do bookbinding whenever I could. Our place in Idaho started with bare land, so I had things to do there too, like building a house, keeping the truck running, raising a family, and making a living. I was able to work at tree planting for roughly two months a year. We could live on that plus crafts for the rest of the year. We didn't have a lot of need. I was living on $4,000-$6,000 a year then, with one kid. In 1981, we had a second kid. We didn't go hardly anywhere, didn't spend much money; we did a lot of stuff ourselves so we didn't need a lot of money.

In the meantime, I was passionately working on perfecting my book structures whenever I could, which was mostly in the winter. In 1985-86, Jack got a huge amount of money to work on the Mt. Angel's [book] collection in Oregon. He brought me down to help as his medieval specialist. I knew how to work wood and I learned to make clasps—all self taught. I had the models; I had the tools. We worked together. He taught me a certain aesthetic and a lot of historical facts. He has a library on materials and history that is one of the best in the whole country, especially on historic materials, binding, and papermaking—anything that a museum conservator would want. We spent a lot of hours jamming on those subjects. He was out in the world; I wasn't really. I did join the Guild in 1974, but I never went to a meeting. I let that peter out. In 1985-86, I spent several months working for him on the Mt. Angel books. Most of those had broken wooden boards, needed clasps or clasp repair. That is when I really got into clasp making. That was the perfect addition to my book form because most old books had clasps. I discovered the beauty of clasp-making. That became part of my whole repertoire.

In 1987, we had the idea to teach a workshop at my place on the technology of the medieval book where people make their own thread, make their own paper, do their own wooden covers, and make their own clasps in two weeks (the first one was ten days). My place was the right setting. He and I did that for ten years. He was the public relations man, and I was the site host. Melody was the cook. The first eight years we averaged maybe $200 or $300 each; in other words we didn't have that many students. The first year we had six or seven, but some years we only had two students. We still ran it because it was so much fun. We thought it was a cool thing, and we wanted to keep it going. A lot more people said they wanted to come than actually came.

Did they camp during the workshop?

They could stay in pretty rustic houses but there was no power and they had to use outhouses. But if they were initially afraid, they soon became very comfortable and realized, "Hey, this isn't that much different from what I'm used to. In fact it is fun." Just about everybody loved it. It got pretty good reviews.

Then the Internet came along. By 1996, we had a full class of ten people. In 1997, we had 17 people there including Jack and I. You can see how it began to be a popular thing. A lot of it was because of the Internet. We didn't even have a phone until 2000. Melody and I had been without a phone for 30 years. All we did was done without a phone. Jack was the contact person in Portland, so a lot of this was associated as his deal. If I was mentioned, it was as site host when I was really the co-teacher. I ended up running around keeping the place running while Jack was doing a lot of the teaching. He'd bring me in for the woodworking since I was the woodworker and knew how to do it. For various reasons, that was the last year (1997) we did it together. In 1998, I started to do it on my own calling it Old Ways. I'm not a real good marketer.

In 1994-95, I started teaching on the road. My toolmaking was coming along in a really big way. Hugo Peller started selling my tools in 1985, after I took his class. Jack was bringing these really good people to Portland to teach. I'd go down there and take classes. Bernard Middleton came in 1979 for a three-day rebacking workshop. That was great to meet "the man" after studying his book—literally taking his book to bed with me. There was so much in there. I had bought his other book, A *History of English Craft Bookbinding,* before I took the Middleton workshop. After meeting him and being more into it, I realized what a great reference book that is. Before Szirmai came along, that was one of the single best books out there on historic bookbinding. In 1985 I took my classes from Hugo Peller. Hugo was there for four weeks.

Jack was dropping out in 1997. He was getting more reclusive. In the 1980's, he was all over the place—AIC, GBW, Dard [Hunter conferences], Oxford. I went to PBI [Paper and Book Intensive] as a student in 1994. That was kind of my big coming out. I was teaching people how to make bone tools at night. The next year, they asked me to teach. I started touring once a year, going to meetings and selling tools. I started teaching tool-making in about 1996 as part of a circuit (besides PBI). I do that generally once a year. People began to know me as a toolmaker. They didn't know about my books.

I continue to do book repair and book restoration, especially in the winter. I told people I couldn't do them until the winter, unless I was totally broke; then I would do it whenever I needed the money. Most people who gave me work knew I wouldn't get around to it until the winter; that was my inside time. When the weather was nice, I was outside doing homestead stuff.

I had a pond. Around 1990, Jack said, "Let's build a stamp mill." That is the golden age of papermaking—paper made with a water-powered stamp mill. I was reluctant. I said, "I am up to my eyeballs in projects. I don't want another animal to feed like a paper mill." He kept on with it, to his credit. He brought his son and two other friends of ours, Lou Flannery and Ed Gordon, and we built a stamp mill. That is the way paper was made in 1700 in Europe, before the beater was invented, which is used now if you want to make a living at papermaking. Everybody has this nostalgia for paper made with a stamp mill, but can anybody make a living at it? I doubt it. Jack said, "Let's build a stamp mill. It's a perfect addition to all this other stuff we have going." We took a year off from the medieval book thing and instead of teaching a class, which never paid anything anyway, we built a stamp mill. Basically, it was my animal because he was hardly ever there. He would come up for a week or two. It was a wonderful gift. 1992 was my first year to really make it run. The first year we were just making a foundation, getting the pieces together, figuring it out. He did most of the research and then left it for me, so it was really my baby. I was the one who ran it. My pond is seasonal, so I ran out of water, just like Dard Hunter. A lot of historic paper mills would run out of water in the dry season. They were not necessarily running year round. I had already made paper and gone to some papermaking workshops.

In 1992, I realized that with the addition of the handmade paper to my books—that would be the whole book. Now I'm making the whole book. I thought I would be 60 years old before I would finally make the whole book. I was only 45 years old, 15 years ahead of schedule. I wasn't really excited when Jack wanted to build the stamp mill. Here I was trying to homestead, raising a family, making a living, hardly getting paid anything for all the book repair I was doing. I did the book repair just to keep in practice, not really making much money. But I didn't really need much money. If I got paid $75 for a book, we could live on that for quite a while. We weren't in debt; we didn't have bills; we didn't drive very much. But I began to need more money as my kids were growing up. We needed to drive them around; I wanted them to be out in the world. I started driving more, getting a modern car. It cost more money. I'm still doing some local tree planting even now in 2007. I make more money doing that than anything. It is fun. It's kind of like a little vacation that I get paid for.

So I'm making the whole book now. And I'm raising flax. I've been doing that since the early '80's. I've always been a lover of hemp. Hemp and flax are the dominant fibers in Europe's Gothic Age.

Aren't they the same thing?

No, they are very much different. But when you get to fiber, it is hard to tell the difference. The plants themselves are very much different, but when you get down to the fiber you sometimes have to do the twist test to identify is this flax or hemp? Hemp will twist in a Z when it is drying; flax will twist in an S. They twist opposite ways when they are drying. I've done this twist test.

I've always been interested in flax because of its historic use in bookbinding throughout the world. Flax is more dominant in Europe for the aristocrats, hemp for the peasants. Linen was often made of hemp if they could get away with it. It takes a lot more work to grow flax than hemp. I've experimented in making fiber from both of these plants over the years. I'm good enough now to know how to do it, though I've never gone into production. I make thread and papers with it. Ninety-nine percent of my paper is from flax and hemp. I've immersed myself in this gothic book, and that includes using only flax and hemp, which is not exclusively what they had, but the most common fibers used in that time in papers, thread and cord. Each year, I've gotten a little bit better at growing it and processing it. I've done a lot of reading on it. I could go into production if I had to, if there were enough people who wanted it. That would be a lot of fun.

Are you still doing the Old Ways workshops?

Yes, last year I had two people. The year before I had ten people. I don't use the Internet like I could. If I wanted to have a presence, I would have to make better use of the Internet.

But you've been traveling and that helps spread the word.

That helps. People have heard of me. People say they really want to come, but I still don't see them.

Most of the money I make is from being on the road, selling tools, and teaching. In the winter I do books. I'm doing better. I don't do three-dollar books anymore. I'm making maybe five to ten dollars an hour at book repair. I can live off that. If I make ten dollars an hour at home, that is a great wage. That is all I need. It would be nice to make more.

Where do you get your clients?

Most are local. They bring Bibles and old books. I've got a good client in Boise who lets me charge him by the hour. Everybody else wants an estimate. They want to know how much.

So you are making money doing the circuit, which is really important to your livelihood.

Yes, and now I'm teaching the gothic book on the road, which is new to be doing it as a workshop. I've done it at Penland a couple times. I did it at PBI once, and that was my first on-the-road disaster. Other than that it is all teaching toolmaking. When I was called about participating in the Penland book, they wanted me to do a chapter on toolmaking. I said, "Yes, but I'd rather talk about my binding." When I told them about that, they said, "Let's do it on that." People know me as a tool seller. They don't know me as a bookbinder. People may know me for my Old Ways classes, but mostly in reference to outhouses, living in dirt, rustic accommodations. People dwell on the outhouse thing.

Since I started the papermaking, my whole book has taken off. I used to never try to sell any of my books. Now I'm in a new mood. I could have approached it differently and tried to market myself earlier, but I decided I want to get a body of work and have a show. Now is that time of my life. It is a big change. I've always been doing a little bit here and a little bit there. Some of these books I've been working on for ten years, from making the paper to the point when the book is actually finished. I would work on it in the winter and then skip a couple years and then work on it some more. Now I have $50,000-$100,000 worth of books that are ready to sell.

Are they all blank books?

No, one of them is a Dard Hunter book combined with Edith Diehl's book. One is the Tao Te Ching that I calligraphed and Melody did artwork in—all done in the classic style I love. Daniel Essig [who is featured in the Penland book] traded me 28 Penland books and some money for one of my books. He is one of my big fans. He came to the '97 medieval book class at my place. And Shanna Leino, the woman I taught with at Penland also came [in '97]; it was her first time there. That is where she really got into book making.

You are influencing people, even if your Old Way workshops are small.

I think so. I think people know about me. They would like to come. They are glad someone is doing it. My second daughter, Nara, and her husband, Brandon, make some great books together. Recently we had three generations all doing a long-stitch workshop.

You are one-of-a-kind. You have uniqueness, a signature about you.

Toolmaking empowers people. And now having the gothic book on the road is a cool thing. It is a huge breakthrough to bring this to people because not too many people are coming to my place.

What do you want to do next? What have you not done that you want to do?

I want to go to Europe and study and probably teach.

You want to study more?

Oh yeah! And hang out with people who know more than I do about a lot of stuff. But I can bring something to it too. I haven't met anybody who does the whole book—the traditional wood, the traditional papermaking. If there is anyone out there who is even doing one of those things, I want to hang out with people who do that. I can educate them, and they can educate me. I am interested in wooden boards and clasps, and especially the gothic style. There is a lot of nostalgia for that too.

Jim Croft's 1952 traveling truck.

Chris Clarkson is a mentor of mine because he is so into rediscovering the materials; so is Tony Cains. I'd love to get a Fulbright and study and teach. There is no toolmaking teaching going on over in Europe.

So you would live over there for quite a while?

Yes, Melody and I. That's the plan. And the kids too. It is a never-ending thing. I've worked out things on my own, but I've got a lot to learn. I haven't really been around historic books that much. Someone like Chris Clarkson would know what to show me. That is his life—materials and historic book structure.

He and I are so linked in what we love and what we study. I really should spend some time with him if he would allow that. I did go to his class once in Iowa. I wouldn't say we hit it off really great because he is not a woodworker. But he is a fiber worker, and he is a leather worker, and I certainly want to do more work with leather.

I am learning leatherworking, and I am learning blacksmithing. I want to make more of my own leather the old way. People should be making bark and water leather—the heck with this modern plastic leather that is getting pawned off as so-called historic leather. I can't say I know how to do it yet but I'm close. I've made some, but I haven't put it on a book yet.

Is there anyone in the States making leather like that?

I met a guy in North Carolina that did the buckskin. I talked to him about buckskin, which is a good historic leather. It turns out that he had been doing bark tanning also. I traded him a book for some of his leather and tools. He is a blacksmith too. He was thrilled to get this little gothic-style blank book. I was thrilled to get actual bark-tanned deer skin, some buckskin, and a bunch of tools.

You seem different from other binders in that you might not have a typical routine each day. I remember your saying your life is seasonal, so you may not get up and bind books each day. It depends on what part of year it is and where you are.

A lot of it depends on the weather. If it is a nice day, I will go outside. Some things I do when the weather is good have to do with the book, not to mention the bone work: cooking bone, cutting bone, sanding bone, and hewing bone. I make bone tools at least part-time. Most days I do some bone tool making. I do things related to making the books since I make the whole book. I may be doing some process of making paper since I clean the fiber, cook the fiber, and wash the fiber. That can happen a lot of the year.

It might be an hour or two; it may be just keeping the fire going or getting the wood to keep the fire going. I am doing more leather making and that is ongoing—tanning fleshing, de-hairing, soaking. I haven't done that much, but I want to do more of that. There are the wooden covers. I am always doing something with wood, whether it is heating with fire so I can do bookbinding or something to do with bookbinding.

Now I am selling covers for my classes or just on my route of teaching. And since I am teaching bookbinding, I am doing prep work. But the main time for me to be in my shop is when the weather is rainy and cold, or just plain winter. I am one of the few people who want to see a late spring. If it is April and snowy I am really happy because I am just getting the books going and I want to still pretend it is winter. If it is warm, I usually go outside, unless I am totally broke, and then I'll work on books since that is my main winter income. If I am on the road it has to do with bookbinding, whether it is driving or working on the car to drive, since I work on my own vehicles. You do that when you need to. It all ties in since I need that to work.

You are like the frontier family that keeps the fires burning, and you do all the work to keep the place going.

It takes a lot of work to just keep that place going. But on the other hand, you are not paying a large overhead in rent or power. Cutting wood is a form of making your own power, or fixing the truck that hauls the wood. It's all tied. It's a lot more time than it is money.

So instead of doing binding 12 months of the year and paying a lot of bills to someone else, I am doing a lot of my own work and not paying bills to someone else. There is a trade off there. That takes a certain kind of person to even want to do that. It can be romantic to some people but there aren't that many people that want to do it when it gets down to it.

They can always go to the Old Ways workshop and see if it is for them.

Yes, and I really wish that I would have more people to talk to about it. That is the nice thing about being on the road—I get to talk to people about books and tools and meet people who really want to talk about what I think about. That makes it really gratifying. Not only do I go on the road to make money, but I also get a lot of book socialization. That recharges me to go back home and go for another round at home. I am always glad to get home.

I am impressed that you know so much about what is going on in bookbinding. It seems you know everyone I've ever talked with or heard of and you know what is going on in the book world. You are not in any way secluded in that sense.

I'd like to get more involved, be a Guild [of Book Workers] member. I have kept up my Dard Hunter membership. If I want to market at a Dard meeting, I have to be a member.

What is your favorite part of being an independent bookbinder? And what is your favorite type of project?

What I would like to do the most is to get paid to do the kind of books I do now in my spare time—going the whole route, making my own replica with thread, paper, and as Gary Frost says, "building the book from the ground up," which is making everything myself from local or salvaged materials and not being dependent on anybody. Chris Clarkson says that if you want something good, you've got to make it yourself. People continue to accept and pay more and more money for increasingly inferior materials. People like he and I would like to change that. The only way to do that is to research how to do it and show other people how to do it so they can at least demand high-quality materials. Like the old days and the old ways, we are high quality. I'm part of that movement that wants to preserve that, recreate that.

I think that is something a lot of people would like to happen. So building a book from the ground up is what you really want to do.

Yes, that is my life work. The tools are kind of a sideline, but they are a way to pay for all that other stuff. My idea is that I have a body of work now, and I am ready to ask for some help. Maybe the help will be people buying one of those books or giving me a grant.

What about the least favorite thing about bookbinding?

I think it is trying to estimate the prices for book repair. Most people that I run into don't want it to be an open-ended job; they want to know how much it is going to cost before they give you the work. I'm getting better, but I still work way too cheap. If I get a job I'll do it the best way I know how no matter what I told them for the price. I always stick to my price no matter how long it takes. Even though I have written stuff down and kept records of time, I still give bad estimates. That is the worst thing about binding—and finding the work. I don't really try to advertise, it is a word of mouth business.

All those years I worked without a phone, so isolated people couldn't even drive to my place. They can't call you. It is a hard way to make a living in book repair. That eliminates a lot of people right there. That has changed now, but I went for 30 years like that—not the most conducive business-building atmosphere. I was seasonal too. To tell someone "I might not get around to it for six more months, when winter comes" is not what people like to hear either.

Are you still doing book repair?

Oh yeah, just in the winter. I do just enough to keep in practice. I do it on an average of two to six months; it varies.

What advice would you give to someone who is interested in becoming a bookbinder, regarding the reality of making a living and how to learn?

That is a tough question. In describing bookbinding, to me that means sewing, so that eliminates a lot of what we call book art, a big part of the book world. I know a lot of people who make a living at book arts but have never really bound a book. It is all book related. I used to be more bitter about people who could ask a lot of money for more of a sculptural book art piece, and you could see that there wasn't a whole lot of time in it. There is a certain clientele that wants that kind of stuff. I was struggling with the strict traditional stuff. I used to be a little bitter about it, but when I went to Penland [School], I suddenly made peace with that and decided that anything that enhances a book—if they want to call it a book and it doesn't look like a book to me, it doesn't have pages, it doesn't open, whatever—then that is fine with me because it all contributes to the wellbeing of the book arts and the prosperity of the book itself.

I don't consider the book to be endangered in any way. I think the appreciation of the book is growing, especially the handmade book. It doesn't seem like books themselves are declining, even machine-made books. I am not worried about that. I think it is one big happy family now. I even got my own wacky book, *The Dump-Truck Book,* that will go on the road someday.

I'm trying to be all-inclusive. There are so many simple, lightweight ways of making books that people can make a living at. You don't need all the cast iron and complicated equipment and a big heavy-duty shop. I'm famous for portable bookbinding. I've done it in the back of trucks; I've done it in tents; I've done it anywhere. I like doing things outside. You don't necessarily need a real complex building or equipment to do a lot of good stuff. The Keith Smith books talk about binding in that way, so unintimidating. When I started, what you would read would be strictly traditional that required a lot of complicated tools and was really hard to learn on your own.

I would encourage people to start simple and start playing with it. There are so many things you can do really quickly and get good results that can even sell. Start doing it. Don't worry about the equipment stuff. There are all kinds of cool stuff you can do without a huge commitment or getting in debt. You don't need a separate building to do it. Do it on your table or on a piece of plywood—long and link-stitch for instance!

For more information on Jim Croft, and to see examples of his work, go to http://www.traditionalhand.com.

Cris Clair Takacs:
Aviator Bookbinder

Chardon, Ohio
September 2007

I arrived in the small mid-America town of Chardon, Ohio, home of the annual Maple Syrup festival. Upon arriving, Cris and I took Annie, their adopted Corgie, for a walk through the cemetery across the street—crisp leaves were underfoot from stately old oak trees and vibrant orange colored maples. The cemetery was storybook idyllic, with headstones of all sizes, shapes and vintages, some designed and sold by Sears and Roebuck over a hundred years ago. As we walked back to the raspberry painted house that Cris and her husband, Bob, share, with the big "barn" behind it, I felt like I was walking through a Norman Rockwell calendar.

Cris and Bob both live and work at home. Cris' bindery is divided between a renovated upstairs with good window light and clean worktables, and the darker basement where she does paper washing, leather paring, cutting, and tooling. Cris spent days in the Cleveland Public Library learning bookbinding from every book that she could get her hands on that related to bookbinding. Self-taught, she also made her own decorative marbled papers. It wasn't until Czech binders Jan and Jarmila Sobota immigrated to the area that she received hands-on instruction. She went from being self-taught to learning from an internationally known master bookbinder.

Cris and I were both fortunate to have lived close to and spent much time with Jan and Jarmila Sobota. The Sobotas immigrated to Cleveland when they first came to the USA, before they relocated in

Dallas. Cris was ripe for hands-on instruction. She was a sponge to all the Sobotas taught her.

Cris now focuses primarily on restoration and conservation work for local clients and book dealers, specializing in children's books with pop-ups and sliding features. Her unique and whimsical design bindings incorporate movement and are often sculptural bindings. Cris has continually supported the Guild of Book Workers, most recently as membership chairperson. She also works part-time at the International Woman's Air and Space Museum, with a dedication to preserving the memory of American women pilots. Cris is a licensed glider pilot.

With her intelligent sense of humor, an uncanny ability to communicate with dogs and cats, and a devotion to aviation, Cris is quirky and endearing. She brings to the world of bookbinding a zealous enthusiasm for the craft.

Why did you choose to go into bookbinding?

I didn't want a real job, which is still an issue. I wanted to be able to travel with my husband [Bob] when he went on business trips. I wanted to have a job that I could leave for a while and come back to a few weeks later. I wanted to be independent. Bookbinding seemed to fill that need. It was something that I liked to do because I liked to repair things.

My husband and I both liked tools. We couldn't go down to the local hardware store and get bookbinding tools, so we had to make our own. Some of the books had instructions on how to do that. We also got to hunt in antique stores for tools that were related to bookbinding.

I learned how to do paper marbling first. There was usually a chapter on that in the books on bookbinding. I was thinking, "This is so neat, I didn't realize I could do these." I had seen marbled papers in old books and didn't know that it was something a person could actually do.

So you learned from books to do marbling and bookbinding?

Yes, and some of my experiments with glazes actually worked out. Unfortunately, I haven't been able to replicate them.

Arthur Johnson implies in his book, *The Practical Guide to Craft Bookbinding*, that women don't have the talent to be bookbinders and shouldn't try. But he has good descriptions on how to sew a book and the different types of sewing. You have to not let this man discourage you. Get Laura Young's book. Sit down with Laura and have her talk you through it. Mary Schlosser once said that my comments reminded her of Laura Young. When I was sitting up with her and Margaret Johnson in Margaret's room [at a bookbinding conference] drinking bourbon, I felt like I really had arrived! My mother would be amazed that such women would even speak to me.

You told me why bookbinding was a good fit for you. What made you even think of bookbinding as a career?

Bob and I were sitting in a bar one night with a friend, and Bob asked me, "Why don't you take up bookbinding?"

And I said, "You mean like General Bookbinding?" That is a plant about 15 miles away from here that does bookbinding. I've never been out there. They advertise for employees 365 days of the year, a real sweatshop kind of place. Bob said, "No, don't do that." I don't know why we thought it would be a good job but I said, "Yes, I've always wanted to do that."

I had learned how to do stitching. My good friend's husband wrote a masters thesis and brought it over to me because he didn't want General Bookbinding to do a "perfect binding" on it. So I whip sewed it and made a nice case for it. I had to use press-on letters [for a title] because I didn't have any other kind of tools. I began a quest to find tools. The first time Bob and I went to Europe, we spent a weekend in London. I went to an art store where I bought gelatin and brought it back. I had already tried using Jell-O gelatin to restore a picture. It was a picture we got in a bar, like a fan picture. It was all spotted from hanging in the bar. That was the first time I washed and resized paper. I soaked it in Jell-O gelatin to clean it up. It wasn't valuable, so I wasn't losing or hurting anything. I don't do resizing like that now.

Was there anything in your past that would suggest you would go into bookbinding?

I was a second child. My mother always repaired things. She would attach oilcloth on my sister's books using contact cement. I would peel it back and get yelled at for doing that. But I was thinking, "Isn't there some other way we could fix this?"

I liked crafts and knitting and crochet. I liked to play with chemistry, mixing things. When I read about marbling, the book said to use hide glue as a size, so I went down to the hardware store and got liquid hide glue and used that to float oil color paints on it. When I was growing up, my mother worked for Manpower, a temporary employment agency. One of the things she did was to demonstrate various foods at trade shows. I remember she was demonstrating Swiss Miss, the first hot chocolate that had teeny tiny dried marshmallows that reconstituted in hot water. I spent a week with her at the sportsman show in Toledo while she was demonstrating Swiss Miss. I was walking around and saw a guy who was selling a marbling kit. He had a bucket of water and he said, "You dip a toothpick into the paint and then onto the water and the paint floats. Then you take your pencil or your bottles and spin them down into the bucket of water and marble them." I got the kit. I've always been fascinated by that kind of thing.

In our house if you needed something, you would first try to make it yourself. When my mother was taking care of the neighborhood kids, she would mix up some paste, cut up some newspaper, and send us out into the backyard, telling us to make something. "If you want a pony, make a pony!" So we played with papier-mâché. Now I work on books.

It sounds like you were encouraged to make things without worrying about whether you made mistakes.

We did it right! We were German. German children were given buttons to play with—playing means sorting the buttons by color, size, and number of holes. That's fun. I still have some of those buttons. We would save everything because we might need it.

I think I did all these little things to become a bookbinder. My sister started off her college career in chemistry and switched to art. I started off in English and stayed in English. I developed a love for research. I got that from my mom too. I remember my mom taking me to the library one day. She said she was going to be the weather lady at the Girl Scout day camp. I said, "What do you know about weather?" She said, "Nothing, that's why we are going to the library!" So that's what you did. If you wanted to learn something, you would go to the library and learn about it. So I got every book I could find on bookbinding.

I needed to get a teacher. I wanted to find a teacher. Going back to what I said about England, I saw an ad in one of the art stores for the Guilford School, where Gabrielle Fox went and where Maureen Duke taught. Now, thirty years later, I've met the people who I would have been in class with had I gone there, which is cool. I had done all these different crafts, and bookbinding encompasses them all. It is also unique enough that nobody else is doing it and hard enough that nobody in their right mind would want to do it. It had that snob appeal. I used to think I wanted to invent something for bookbinding, expressing myself in bookbinding as a book artist, but now I think maybe I already have but I don't know what it is, if you know what I mean.

Having read so much, I learned many different ways of sewing instead of one way of sewing. I had made thirty blank books to sell at my first craft fair. Every sixth one was a different style. They may not have been perfect, but I followed the [instruction] book as closely as I could. I did that many so I would know how to do them, and I did five different styles so I wouldn't get bored. I'll never do thirty of anything again; ten is my limit, or twenty if the pay is good. I don't want to do edition work.

You really learn how to do something if you repeat it.

Yes, I taught myself how to do it. I did blank books, and I marbled paper. A lot of people didn't know what marbled paper was then.

Then Jan and Jarmila Sobota arrived. There used to be something in Cleveland called the May Show. It was the local artist show held at the Cleveland Museum of Art. One year, I was working in a frame store for a watercolor artist. The only judge for that year's May Show was going to be the retiring director of the art museum, Sherman Lee. I thought, "This is cool because this is his show and he would want to make a statement." I had been exposed to things like Tony Caines' books with the puckered leather. I had tried that technique using sheepskin leather from Tandy and using Rit dye.

I was also doing things with the marbled paper. I chose a book that I always loved, which I had heard of from the movie *The Horse's Mouth*, about an artist and his patrons in England, and about art galleries— who should own art—and about life and laughter, basically. I was sure that Sherman Lee would have read this book. My book had blue-dyed leather and a nice design, and even with its faults, I thought he might want the book in the exhibit as a statement. And he did. It was displayed nicely but laying on its back when it should have been standing open.

I had the horse laughing. There were a lot of images and colors in the book that I used in my design binding. The label was horrible. I did it three times. I was using gold leaf on a tape and a handheld pallet, and it was kind of wonky. I had tools at that time, but I still didn't know where to get good supplies.

The next year, I didn't get in the exhibit because I had a miscarriage. But the following year I thought I should enter. I used a library copy of David Balasco's *Through the Stage Door.* David Balasco was a set designer and a director, and he believed in three-dimensional set design. I did a relief of one of his famous sets on the front of it. As an English major, I also had a minor in theatre. The book was stabbed sewn and had wings that folded out so it would stand up on its own. I used marbled paper to look like theatre curtains. I took little bits of leather and made little curtains on the stage design windows.

The reason I picked this book was there was a blackboard in the back of the stage where the label would be. It was well displayed. It was a sculptural binding I called "Off the Library Shelf and Back on the Stage." The show had two floors. The judges were from the American Craft Magazine. The rest of the show was mostly good pottery and craft items. You could see my book while you were either walking across the floor or looking down the stairway. They liked it. I went upstairs and there was another book in the exhibit. It was by some woman named Jan Sobota. I went, "My God, why did they let my book in? This is someone who really knows bookbinding." It was a cross where the book is pulled out and stands on its own. I ran and hid.

That was the year my mother died, and I wasn't doing anything, feeling depressed. There were open studio days at an artist organization called Nova. Jan Sobota's name was on the program. I thought, "I'll go up and talk to her." Jarmila was there, and she asked me who I was. I mumbled my name and that I had a book in the exhibit. She started screaming, "Jan wants to meet you! Nobody knows who you are, but he says you are a bookbinder. Other artists try to do books, but you are bookbinder!" And that was the start of my relationship with Jan and Jarmila Sobota. Jan was out of town, probably at a Guild of Book Workers meeting or a workshop that he was doing. She called him immediately.

I would go up to Cleveland to see them sometimes. One time I went up after Jan had a heart attack. Jarmila had let the car freeze. She didn't know about putting antifreeze in a car. She was really depressed when I walked in. We talked. That is when we became good friends. She taught me a lot about business. From there, they moved their gallery out to Geneva. I thought, "This is what I prayed for." I wanted to meet a European binder and one came to Cleveland and then moved to Geneva, which is only 12 miles away from me. Whenever I would get depressed, I would hop in the car and go to their studio.

They would always be working on dozens of things for a show. I would offer my services, and they would pay me minimum wage, and that was fine! If we were sewing books, Jan would sew one and tell us how long it should take us. We would try to work up to his speed but never got there.

My grandmother was Polish and spoke broken English. So broken English is like a second language to me. The problems that most people had in understanding Jan, I didn't have. But I would tell him to, "Just show me. You don't have to explain it to me. Just do it, and I'll watch." He would smile and do it, and he would come back in a few minutes and say, "You have some such problem here." And he would show me where I wasn't doing it right. I also took workshops from him.

You learned on the job with him.

I did. He started The School of Bookbinding and Restoration, and I took classes. That was cool. I got a certificate from him. Then he got the offer to go to Southern Methodist University. People were mad that he left town. We used to meet on Tuesday nights and do a lot of drinking afterwards.

Sometimes the roads were rather interesting—freak snowstorms would come up. I didn't like drinking and driving. And I didn't, I didn't! I would stay late so I would be sobered up. Those guys do like to drink. I got to see him do some of his most fabulous work—watch the big guy work. Before they left, he went to the marbling tray. Jan doesn't do that very often. When Jan marbles, I am amazed. "How does he do that?!"

I saw Jarmila marble but not Jan.

I got to see her marble too, and I got a whole bunch of her scraps. She did double-marbling, which I had never heard of. It was so entirely different from the formal way that I learned. I taught myself not to throw away anything you did just because it wasn't right, because even though it was not right then, it was going to be perfect for some project down the road. Even though I made these papers a long time ago, a lot of them are still really good. I did a lot of work with them, especially on boxes because boxes can make a bad book look really good.

It sounds like you learned on your own and then honed your skills with Jan and Jarmila. How long were they here in Ohio?

Must have been about five years.

Did you take classes from anywhere else?

No, not a series of classes. I heard that there was a book fair in Akron and they were going to have a bookbinding demonstration, so I went down and that is where I met Andrea Kline and Ellie Strong. Meeting them was like meeting sisters. They told me to join the Guild of Book Workers. The first Standards seminar I went to was in Chicago at the Newberry Library where Karen Crisalli showed up and was selling leather in her hotel room. They didn't have a vendors' room back then. That became the beginning of the vendors' room. This wasn't in the centennial celebration history [of The Guild of Book Workers] because they didn't really cover the Midwest chapter in the centennial.

The following year, we went to Columbus or Cincinnati for a Midwest chapter meeting. Ellie and Andrea and I offered to do the meeting in Cleveland. We thought we would set it up just like Standards. We decided that we would have a vendors' room with around seven to ten vendors. We had Karen Crisalli there, and we had Peggy Skycraft's husband [sell her marbled paper]. He was coming here anyway for a wedding—everybody is connected to the Midwest in some way. We had a tour of an ink factory. Jan Sobota did a demonstration of relief under leather or bookcloth. I think we charged $15 for Jan's workshop. That is where I met Peter Verheyen who had come just for Jan's workshop. After that, the GBW started having a vendors' room. It started here.

It is interesting that you were almost completely self-taught except for the time you took classes from Jan.

Yes, that is why Standards is so important to me. I was working with a dealer at one time on Civil War books and working with leather, lifting leather and trying to pare it and get it underneath. I went to Standards at Bloomington, and that is where Don Etherington introduced the Japanese tissue repair and tissue hinge. It was like, "Yeah! I was wondering why there wasn't something like that." People were outraged by the paper technique then and some people still are. But it made sense to me.

Phillip Smith came here when Jan was in Geneva and talked about the Florence floods. At the time of the floods, in 1966, my sister was in

Cris Clair Takacs' studio.

college and learning art, and she wanted to go to Florence. I did too, though I didn't say anything. My mother said, "You go, you are never coming back. You definitely aren't getting more college money if you run off." So once again, I didn't do that, and she didn't either. But now I am friends with the people who were there. Philip Smith said it was the first time binders from different countries sat down at the same worktable and said, "That is not the way we do that. How do you do that?" They also developed some new techniques. They saw how wet leather reacted with the bookends on bindings. The metal impressed into wet leather and left a pattern; that was kind of neat! That was where Philip Smith got the idea to press objects into wet leather. I read that in his book. I thought that was cool. I was meeting these people.

I think Standards is most useful to people who already have some knowledge.

Yes, I knew what they were talking about. There were things I read in the books about bleaching paper, and I thought that didn't seem right. But when I saw it demonstrated, I had the background and suddenly it became clear.

Everybody learns a different way. This spring we had a workshop with Martin Frost who does edge painting. I just audited it. I could run around and see what everyone was doing without the sweat of having to produce something. I could look at 20 people's work to see whether it was working or not. I could see something going on in somebody else's work instead of being involved in it myself. I could learn from watching. Some people can't; they like to actually sit and touch. I like to be learning when I am out in public, and I like to be alone when I am actually working.

What are your favorite parts of being a bookbinder?

My least favorite part seems to be calling up the client and telling them their book is done. Isn't that strange? I'm afraid they aren't going to like it.

Do you ever find that you want to lower the price? I sometimes finish a book and think, "It isn't perfect. Maybe I should knock a little off the price."

I think most bookbinders will look at their work later and think, "That is pretty good." But right after you made it, you have been so into it that you don't see anything except your flaws, like when you know that the endpaper slipped or you pressed it too hard.

A couple of the first books I made were book boxes, before I even met Jan Sobota [who is known for fabulous box bindings]. I saw them in the 20th Century Binding book and I thought, "This is such a great idea." But I didn't really know the full mechanics. You need to do several.

I won an award on one that I thought I destroyed. I pressed it too hard and it slipped. I ran away and didn't look at it for two weeks. But I entered it in an exhibit, and I won an award of excellence in any craft, and then somebody bought it, so I made a lot of money on that one.

How long have you been bookbinding?

I hate to say it—30 years. I should be further along. If you are teaching yourself, you have to be an apprentice (to yourself) for a long time. I don't consider myself a master—on some days, maybe.

You weren't doing it day and night.

No, mainly at night. If Bob was going out of town, I would do a 40-hour workweek in three days. Those were late nights.

What is your favorite part of bookbinding?

Doing it. I put on a book-on-tape or CD—usually something that I have listened to several times so I don't really have to listen to it that much and it is just running through the head, taking care of the brain that wants to go off and do something else—and the fingers take over. I like cleaning paper, if it is working and my back doesn't hurt. I may have to be sitting in the same position for a long time, in pain, so obviously I'm enjoying what I'm doing.

That is one of the threads I find in common among independent bookbinders: physically painful, financially painful, lots of time put into it. Yet they still do it.

So many people complain about their work. They get a job just so they have something to complain about. They hate the people they work with. They can't wait to get away from their job. I have to fight a lot of things to get to my job. When I start working I don't want to stop. Sometimes when it's really working well, I find that I haven't worked that long.

You say you have three basic clients and they are booksellers.

Yes, I've had more. I don't like doing Civil War books. I like children's books.

I had this book for a number of months that I was working on. I learned that the ink wasn't going to run, so I colored it in as I thought the rest of the scene would look like and gave it back to him months later. He was thrilled. I just couldn't possibly charge for the amount of time I put into this because it was a learning experience for me. But a couple years later, I got the same book. That one I repaired in half an hour because I knew what I had to do. Some of them you can't charge the same for if it is a learning experience, but it all adds up eventually to fast repairs.

I do like doing repairs. Probably 80% of what I do is repair. I have a whole shelf of books that I bought, figuring I would bind them—things I want to do for friends and for myself. *David and the Phoenix* is one I want to do for me. That is one I've always wanted to put a design binding on, even before I knew what a design binding was. Phoenix rises out of the flames of its own death—you can't just do a flat book. But I'm not good enough to do what I want to do yet.

People may show up with a self-published book, and they only want one or two. I see myself as the village bookbinder. When I was in the craft store with ten other artists, there was a blacksmith. He was the village blacksmith, and I was the village bookbinder. People will show up with a Bible. There is a lady who does the newsletter for Phi Kappa Gamma and whenever they get enough, I sew the newsletters together and put them in a binding, two copies. Librarians tell people about me. I've had people show up with books for whom I repaired something for them 15 years ago, or 30 years ago! A couple showed up last year that told me I did their family Bible 30 years ago—the first one I ever did. I have repeat clients. I get library referrals, bookseller referrals, and friend referrals.

Do you have a website?

No, I couldn't deal with that. I have a backlog of work.

What is your turnaround time?

I ask the client, "When do you really need this? Would you call me a couple weeks before you need it and remind me?" I've always been bad about deadlines. Douglas Adams had a line about deadlines: "I like the sound they make when they whiz by." On the other hand, if I do have a deadline, I'll stay up all night and finish it. I'll sit there for three hours to make sure I'm closer to the deadline before I start. It is usually that I don't know what I'm going to do. But once I've started, I don't like to stop.

What would be your favorite job you have ever done?

I've done three books that involve aviation. That is when it all comes together for me. I love my Ruth Nichols book, *Wings for Life* (which didn't get into the GBW In Flight exhibition). Another favorite was the first book I did on flying, *Cold Comfort Farm,* which I got from a couple who are still my clients. I first met them at one of Jan Sobota's workshops. They deal with 20th century children's books. That is my favorite book! I won an award on the binding, "Award for Excellence in Craft of Any Kind," at the Toledo Museum of Art's annual artist show. The next year my binding on *The Doors of Abu Dhabi* was rejected from the same show. I showed Jan Sobota, saying, "I'm not faking it anymore. I know where to buy the leather; I know how to do the tooling." There was going to be an exhibition in Switzerland that was open to everybody. So I sent my book. It is pictured in a beautiful catalog. We went to the opening of the exhibit in Switzerland. The train stopped. Swiss trains always run on time, but our train stopped and sat there for two hours, and we missed the opening of the exhibit. So there is the story of my life, in a nutshell. That is why I don't try to succeed. There will just be a train that stopped and you'll just have to sit there, politely.

Have you ever had any jobs other than bookbinding?
    Not really.

Don't you work at the Women Pilots Museum?
    That is part-time and no benefits. It is not a real job that pays benefits and with a retirement scheme. One of the reasons I got into bookbinding was because no bookbinder ever really retires. I used to say, "After I am dead they will still be pushing around the body because I still have a few more things to finish. Give me time to catch up." But I also admire that; I've met people in their 80's and they are still working. I've found that, too, with the women pilots at the museum. One of my favorite movies growing up was *Holiday*, with Cary Grant and Katherine Hepburn. Cary Grant makes a bunch of money and then goes on holiday because he wants to work when he is old. He wants to enjoy himself when he is young.

How did you get involved in aviation? One of the questions I like to ask is about other things you enjoy doing in life besides bookbinding. You seem to have an equal passion for aviation.
    I always seemed to. When I was ten years old, I read a book about the Wright brothers, actually about their mother and how she inspired them. Their sister helped them because their mother died when they were very young. We have that book in our library at the museum.
    My husband was always interested in aviation because his father had learned to fly airplanes in the Navy, at the end of the war. Both my husband and his brother were interested in aviation. One of my husband's co-workers moved out here and flew airplanes. I was 36 and just learning to drive at that time. I didn't like cars. I liked public transportation. I grew up in Toledo where you could take buses and meet people. My mother didn't drive either.
    Not driving was one of the reasons I could learn bookbinding. I would drive with Bob to his work and then take a bus into downtown Cleveland, or I would carpool with somebody who worked in downtown Cleveland as just a ride-along. I would spend the whole day in the library in Cleveland researching bookbinding and learning about it. I still have my handwritten notes on marbling. I learn by writing things

down.

There was a line in the movie *Repo Man:* "The more you drive, the less intelligent you are." I had time to do bookbinding. Somebody once told me, "You get your license, and you won't have time to just sit." Now that I drive, I am running more errands than I used to. I used to walk down and get my groceries just a few times a week. Now I go get groceries every day!

A friend took us down to a glider field, just a mile outside of town. Bob went up for a flight. I thought I wouldn't get a chance to do this. But there was a man there that asked me, "You want to go up too?" So I got to go up after Bob came down. Our friend said, "Just imagine you are in a comfy chair." I sat there looking out over this canopy. He said, "You want to try flying it?" I said, "Comfy chairs do not have controls. They do not fly. I'm just going to sit here. One image at a time please."

Bob started going out of town a lot on business. He was always out of town on Wednesdays when the glider club met. I used to drive myself down and just hang out and help. Bob joined but then got ulcers and dropped out. I thought he would get his license first. I realized that I always wanted my license, and he wasn't going to do it. So I joined, and I did it on my own. I discussed it with his brother. Now his brother is taking lessons. It is real seat-of-the-pants flying. I found out that Deborah Evetts has her pilot license, though she said she hasn't flown in years. Roger Powell was a pilot in WWI. When his plane crashed in France, he got out and re-sewed the cloth on it. A French farmer's wife came out to see him and was amazed that a man could sew.

I was in the club for about ten years, and it was taking up three days a week of my time. I would wait around all day just to get my 15 or 30-minute flight in. I thought if I concentrated on the bookbinding the way I was concentrating on the flying and spent that much time bookbinding that I could make the final push into the big time.

My friend Ellie Strong told me about a museum of women pilots that just moved to Cleveland. So I went down. At that time in my life, I really needed to meet other women pilots who didn't have ego issues. By that time my mother was dead. The women at the museum were about the age my mother was when she gave up living. I have enjoyed it ever since. I started off as a volunteer and then they asked me to work. I would go in the corner and work on whatever project they needed until it was finished. I am the collections manager there.

We have a small staff. There are only four of us working there. I accept donations, write the letters, and do the housing. Luckily we don't need a lot of repair work on things, though I have fixed books and made sure everything has dust jackets. I work two days a week. I've done at least three exhibits a year at the museum, so I am doing something, but my creative juices seem to be going to that more than the bookbinding.

If you had your druthers, if you could paint a picture of your life, what would it look like?

Somebody that I trust would take over the museum, and I wouldn't have to worry about it any more. Then I would devote myself to bookbinding and be here working on things, getting things done, not have the frustration of not getting peoples' books done.

Would there be any other angle of bookbinding you would work on or is there anything you haven't done that you would like to do in bookbinding?

I have a few books on the shelf behind you that I want to put design bindings on—and the design binding using the whiskey and bourbon bottles down stairs. I want to use them to do *Our Man in Havana*.

Would you say you earn a living doing bookbinding?

I've never advertised and I've never pushed. There are weeks I make my living and there are weeks I don't. But if I have enough repair work to do, I am making a good amount, at least more than an autoworker makes in strike pay. I would like to do that and balance it with working at the museum. One idea of working at the museum would be so I have a steady income that would pay for bills. I'm still not doing that. My husband is still paying for things.

What is your favorite type of work in bookbinding?

I like doing repairs; I work mostly on old children's books and pop-up books. They are so interesting. I am learning things, mechanisms from them that I can apply. The two books I had that sold recently both had some kind of mechanism in them. One was about classic typefaces. Gabrielle Fox found the miniature book. I made it into type drawers with faux wood grain on the paper. It was all made out of paper and binders materials. The books were actually drawers that pulled out with little brass handles on the spine.

I put a little label title on it like a label on a type case. Nancy Jacobi from Japanese Paper Place saw it and said, "I like your book; it's full of whimsy!" That is what I'm aiming for! There is not a lot of whimsy in this world, and it is one of my favorites.

The other one that also sold was *The Pit and the Pendulum*. I wanted the book (under 3x3x5) to pop out when the pendulum was pushed. Bob made me the pendulum. I wanted to keep it sharp, but he said I couldn't because he said people would hurt themselves. So it has a dull edge. He was trying to figure out how to make it work. This is where all the paper mechanisms I have worked with helped.

Bob and I build things together with tinker toys, as models; we always build models. It took me 15 minutes working with cardboard to make slides to have this platform come up. Then I handed it over to Bob, and he did it with thin sheets of plywood. He cut them out for me, and I sanded them down, and we built it and built a cardboard box around it. I knew it could be done, though I hadn't known how I was going to do it.

What are your gifts or abilities that make you a good bookbinder?

The ability to play.

You have a curious mind.

One of the reasons I got into bookbinding was because I didn't have to drive to work, and I could do something I loved. Around here everybody has a winter project that they are working on. In the spring everybody's projects come out. You have to [have a curious mind]. One of the craftsmen in my co-op complained that when it wasn't snowing we weren't getting as much done. Staying in is a talent. I'm using myself. I like listening to books on tape, working on books.

What advice would you give to someone who is interested in pursuing bookbinding as a career?

As membership director of the Guild of Book Workers, I have collected information on what schools you can go to. I've talked to people that have gone to those schools. I would tell them to go to one of the schools. Now that there is a school up in Ann Arbor, I want to save up my money and go take courses there with Monique [Lallier] and get a certificate. I tell people to do that. I tell them not to buy a lot of equipment at the beginning. You can add on equipment. I have spent a lot of money on my equipment, but I didn't just buy somebody's bindery. That is a huge investment.

The only time-payment I did was when I bought a piece from Frank

Lehmann. He was just starting his supply business, and he said it would help establish him. Buy the tools you need (unless you get a really good deal, of course). I think it is good to go work in an institute or library if you can to find out if you like it. When I was starting bookbinding, someone asked me if it was something I could do eight hours a day, seven days a week. That was a good question to ask.

I mentioned to my friend, a potter, divorcing from an engineer, "So why are we working so hard to learn something useful that we love when we could just be making money somewhere? Because we wouldn't be happy, really, doing that. But we won't knock anybody who does it, God love them."

Don Rash:
Perseverance of a Dream

Plains, PA
September 2007

A pivotal point in his life directed Don Rash toward bookbinding. He was a laborer on a construction site when a friend showed him an ad for a bindery assistant job at Haverford College. He had already developed a love for printing on a tabletop printing press that he and his wife bought. He thought working in a bindery would be cool, bringing together his interests in printing, calligraphy, and the arts. The job at Haverford would make far less than construction work, even less than a janitor was paid. But with his wife's encouragement, he applied and got the job. Thus began the journey to become the master bookbinder that Don Rash is today. Those were the days when no formal instruction was available in the US. He learned from bookbinding manuals and on the job. Eventually he and his wife, Pam, took bookbinding lessons from Fritz and Trudi Eberhardt (1979-86). Though the Eberhardts tried to dissuade them from following in their footsteps into a financially challenging career, the Rashes decided they wanted what the Eberhardts' had—the freedom to be independent bookbinders, working together.

They set up their bindery in a part of a small cottage in Lake Harmony, PA and began work. Tragically, Pam was stricken with cancer, eventually succumbing to the disease. Don persevered, trying to fulfill alone the life they had chosen together. The journey was tough. He ultimately left their little rural home and eventually moved to Wyoming, PA where he rented a larger space and expanded his business. Now married to Elaine, a librarian in Wilkes-Barre, and living with her and their dog,

Max (after which he named his press, Boss Dog Press), and several cats, he works right across the street from their house, in a building they now own.

Not tall but with a solid build, wearing a black t-shirt and jeans, Don could easily be mistaken for the construction worker he was long ago and whom he thinks he would still be if that pivotal event hadn't occurred. Don is good-natured as he talks honestly about life and living, its hardships and pleasures. He seems content in this small town.

Don walks my friend and fellow bookbinder, Bill Minter, and me across the street to the building that houses his bindery, once an old pool hall. A massive Washington press dominates the first floor. Upstairs is the office and bindery with a wall of windows that overlook the street and their house. Several times during the interview Elaine arrives home and then leaves again. Each time she leaves, she looks under the car for cats, and then she and Don wave to each other.

The building includes a spacious, two-bedroom apartment with access through an outside entrance in the back where Bill and I stayed. Mona, Curly, and Larry, their cat family, are our apartment companions. There is a sitting room that has a TV and lots of movie videos, a kitchen and eating area, and even a washing machine. The accommodations are very affordable and convenient for students who take classes from Don. He has since acquired another neighboring house to accommodate more students.

Don's easy-going manner and gentle kindness are appealing. I respect his perseverance as an independent bookbinder, in achieving a dream that presented challenges along the way. I applaud his willingness to share the craft by offering classes (complete with accommodations) at his School for Formal Bookbinding. He wouldn't consider doing anything else. As he says, "In the end, if I can just keel over working at the bench, that would be fine."

What is your background in bookbinding? I know you have studied with the Eberhardts. What made you interested in bookbinding?

I started off as a calligrapher in college after I was a failed art student. I was an art major for a year; it was a bad year. I had done some calligraphy. I wandered down to the Z's in the library and found all this really cool book stuff—books about books. I got interested in printing but I didn't know how to go about it, so I did my own thing.

I was heavily into science fiction at the time. I really wanted to do science fiction art. But after I graduated from college, I was teaching an extension class in calligraphy for the university and met a woman whose husband was editor of the DuPont papermaking magazine called *The Papermaker.* He was a friend of Henry Morris. Henry had set him up with a whole papermaking set up and a little print shop in his basement. After suffering a heart attack, he sold us (my then wife and I) a tabletop printing press and some type. So I started playing around with that. Probably a year or so later, a college friend of mine who knew I was into this stuff called me up (he was living in New Jersey; we were living in Delaware) and said, "There's this place called Haverford College. They've got an ad in the Philadelphia Enquirer for a bindery assistant. I thought, "Well, that would be really cool because it all kind of ties in." So I called them up, but the assistant job was only part-time. But they said, "The bookbinder's job is open too if you want to apply for that." I said, "I don't have any qualifications." They said, "That's okay." So I drove up to Haverford, about a 40-minute drive, and I interviewed for the job. I was going crazy because there was all this stuff there that I had read about. They had a print shop around the corner, with a Chandler-Price and a big old Washington. I was so enthusiastic. The associate librarian that was interviewing everybody, for whatever reason, saw something in me. It could be that nobody else really wanted the job the way I did.

At the time, I was working as a laborer on construction jobs making $9,800 a year. They would lay us off for two or three months in the winter. This job made $7,200 for the whole year. That is less than the janitor was making. I went back to my wife and asked, "Should I do this?" She said, "Yes, go ahead." So I said yes, and they hired me.

The associate librarian, David Fraser, taught me what he knew from the two women who had been the bindery people. Then I was supposed to teach my part-time assistant who didn't know anything. When the semester started, I had ten students working ten hours a week each. It was not a good situation because I didn't know squat. I had read a lot, but I hadn't done anything. This was 1978; I was 26.

My wife, Pam, had ten horses. She had hurt her back just before we got married—screwed up both sciatic nerves—so she couldn't ride professionally as an exercise rider anymore. So she started teaching riding. When she couldn't ride anymore and teaching started to get sour for her, she sold the horses. She got a job at the library doing processing. She got into the bookbinding. It worked out well. The red book with the eyes that was in the last Guild of Book Workers show was the last book that we collaborated on. I feel bad because I didn't say that in the catalog. She was good.

Fortunately, all we were doing at that time at the library was to take in paperbacks, take off the covers, cut cardboard, glue that to the inside of the covers, put plastic on them, stick the textblocks back in with Gaylord's double-stitch binders, and then cut the fore-edges off. The only cutter we had was a 36-inch power guillotine. Every time we ran it the whole library would shake. It was not good. We ended up trading the guillotine for a Jacques shear.

I had heard Fritz Eberhardt talk at an exhibition in Philly in 1978. I knew it was a big deal. I heard that Trudi Eberhardt was offering a class at Montgomery Community College called "Fun with Paper and Cardboard." So I called and talked to their daughter and told her I was working as a binder. She said it was a really, really good class, because it was the start of what they would teach their early [bookbinding] students. My wife and I both took it. It was great because it taught how to cut, how to paste, how to fold—basic stuff you really need to know to do this stuff even halfway well. We decorated papers too. At the end of the class, we all made a single shell clamshell box structure—a single shell with a case on it that ties in the front. The very last class, Fritz came and he wandered around and looked at everything. He was really gracious about the whole thing. What they intended to do was continue on and actually have a curriculum to teach at the community college. But they had bad experiences with students. Fritz swore that he would never teach again. The administration of the community college decided that anybody with half a grain of sense wouldn't take a class like this so they got rid of it. Pam and I had intended to take it again. I made her call because I was too scared. She called Trudi and said, "Look, we'd really like to continue to study. If we get the students you want, and you tell us how much you want us to pay you, will you come and teach on Saturday mornings?" She was really leery. She said, "If it is not more than an hour drive. I'll come down and look at your situation and I'll think about it." She drove down in 55 minutes. We showed her the shop and we talked. She said, "Let's give it a try and see how it works." We did that for four or five years. She would come Saturday mornings. There was a really good bakery in Haverford at the time, so we would get croissants, and bring them back. We'd all get there at 8:30 and have a croissant and at 9:00 we would start to work. We worked until noon. She would bring her lunch, so instead of driving back right at noon, we would all have lunch together. She was lucky if she got out by 2:00. It was fabulous. She and Fritz were super people.

After we reached a certain stage, there was Pam and me and Jane Aaron who was a librarian at Swarthmore, and Bruce Bumbarger who took my place at Haverford. There were the four of us. Then Trudi brought Fritz in and we started going to their shop. We started going to Harleysville on Saturday mornings instead of coming down here. We did that for a couple of years. At that point, we were doing better quality work at the library. Primarily, the situation down there was mostly dealing with circulating material. I really wanted to do something more.

We looked at what Fritz and Trudy had and really thought that would be the way to go. They said, "You really don't want to do this (from a business point of view)." But we wanted to do it anyway. Pam's parents had a really teeny cottage, one-and-a-half floors, 800 and some square feet, on a lake just south of here. They sold it to us for what they had paid for it. So in 1986 we moved. We didn't have much of a shop. We had been living in a one-bedroom apartment. We had the biggest table model Kutrimmer, and a couple of nipping presses, and a German backing press, and a sewing frame. We kind of shoehorned everything into this little cottage and kept working. Then in September of 1986, Pam got cancer. After we moved up there we didn't have the really good health insurance from the college. She got better and she got worse and she passed away in January of 1989. Everybody at Standards in 1988 got this big piece of construction paper and signed it. I still have it somewhere. It was really nice. We appreciated that. I hung on there for a while and then I had to make a decision, which way I was going to go. We had made the commitment to make it on our own, so I wanted to keep the business going.

I grew up in Delaware. My choice was whether to stay here in Northeast PA or go south. I ended up staying here. There was an old industrial building over in Wyoming that is only about three miles from here that had a "For Rent" sign on it. I thought maybe it was time to have a real space instead of working out of one half of the first floor of the cottage. The price was really good, and it was a big space—$250 a month for a huge, huge space. So I moved the shop down there. It took a month to get the place all fixed up. It was really nice. I was there for eight years as an independent binder. We had gotten to know a guy named Barney Taylor who, after he retired, set up his Press of Appletree Alley in Lewisburg, PA. I bound his editions for about 20 years. That was good steady work. I was doing a lot of that kind of work, getting work here and there, and getting the all too frequent Victorian Bibles that we have around here. Then Elaine and I started dating, and we got married in 1994. We bought this place in 1997, and I've been across the street from the house ever since. It works out really well, especially with the price of gas the way it is. Not having to commute is nice. Unfortunately it means I don't get many snow days.

So you worked in the library and then you left to set up a business like the Eberhardts had. What kind of clients did you have and what kind of work did you bring in?

We had been doing work for Philadelphia people. We had done work for some of the Philadelphia book dealers. When I moved up here, I swore I would not do work for another book dealer, but unfortunately I got to know a guy who is related to someone that my wife knows. He is a book dealer, so I'm doing his stuff. Most of it was Barney's. We were lucky that our overhead was low in the cottage. We kept ourselves afloat, but it wasn't a lot of money. Since I've been here, I've done some institutional work for the larger special collections; I've done work for Lehigh University and Lafayette College. I've got a piece for the University of Scranton, a dummy of a gothic binding. I've just won a contract to do some bindings for Independence Park down in Philadelphia. They have all these historic buildings that are full of historic books. Fritz and Trudy used to do work for them. It's funny because even though there are a fair number of book people in Philly, there are no freelance binders like us. They are either all book artists or they are institutional people who don't do outside work. Even though the population of people that do this kind of stuff has increased, there is still nobody to do it.

Can you explain the difficulty you have had with the book dealers?

I know their profit margin is thin. Mostly, it is the fact that what the book needs and what the dealer needs are two different things.

Where do you get most of your jobs? How do people find out about you? Is it word of mouth?

It is pretty much word of mouth. After I moved down here, I took the advice from someone here and I put my name in the yellow pages. I actually got work from that—mostly family Bibles and cookbooks. I have been trying to slide out from under that. I took my yellow pages ad out a couple of years ago and it doesn't seem to have been a problem. At this point it has primarily been word of mouth.

Do you do edition work?

Not now. Barney was the only one.

It seems like your visibility has increased a lot in the last few years.

It has.

I see you on the book arts listserv and other places, and you spoke last year at the Guild of Book Workers' centennial celebration. You are obviously trying to be more connected to others in the bookbinding world.

It's happening. When Pam and I tried to figure out what to do, we decided we wanted to start showing consistently and that happened. Then in about 1996, Frank [Mowery] saw one of my bindings and he was impressed with it, and he told [bookdealer] Josh Heller about me. So Josh was selling my stuff. Then I slacked off doing the design bindings. It is another one of these deals that if you stick around long enough, people know you are there. A lot of people come and go. The guy who lasts the longest is the guy who you see.

So you were in institutional work when you first learned. Then you left institutional work because you wanted to do kind of what the Eberhardts did. Are you devoted to staying independent now? If so, why?

I think at this point I probably am chronically unemployable. There are times when the cash flow gets bad and I think, man, I should find an institutional job. The benefits are a big thing. Fortunately, Elaine is a librarian, so she has benefits. She has been there as long as I have been binding. We both started the same year: 1978. Next year she'll be 30 years at the library, and I'll be 30 years doing this stuff, which is kind of a scary thought. I'm used to working by myself. I'm a really bad boss, which I found out working in Haverford. So going into an institution with the idea of running a shop would not be a wise move for any parties concerned.

Have you had any individuals work for you here?

Yes, I had a woman who worked with me over in Wyoming. There is a local family, and she was a friend of one of the daughters. There was a nice spread on me in the local paper right after I moved down here.

The daughter called me and said, "I have this friend and she is really interested in bookbinding. Would it be okay if she got in touch with you?" I said, "Yes, sure." So she came to see me. We talked it over, and I told her, "I can't pay you anything." She said, "That's okay." She stayed with me for most of the eight years I was over there.

Eight years and you never paid her?

No. She was very good that way. At the end, she kind of slacked off and disappeared. I feel really bad about that. It had reached the stage that I tried to pay her, but she wouldn't come into work. It was not a good situation.

When I moved here, Peter Verheyen introduced us to a young woman who had just graduated from Syracuse who wanted to learn bookbinding. We worked it out so she paid token rent to stay in the apartment [in the bindery] and she worked in the shop. A little later she got a job at one of the local bookshops and continued to learn and help me in the shop. She met a guy who she married. She was with me for about a year-and-a-half.

What qualities make you a good bookbinder?

Oh man, I have no clue. I think there is a certain personality though. You have to be willing to do a lot of fiddling with little details without losing sight of the big picture. You have to be dedicated, especially to do it [as an independent bookbinder], through the good times and the bad, because the bad times come pretty frequently. The other thing is that what we do is not glamorous. Guys that turn wooden bowls are glamorous in their own way. But generally, a book is a really sophisticated artifact, and a really subtle artifact when it is done right.

I think that you need both the people who do it and the people who appreciate it to understand these little teeny things. Fritz would say, "There is not a single thing that goes into a binding that is not important." The very smallest thing is as important as the big thing. That means when we look at other people's work, we get our noses right down in there because we really want to see how they did it. That is one thing about artist's books. I'm not trying to be demeaning here—artist's books are kind of upfront and straight-forward in some ways, so they are much more accessible to people outside the field. A really well done binding, not necessarily a design binding, is a subtle thing. It is the details that either make it or break it. For me, if I look at a binding and if the tooling is just on the surface and isn't impressed, or if they didn't bother to letterspace it, it loses points in my head.

Is that the letterpress printer and calligrapher in you?

No, I'm sure that every craft is this way, but I think that books especially need an educated audience.

After your wife passed away, you did independent bookbinding on your own for a couple years. Did you make it without a second income?

Yes, but I had a line of credit that was maxed out!

The criteria I used when choosing people to interview is that they make a living as independent bookbinders, but most of these bookbinders live with someone who also works. I am curious about whether people can really make it on their own as independent bookbinders.

I think that it is possible, but you have to accept a relatively low income to do the work that you want, and to understand that what makes a good bookbinder doesn't necessarily make a good businessperson.

Well it is certainly not a 35 or 40-hour-a-week job.

No, never. In fact, I was talking to a client the other day. Actually, I had been avoiding him because I don't have his work started. He is a really nice guy. I was telling him, "You know I'm getting kind of burned out." It's true. I mean you do six days a week for 30 years, and it does tend to get to you after a while. The weird thing is that things in some ways are going pretty well right now. But yet this is after a very long time. A lot of those six days a week were 12 hours a day; now I've gotten down to about ten hours a day.

What do you like about being an independent bookbinder? And what do you not like?

There are fewer things that I don't like. Most of it is the financial insecurity. If I had my druthers, I wouldn't have to do a lot of work for people, which may sound counter-intuitive since obviously I'm trying to make a living. But what I'm shooting for now is to teach about half the time, have one or two conservation clients, have time to do a couple design bindings a year, and print one edition a year; that would be an ideal situation I think. Whether that will happen, I don't know. Part of the thing about teaching that is really nice is that people come, they pay you money, you teach them, and they go home. I'm not by nature a self-starter, even though this is the kind of business where you really need to be a self-starter. One of the reasons you see all these books hanging around here is this is stuff that should have been done a while ago that just didn't get started.

Basically, I am trying to keep other people happy. It is really weird because I know in my head that pretty much anything I do for people at this point in my career will be acceptable if not pretty good. But there is still this little thing inside me that says, "They are not going to like this. This isn't good enough." Then you hesitate. But you show it to someone on the street and they say, "Wow, that is really wonderful! How do you do that?" Almost everything that goes out of this shop, I'm afraid to show the client, which is really stupid. Not all jobs, but all too often, especially a conservation job or a restoration job. You do it and you can see what you've done. It doesn't mean the client can see what you've done. I'm no Bernard Middleton who can repair to the point that people think it has never been repaired.

You have told me your ideal scenario. What are your favorite things about bookbinding?

There are very few things I don't like about the actual process. It is fun work. I like being my own boss. There is something about it that would be hard to beat somewhere else. It is funny—when I first did the announcement about the school back in late spring, one of the first emails I got was from Sam Ellenport [Harcourt Bindery]. He said, "I'm on the board at North Bennet Street. We are looking for someone to take over the program. You may want to think about applying. It's nine months, benefits, etc." If circumstances were different and I hadn't needed to move to Boston, I might have considered it. But I thought about commuting in Boston. I thought about this commute [crossing the street]. There was no comparison.

I have an old friend; he has his bachelor's degree in chemistry; he's got his masters degree in business administration. His wife is a graduate physicist. Probably four times in his career somebody has come into his office and told him to clean his desk out, "You've got to be out by noon." His wife has multiple sclerosis; she got it about the same time Pam got

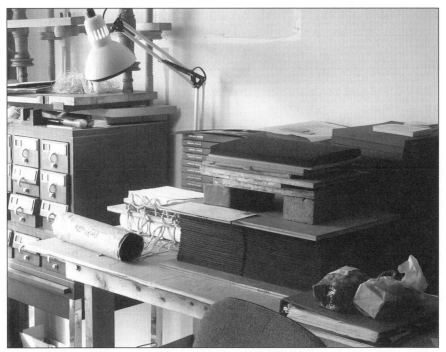

Don Rash's bindery.

cancer. Now she is in a wheelchair and has been for a couple years. This guy tells me that I'm the smartest guy he knows because I don't work for somebody else. In these unsure days, that is actually not a small thing. I can go out of business and all kinds of bad things can happen, but at least nobody can come in on a Friday and say, "You're gone." That counts for a lot.

Are you enjoying teaching?

Very much. The students seem to go away learning stuff and being happy. What I have to do now is redo this space. I'm going to build benches along both walls and a bench in the front here. That will give me enough room. I will take a maximum of five students—small classes. I've been charging $20 a night for a bed here. It's got to go up next year, but it will still be affordable and everybody will have a place to stay.

Is there anything in your childhood that might suggest that you would be interested in bookbinding?

Just that I read a lot. My mom was a crafty lady. My dad was not a patient man. I didn't realize until after he passed away and I was talking to my mom that he had actually worked as a carpenter. But for whatever reason, probably because he was not a patient person, he ended up being a middle manager for the state of Delaware for much of his career. I built model airplanes. I drew quite a lot. I thought I would end up doing some artsy sort of a thing. My dad wanted me to be an engineer. I had no past experience doing this, so I was a step behind. Bruce Bumbarger, who is at Haverford, had been a cabinetmaker before he started studying from the Eberhardts. So much of this stuff was second nature to him—keeping his hands clean and having worked with his hands. It was a struggle for me for a long time to get to that point where I was comfortable doing the work.

When I looked at the job at Haverford and had a vague idea of what the potentialities were, I focused. I put my printing press away. Pam was the same way. We did a little bit of printing, but we focused on the binding for six or eight years. It made a difference; we were studying and we were practicing. I was doing the work full time. After a while, we started taking in work too on the side. It was pretty much bookbinding 24/7.

I wonder what would have happened if you hadn't been given that opportunity.

I would probably still be working construction. It is odd because my friend Terry, the chemist, is a pretty hardcore libertarian. I was too; it is kind of trendy for science-fiction people to be libertarians. But it really hit me that as much as you want to be in control of your own life and be left alone to do your own thing, so much of how we end up is fortuitous. Somebody calls me up and I jump on it, and I happen to be interviewed by a guy who thinks I can do the job. The people at Haverford were extremely supportive. I knew the work I was doing wasn't particularly good, but they were thrilled that somebody came in and was serious and was trying. It could have all gone south at any point. A lot of it is pure dumb luck.

We went to PBI [Paper and Book Intensive] in 1984. Pam had an assistantship so we went there a couple days early. I remember driving to the airport with one of the guys from Oxbow. We picked up Hedi Kyle and a few other people. We were having a really nice talk on the way. I was saying how I came into bookbinding through the back door and she said, "Hey, that is how it happened to me too." She kind of fell into it. She wasn't looking to be a bookbinder. I don't remember her story now, but she didn't grow up wanting to be a bookbinder. All of a sudden the possibility was there and she took it.

I am always fascinated to learn how people hear of bookbinding because it is such an unusual career.

Actually, I can say there was one thing that led me to wonder. Remember the psychological tests that they give you freshman year of college, or maybe senior year of high school? "Do you prefer your carrots cooked or raw?" Did you ever get that test?

No, where did you grow up?

Delaware. I remember taking this test. They give you a list of things you might be good at. I remember bookbinding. That was the first time I'd ever heard of bookbinding. It did make me perk up my ears, and at some point, I remember going to the state library and looking it up. The first book I ever read was Bernard Middleton's. I remember taking it home and getting into it thinking, "This is really interesting stuff." That was in college I guess. That was the only indicator.

Where did you go to college?

University of Delaware. I graduated with a degree in American Studies, which made me a perfect candidate for becoming a construction worker. I didn't have a real good average.

The last job I was on, I had to join the steelworker's union. I thought, this is going to be great, I'm going to make some money! They put me to work raking topsoil, which was fine. I didn't have a problem with that. That would have been 1975 or 1976. I was making $3.15 an hour. When you joined the company, they took $75 right off the bat for the union. Then the union got $.57 an hour before taxes. It was brutal. I was making just over $2 an hour. I made $75 a week and I was renting a room for $75 a month, so I was okay.

I think you answered this question. What would you like to achieve in bookbinding that you haven't yet achieved? I think that is that ideal scenario you talked about.

I think so. In the end, if I can just keel over working at the bench, that would be fine. Fritz finished his last binding six months before he died. It was a good binding too. I really just want to be able to work until I can't work anymore. It's funny, the first book I read was Middleton; the first book I bought was Philip Smith's, *New Directions in Bookbinding,* when it came out. I was making $75 a week; I paid $30 for the book. It blew me away. I would like to do more design binding, and it is always nice to have people like your stuff. I don't know how important it is, but it is there.

Is there anything you would rather be doing than bookbinding as a career?
    No, no way!

Is there anything you do besides bookbinding? Do you have a life outside of bookbinding?
    We both work pretty long hours, but we really like spending time at home with each other and the critters. In the summer, we have a garden and a couple of fruit trees, so we're outside a lot. We travel occasionally. This past year we've been going regularly to local auctions, which is a lot of fun. There are a lot of good restaurants around. It's a good place to live.

You also have an artistic ability.
    Yes. Fritz and Trudy were emphatic about this. Even when we do ordinary work, aesthetics are a factor, even if you do just a quarter cloth binding. The choices that you make will either make it a successful binding or not a successful binding. These are parts of the education that need to be addressed as well as the technical aspect.

What advice would you give to someone who is interested in pursuing bookbinding as a career?
    Don't! Run, run like the wind! In some ways it is easier now than when I was getting started. There are schools; there are people that are teaching. Just the awareness of books as artifacts is much higher than it was 20 or 30 years ago.
    Opportunities for study aren't as limited as they were, although they are a little different today. There are still very few places that teach traditional (I hate the word "traditional;" that's why I call my school the School for Formal Bookbinding) skills, the basics, the real fundamentals of making a book that really works. You can go to a lot of art schools and get an MFA in book arts, but it's not the same thing.
    The problem becomes, where do you go to get your bench experience? That is still a problem. People reasonably expect to be paid for their work. But to people like you and I [to Bill Minter], the cash flow just isn't there to pay a real salary. To try and go out and get grants

to fund having people come and work, that is just a whole other rat race.

That is probably the biggest problem—finding places to apply your trade in the early stages. There is still not an easy way to do journeyman work.

Let's say an aspiring bookbinder gets his or her education and wants to go into private practice. What advice would you give them? Bill and I had this conversation about not getting advice in school on how to run a business.

That is something that I should have someone come in and teach—how not to go out of business being a bookbinder. That is something we don't get. You need it early on. One of the things I do tell people in the early stages of their careers is to not undercharge. They assume rightly that their work is not up to the standard they want it to be, and they undercharge.

But once you get that mindset, it is almost impossible to get rid of it, and you underprice your work for the rest of your career. I swear to God, I do it all the time. A little old lady comes in and brings a Victorian Bible. I quote $150, and she says, "Oh, that's fine." And she drives off in a Cadillac or a Mercedes.

Do you give a quote on a job up front? Do your clients accept your fees?

I have been really lucky with my clients that way. Part of it is I don't charge enough. They are always happy when they see the bill. Sometimes they will say that I don't charge enough.

Fritz and Trudy said if you have to give a quote up front, you should always add 40%, which is probably a smart thing to do. The thing that has really helped me is that I found a really good timekeeping program for my computer. Basically, I let the computer keep track of the time. If the computer said it took me ten hours to do this job, at least I know it took ten hours to do the job.

Another question you had was about clients. A lot of my clients become, to some degree, friends. Once they are your friends, you don't want to charge them. It's this insidious circle that you can't get out of. One of my clients who has become a friend owns an animal emergency hospital up the road. He is a really nice guy. He has neutered cats for us for a really low cost. We barter, which is not something I do with most of my clients. But we are able to do that. That has worked out well. But that is an unusual situation.

Is there anything else that you want to share?

Oh boy. Bookbinding is about the best thing I can think of to do. It's a good time. Even when things are bad, I don't think I would be doing anything else.

If you work for yourself, you never know what is going to come in the door. There is a huge variety. I like the variety, doing a little bit of everything.

For more information on Don Rash, and to see examples of his work, go to http://www.donrashfinebookbinder.com.

Daniel Kelm:
Empowering People Through a Community of Bookbinding

Easthampton, Massachusetts
September 2007

Daniel Kelm is a body of peaceful, loving energy. Snow-white hair creates a band around his head from which a thin braid cascades down his back. Furry white eyebrows cap clear blue eyes. His smile is of a twelve-year-old that is excited about stuff.

He named his bookbinding business, The Wide Awake Garage, in memory of his childhood years when he would do experiments and make things. His love of chemistry and science is evident everywhere. Walls of antique, glass-fronted display cases are filled with antique scientific equipment; brown cardboard boxes, stacked on the floor, hold carefully wrapped scientific supplies. Many of these items may become part of his Poetic Science sculptures, a direction he is passionate about. On the other side of the floor is Daniel's bindery. Inside, a stairway leads to a partially enclosed nook, surrounded by books, with a comfy chair in the center—a haven.

Daniel's Garage Annex School and bindery are located at One Cottage Street, in Easthampton, a charming little town afire in color on this September day. His bindery and school are located on the floor above bookbinder Peter Geraty. The building is infused with creative energy from the diverse artists and craftsman that also inhabit the space. A long classroom is on one side of the hallway where visiting bookbinders and book artists teach. Today Linda Lemke is teaching boxmaking to 12 students who traveled from all over the USA to attend. High rows of raw wood shelving line the perimeter, supporting hundreds of brown cardboard boxes with labels like, "Wire-Edge Binding." At the end of the large classroom is a little staircase that leads to a landing full of books about books and models of book structures. At the other end, beyond a partition, is more workspace and equipment, as well a round table, chairs, and a sink.

Daniel is a scientist who taught chemistry at the college level before focusing on book arts. He is still strongly tied to science, alchemy, and philosophy. His recent Poetic Science exhibit at Smith College (www.smith.edu/artmuseum/exhibitions/kelm) featured his moving, sculptural bindings as well as videos that showcase the movement of each book. His books are interactive works of art. In order to begin the bookmaking process, Daniel asks his clients to tell him a story about the project. "Books tell stories beautifully, and I want to know their story so the book that I create can faithfully relate their story."

Daniel is going through the process of making the school into a non-profit organization. He hopes to raise funds to provide scholarships for students to attend classes at the Garage Annex School. He thinks of the school as a way of building community, offering an opportunity for people to come together and achieve a goal. "What can I do? We need to come together and help each other. That is what I try to do through my world here. It's community building." Performing alchemy by transforming lives through book arts.

How long have you been in business as an independent bookbinder? I know you were a chemistry instructor in Minnesota. Tell me a little about your history of work.

In general, I was a chemist. I fell in love with chemistry at age seven. I studied it, devoured it. By the time I got to college, I was well versed in it and did very well, so after taking general chemistry the first year, I started getting jobs in the department. As an undergraduate, I was proctoring and grading exams and tutoring students during my second year. I got a job as an undergraduate research associate. Then I got a job in a biophysical chemistry lab. I saw chemistry from that side, from a working research laboratory.

I enjoyed the teaching a lot more than the research. The project I was on didn't grab me. I taught chemistry for five years. I really learned that I loved it, but I didn't know if I wanted to go on in chemistry. I figured if I wanted to teach I was going to have to go on and get a masters or a PhD. I did well in the academic world, but the environment didn't satisfy me. I was up in my head way too much, thinking about things, when I really wanted to be making things.

As a kid, I had always been building things. We had an alley behind the house. Once a week, the trash man would come and pick up the trash. I had a friendship with him. He always left more stuff at our house than he took away. He knew I liked to build stuff in the garage, so he would bring supplies for me to build with.

The name of my studio is The Wide Awake Garage partly because I built things in the garage. So there I was in college; I'd been teaching chemistry for a few years. I decided I needed to get out of academics, so in 1978, I went from working in the chemistry and philosophy departments to the library bindery on campus. That was my first bindery job. I was only there for a short period.

I was living in an old house in Minnesota, built back in the 1880's. There was no insulation in the walls; it was really cold. I can remember winters back then when it was 45° below zero (Fahrenheit). We would put insulation on the windows to make it warmer in there, but all it did was cut the light out. We had a cold, dark apartment instead of just a cold apartment. I felt like Faust—I put my reclining chair in a walk-in closet; I lined all the walls with books and would just sit in there and read all the time. Faust kept warm because the walls of his library were lined with books. That was his insulation from the cold outside world.

Books were it. I wanted to have a career change. I wanted to make books for a living. This was probably 1977 that I decided to do that. My transition from chemistry to book arts was really a matter of me wanting to build things, looking around for what I wanted to make with my hands. Having collected a lot of books and loving my library, I decided books were the thing. Hard cover books were a lot nicer than paperback books; I wanted to find out how to make those hard cover books.

I had a hard time finding someone in the Minneapolis/St. Paul area that could teach bookbinding. There was one fellow who was doing restoration for the local bookstore, but he wasn't teaching and I don't think he knew that much about bookbinding. I did find someone in the library sciences at the university who had taken one cloth binding class. I arranged with some friends who had a calligraphy studio for him to teach a class on cloth binding. That was 1977.

By 1978, I thought I should just go get a job in a bindery, get some practical experience. Bud Weber, the guy who was in charge of the library bindery at the University of Minnesota, knew that I was interested in hand bookbinding. The year before, there had been an article about Sam [Ellenport, owner of Harcourt Bindery], and Harcourt Bindery, and the school in the *Library Scene* magazine. I was at work one day when Bud said, "Hey, Dan, you're interested in hand bookbinding. Look at this place in Boston." It was a little article about Sam and his working museum-type bindery.

So I went to Boston and took classes. I left Minnesota to come to Boston to learn traditional leather binding and gold-tooling and took classes at Harcourt Bindery while I looked around for a job. Sam had a schoolroom in the bindery. Joe Newman was teaching.

I got a job first at Tantalus Bindery in Cambridge, but that turned out to be the front for an SM equipment maker. Both of the owner's grandmothers had been amateur bookbinders, so he [the man who ran Tantalus] loved bookbinding. But his main business was making SM equipment—lots of black leather stuff with silver studs. It was really weird. I felt like a naïve kid from Minnesota. Here I got a binding job from someone who didn't know leather binding except for another type of leather binding. I didn't stay there very long because he really didn't know anything about bookbinding. I hadn't done any leather binding at that point. I'd ask him, "How do you do this?" He would say, "Just do it the way you normally do it." I'd say, "I don't know how to do it." I have to admit there is one book that I did that gave me the most pain, a beautiful little book of common prayer from 1601, a sweet brown leather book. I turned it into a bordello book with red leather, gold edges, and lots of gold stamped on the bright red chrome tanned leather. To the beautiful leather book, if you are out there anywhere, I am sorry I did that to you.

Fortunately, Sam offered me a job doing the edge gilding and finishing at Harcourt. He had been offering me other jobs. I'd ask, "What do you have now?" and he would say, "Endsheeting, but you are going to endsheet 40 hours a week, every week." I would say, "No, I think I'll stay over at the leather bindery in Cambridge just a little bit longer." Then finally he wanted someone to do the finishing. Where else are you going to get that experience—40 hours a week handling gold leaf? There aren't very many places left where you can do that. I grabbed it. That was great fun on Sam's dollar. At first you chase a lot of gold around; it doesn't go where you want it to go. I still do a lot of gold work, more palladium than gold now. I still like leaf work, as a highlight rather than a period cover-all sort of thing. I learned from Woody Agee. Woody was doing the finishing work at Harcourt right after WWII. He took his GI money and bought tools to start his career in a trade. He was even-split between two different trades—one was bookbinding and the other was plumbing. He happened to choose bookbinding. It was a trade for him. He wasn't passionate about books. He decided he would rather do bookbinding than plumbing, so he used his GI money to buy stuff to do bookbinding. He worked at Harcourt full-time from right after WWII until around 1982. By that point, he was wintering down in Florida and just coming up in the summer. Joe Newman was doing some of the gold-tooling also. Woody wasn't around much, so I was the main finisher and Joe was the shop manager and forwarder. Peter Geraty was also a forwarder.

While I was at Harcourt, I continued to meet people. David Bourbeau would come into Boston and we would meet and talk. He came in and showed me a project he was working on for Cheloniidae Press—a sculptural cover of the head of a right whale. I liked that idea and stayed in touch with him. After I had been at Harcourt for about three-and-a-half years, I realized that I needed to move on to find some other bindery where I could do more refined work, a different type of leather bindery.

David was looking for a partner in his business, Thistle Bindery. So I came out for an interview. It happened to be the day Easthampton had its fireworks. That cinched it for me—the great fireworks display. I really liked David's shop, a beautiful bindery. David has an exquisite aesthetic. I worked with him with the intention of becoming a partner in his business. But pretty quickly we realized that we have very different working processes, and so I just stayed at David's for nine months. I set up an opportunity with bookbinders Bill and Elaine Streeter; they were just moving into a house they had purchased in Northampton. They gave me the porch of the house to set up my bindery. They set up their bindery in the rest of the building. I stayed there for two or three years, working on my own projects as well as client work.

Right from the beginning, when I was working at the library bindery in Minnesota, I had my own shop and was doing my own work, picking up clients, developing a business. When I was at Harcourt in Boston, I was a finisher there, but I was a forwarder of my own leather bindings. I was also doing restoration; that was back when restoration didn't have such a bad association with it.

I was doing restoration for the Christian Science Mother Church. It was interesting—during the day I would do the finishing on the first reader's set of the Christian Science Journal. Then I would go home [to my private practice] and reback books from the same set that had been bound at Harcourt's 20 some years before. They were calfskin. It is hard to tool. You have to paste-wash it to get the size to sit up on top; the alternative is to varnish it. Sam would buy Victory varnish, and I would varnish the whole calfskin binding. Then you could put Vaseline on to hold the leaf, and the varnish would hold the gold when you tooled. You had a good chance of getting full coverage of gold, but of course the varnish stiffened the joints and after 20 years, the joints would break.

I would take them home and reback them. So it was good; I was learning a lot. I always had my own business. But it wasn't until 1983 when I hung out my shingle on Masonic Street in Northampton that I had my first public presence with my business: "Daniel Kelm, Bookbinder." Then I moved over here [to Easthampton] in March of 1985. I've expanded as space becomes available. That is the story of how I started and got here.

Is there anything you remember as a child that would have suggested you would be a bookbinder?

As a child I made little books. I did little comic book type things. I would do the drawings. I would dictate to my mother what the voices would say. I would do little adventure stories. I wish I still had them.

Did you talk to Tim Ely about those books? He told me he used to write comic books as a boy too.

Oh yes. When I first visited Tim in NY, it was just before Steve Clay was going to start selling Tim's work. The first time I went to Tim's place on the Upper-West side, there was a bookshelf with three feet of Tim Ely books on it. He had never sold one, well, maybe one. Then Steve started selling them like crazy, and Tim had to start to make books on demand. It changed the way that he worked. Some of those books on that shelf were great; there was one called the *Gama Sutra* with all these flying beans, based on the *Kama Sutra* filtered through Tim's mind. It was wonderful.

Tim is coming out for the opening. [Daniel has a show opening October 2007, at Smith College.] A lot of the books in the museum show have been collaborations with him. A significant part of my work in the show is from the late '80's. Reagan was in office, and Reaganomics was operating quite amazingly in the arts. There was so much virtual money that there were all sorts of projects to be done. Cheloniidae Press was located in this building and was putting out two major books a year. I would do the full-leather versions—between 15 and 35 copies of each book—each with an elaborate box. It was great to get those projects. Then Barry Moser with Pennyroyal Press was putting out one major book a year. There was all sorts of work. Plus, I would come in some days and just play. "What should I make today?" I would start mocking up a book that would turn into a one-of-a-kind or a small edition of three or five copies. I would send them off to [book dealers] Bromer's in Boston or Jim Cummins in New York. They would sell them, send the money back to me, and I would play more.

The show reflects a lot of the collaborations in 1988-91, that era when I was playing and selling books through dealers. Then the Persian Gulf War hit, around 1991. Galleries closed and people held on to their money. The arts were hit pretty hard, so I switched to doing more commission work, which was good too. That is when I started doing books with Steve Clay at Granary Press. Steve would do larger editions than I would normally do, plus he did a lot of them. I ended up doing about 19 projects with Granary over the years. He put them out all over the world in great places, so my work was seen, but it wasn't entirely my work; it was a collaboration.

Was the wire-edge binding a result of your playing?

Absolutely, it was actually a result of a box-making project. It was the box for [a Barry Moser edition of] Frankenstein that had a flap. Rather than a fall back box or a clamshell box where the sides overlap entirely, because this was a thick book, I did a suitcase style of box. It had a flap on the fore-edge side. The way I resolved the closure on the flap was to put a 1/16th inch diameter wire rod right on the edge of the flap because I wanted a hole very near the edge of the flap where I could lock on to another part from the other half of the box. One day, I was looking at that flap with that wire rod buried in the edge trapped by the cloth wrapping around it, and I thought, "You know, I could make book structures like that and use thread and tie off one wire to the next." So I threw together a quick model, and it worked. That was the first wire-edge binding. That must have been 25 years ago now. If I look at the date on Frankenstein (1984), I could figure out what year I invented wire-edge binding.

Right after that, Peter Geraty got married. I did the guest book for his wedding. Rather than doing a codex—just a standard structure—I thought, "I'll use this wire-edge structure and try an accordion." I asked Peter for a story—whoever comes to me wanting to do a project, I ask for a story. "Tell me a story." Books tell stories beautifully, and I wanted to know their story so the book that I created could express their story. Peter said that both he and Daphne were going to wear four-inch-wide silk stoles around their neck that would hang down to their knees, and they were going to ask all of us to make little talisman to put onto the stoles for this occasion. Then they were going to add other talismen for other occasions through their lives. I thought the book should be in the shape of a stole, so I did a wire-edge accordion book—the first finished one I'd ever done—with these shapes that created a finished structure that hung like a stole around the neck. Plus, it folded down into a little square stack of panels. The in-between is what surprised me. You could put it down on a table, and it would form little architectural structures. That was a total surprise. I thought that was really cool. I thought, "I can do sculpture using this." That is what captured my imagination and why I experimented so much with wire-edge binding. There are probably a dozen different versions of it now.

What brought you into teaching bookbinding? How did that develop?

I said I had been teaching chemistry. I like teaching. I just like that environment. I liked Mr. Wizard. I was really struck by that. This guy was a great inspiration to me and to a lot of my friends. When we were young, I watched Mr. Wizard whenever he was on. I had an uncle who was kind of a Mr. Wizard type, Uncle Don. He taught chemistry at a high school in St. Paul. I was always interested in the projects he was working on. He was the one adult who would ask me, "Hey,

Dan, what are you up to?" None of the other adults asked me that question. I thought, "This guy is okay." I had always liked the teaching environment. When I was involved in college chemistry, I did a lot of teaching.

When I got into book arts, I thought about teaching, and I did teach at Harcourt. After I had been doing the finishing for a couple of years, Sam asked me to teach the gold-tooling classes. That is how I met Shelagh Smith from Toronto and a contingent of book artists from Toronto that came to a class. That was before Shelagh founded the Canadian Guild of Bookbinders and Book Artists. Right after they founded the organization, I started teaching classes for them. I really liked the group there. I was thinking of teaching other aspects of bookbinding. I had been working full-time as a finisher, so I really knew finishing, and I could teach that just fine.

Then I started teaching forwarding, and I realized I needed more experience. That was pretty early in my career. I gave myself a five-year plan of going back to my studio at night and weekends doing my own stuff and learning, and then get back into teaching after that. I just hunkered down and made books and boxes. Then I started teaching again.

I taught in my studio in Boston. I would have private students come in. It was good practice to work with the private students first; then I started opening it up to classes. I moved out here [to Northampton] in 1982 and started The Garage Annex School for Book Arts in 1990, eight years after I moved into this space. I started the school here because I had been on the road a lot teaching, and I wanted to stay put and not travel quite so much. I like teaching in my own studio. I use the Socratic method—if someone asks me a question, I very often ask a question back at them to try to stimulate a conversation which they can then use as a model when they are alone in their own studio. If you can ask yourself the right questions, you can move forward in the process so perfectly. When you have someone else who has experience, that other person brings their experience to that conversation and starts directing you in a way that will allow you to understand something that is very personal to you. I hate lecturing. I hate preaching. I never listen to anyone who is preaching to me. That is not the way to get me. I think my dad preached at me a lot. It didn't work.

A good example is where I had an intern here for three months. We

were doing hand-sewn endbands on a full-leather binding. She was up
to the hand-sewn endbands. For the first one, we drew a picture, just a
cross-section of the pathway of the two threads in the style of endband
that I use. She did it, and it worked just fine. She didn't get back to it
for a few days and when she came back she said, "I can't remember
how to start that endband." I said, "Do you remember the picture we
drew?" She said, "Oh, the picture." She went away, and I didn't see her
again for a few hours. I went and found her in the other room. She had
finished the second endband, and it looked great. I said, "So, it worked.
How did you do it?" She said, "I drew the picture and that gave me the
information to do it." So I said, "When you're in your studio and you're
starting an endband, you don't have to call me and ask me how to do
it. Just remind yourself to draw the picture and it's all contained there."
That is what I try to do in my teaching. I try to give people the means
of carrying on that interior dialogue by asking themselves the questions
that bring them to the end point that they're seeking.

*As I understand it, you are doing new bindings, edition bindings, boxes,
playing with new structures, teaching. You do basically all new things?*
    I do. On my own in Boston, I did restoration, but I realized early on
in my career I like new materials. I like the challenge of a restoration,
but I really like to create my own work, so I switched and do just
new bindings. But because we run a school, once in a while I will
have someone come in and teach restoration classes. We do that sort of
thing through the school, but I'm usually not the instructor. I'm out of
practice in terms of restoration.

*What is your favorite part of being an independent bookbinder in private
practice?*
    The greatest strength of being independent is schedule. I love to
come and go as I please. There was a time when I was doing a lot of
all-nighters or working late into the night. I was in a not-so-happy
relationship for a while. I've been married to Greta now for 14 years, and
it has been a great relationship. But the one before this was less happy,
so I would often come over and spend the nights working here.
    Greta asked me when we first got together if my career would be so
far along had I been in a happy relationship for the previous ten years,
and the answer is no. I would not have been here nearly so much. But
I love being able to come and go as I please. There was a time when

I would go to matinee movies and come back and work all night. I would often go out and play during the day and come back at night.

But of course, the other side of that is that there are deadlines and there are cash flow issues. That is the part I don't like as much. It's funny how they go hand in hand, isn't it? The part that I love is the flexibility. Whenever anybody comes here to spend time and work, I say one of the great things we've got is flexibility. Determine a schedule that you want to keep, and come and go as you want. Make it fit your lifestyle. But I've got payroll; I've got 3,000 square feet that I'm paying rent on. There is this constant hustle of making the cash flow happen and keeping people busy. I've become an administrator to a great extent. We filed the papers for the 501C3 status for the school, so we are going non-profit. We should hear in the next month about that. (Update: It has been approved by the IRS.)

The Wide Awake Garage is my for-profit business. The Garage Annex School has always been part of that but a separate entity. It has been part of my business until last year. It is becoming The Garage Annex School, Incorporated, a non-profit corporation within the state of Massachusetts. We are developing new programs.

You asked what I liked best about independent work. Flexibility is a great thing, but it is doing the work, making books, that I've been passionate about for years. My passion is shifting a little bit. I mentioned poetic science—my way of bringing art and science together—which I've been doing through the books. But I'm also doing it in other ways now too. If I could spend my time any way I want to, I would run the school as a nonprofit and do a lot of teaching there, and the rest of the time I would be making books and creating sculpture based on the philosophy of poetic science. I would split my time.

I remember when I first got into book arts, Edgar Mansfield had gone from bookbinding to becoming a sculptor. Remember that book that showed one of his sculptures on the dust jacket? I couldn't understand why anyone would give up bookbinding and go to sculpture. I'm not giving up bookbinding, but my books have been so sculptural for years that I can really see the attraction to sculpture. I often think about that. I would like to know more about his transition in his career. I love teaching. I'm passionate about teaching. I think it is something that our world could use more of. It's not this didactic lecturing that so many of us have run away from; it's more of a community building.

The studio is a lot bigger than I'd need for myself. I created this large studio to bring in a community of people. As I get older, community has become much more important to me. I look at the politics of the world and I think, "What can I do?" What I can do is try to be a sane voice within this society. For years, I've said our society is insane. It's been proven over and over again that we are living within this insanity, and we need to come together and help each other. I get to the point where I wonder, "Why can't we be nice to each other?" It's kind of simple, naïve. But if we are nice to each other, wouldn't that make a better world?

That is what I try to do through my world here. It's community building—bringing people together who want to learn to do something and giving them the means to do that. Giving them the opportunity. It's not like I'm handing anything to anybody. I'm creating an environment where they can come in and thrive and achieve some goal that they have really been dying to do but just haven't figured out how to do.

I like that affirming attitude.

I think that it is the best way. In this country, we have a history of helping each other. There are a lot of great European bookbinders and teachers, but I've also heard of jealousies that have kept some of them from sharing information. That seems to be that old guild type of system rather than what we've got in this country.

When I started bookbinding, Peter Geraty and I lamented the fact that we didn't have the means to go to Europe to study. But we got jobs in binderies and learned that way and did all that work on our own. When our friends would come back from Europe, sometimes I would show them something I was working on, and the response was sometimes, "Oh, you can't do it that way." "Why?" "My master said this is the way to do it." I thought, I'm glad I didn't go. I wouldn't work well if my master really only wanted me to do it one way. It is just not the way I operate.

When people come here, I tell them in the workshops, "What I'm going to show you is a way that works for me. I prepared materials and this is the way we are going to do it, but think about variations or talk with me about variations that might be better suited for what you want to do. It is not chiseled in stone. I made up most of this stuff anyway. You can go home and after you've gotten a good sense for the whole

Daniel Kelm's Garage Annex School.

thing, make it up for yourself. Recreate it." I want to empower people to do what they want to do.

One of the beauties of America is that we can take the best of the European traditions and mold them to whatever we want. We are not bound by the traditions.

But we can look at their traditions, and we should look at them, and encourage everybody to learn as much of that as they can. Even the Guild of Book Workers, early on, was looking at that European tradition and imposed some rules for exhibition that were pretty strict. I think in 1910, there was a list of requirements for a book for exhibition—the leather couldn't be sanded, couldn't be re-dyed, had to be just as it came from the tannery. You could do gold-tooling, but you couldn't scratch it up, you couldn't add your own dye, those kinds of things. And Designer Bookbinders had a list of things that they wanted in their books. I'm glad that the Guild got out of that and opened up.

I love functional sculpture. I've been building functional sculpture for years, but when I hear someone saying that sculpture can't be utilitarian, can't be functional in order to be fine art, I think, "Then I don't want to make fine art."

I don't want to go back in history, but I want to bring a sensibility forward. The gentlemen philosophers' field of study was thought to be broad and inclusive. The different parts borrowed from each other before natural philosophy started fragmenting into chemistry, physics, and the other sciences. There was less territorialism. Now I think we are categorizing things too much, where fine art is so specifically defined. Because bookbinding is considered utilitarian, it belongs in the crafts. I like the idea of art being functional, so books, for me, can fall right in there. Often I get into hot discussions with people who think the contrary.

We get ourselves right down there into the material that we are manipulating, that we are using to represent something. The alchemists did that also. They were intimately attached and commingled with all the material around them. They saw the processes going on around them as extensions of their own inner processes. They called themselves artists, actually. As artists, we are doing the same thing. We are creating environments within which to perform transformations and to be transformed. The alchemists were artists of materials.

As artists, we enter into dialogue, into conversation, into collaboration with the materials. I never ask a material to do something that it doesn't want to do. There is no reason to; it won't do it. Play with the material, talk to the material, collaborate with the material, and you will get a much better result. It is an intimate relationship.

I always understand things best by picking them up and holding them and looking at them. It is physical and slow. Learning to do that with materials is a slow process because it is a body process. Thinking about something is a fast process—it's electronic. So, if you are a creative person you always feel like you are behind because you get these ideas at the speed of light and then how long does it take you to actualize them? It takes you weeks, years. I've got projects I've been working on since the late 1980's, and haven't finished. I think, "I should really go back to that." Well, it's an idea that I had very quickly, then it takes forever to make them. That is the nature of making physical objects. It involves your body learning to work with materials. That is body knowledge. When your body goes through the repetitions to the point where it knows how to handle that tool, then you've got it. It's there. It's like riding a bike.

I like the hand manipulations, the physicality of the books. I use the computer, but I'm not satisfied with it. If I'm searching for something online, that's great, but I often get tired of it and will go back into the studio and just play. That is where my heart is, where my passion is, where I'm satisfied.

Who are your clients, and what type of relationships do you develop with them? Are they mostly people with whom you do repeat-business?

Yes, most of them, though I do pick up new clients every once in a while. I got a call yesterday morning from someone who had seen a portfolio that I had done for another artist in Santa Fe. He called and said he wanted some portfolios.

I don't do any advertising. It's all word of mouth. People see something that I've done and give me a call, but I also do repeat business with the same clients for years—Cheloniidae Press, Granary Books, and most recently one of my big clients is the artist rep for Manuel Neri, a painter and sculptor in San Francisco.

How many people work for you?

I've got one full-time person, though now she is starting to work more on her own projects. One person works half-time. She is doing much of the boxmaking, though she also gets into forwarding as well. Then I've got interns from the colleges around here. They usually come one day a week. I have a full-time apprentice now. A year ago, I started an apprentice program. I wanted to get students to come for longer periods. I get interns coming for up to three months at a time. But I wanted to develop a new program where I work at depth with someone for a longer period; that's what I call the apprenticeship program.

Do they get paid?

Now that we are going non-profit, all of the advice I'm getting is that we've got to charge tuition and then raise money to give scholarships. It can't be just out-and-out payment for the apprentice because donors won't give us money to pay the apprentices directly. What I'm trying to do is raise money through grants to give scholarships.

For 17 years, we have been running this school on tuition only. It doesn't allow us to expand our programs. In a good year we have a little bit of profit that will pay for some of the administration, but in a bad year we don't get anything for the administration of the school. It all goes to paying the instructors and travel and lodging for instructors, with nothing left over. In other regional organizations that I've looked at, maybe 17% of their budget comes from tuition. The rest of it is from grants. By raising money as a non-profit, we can expand our programs. I'm still figuring out how to configure the programs. It can go a number of different ways.

What about the person that comes to you that says, "I want to be a bookbinder." What advice would you give to them as far as education, setting up a business, where to go to work?

A lot of people do come to me and say that. I usually invite them to come to the studio and work on a project. With the interns, I usually have a conversation. "What would you like to make?" Then I help them try to figure out how to make something. They come and spend time. That allows us to get to know each other. I see what kind of hand skills they have. In trade for that, I'll invite them to help—usually roughing up materials, cutting materials, or something for an edition, just so they can get into the production aspect of it.

The strength of our program is that the school is associated with a business, which is a production bindery. We can offer production work to people when they demonstrate a sufficient skill level. I usually tell them that there are a lot of people who are making a living at bookbinding, but being self-employed in this country is a hustle. There is not a lot of support. But it is possible to do it if you really are passionate about it and you want to put a lot of time into it.

I've had people come and say, "I have a family," or, "I have other things going on in my life, and I really only want to put 30-35 hours into it." I say, "You are probably not going to be able to be a self-employed bookbinder." It takes more of a commitment to start the business. It becomes a passion, a full-time employment. It's really hard to set such a constraint and be able to do everything you need to do to start a business. I encourage people to spend as much time as they can at first. You can get to a point where you don't have to spend so much time. But unless you just want to dive in and spend all your time, it's going to be really hard for you to support yourself. So some people go to work for institutions, working from a lower position to something a little more special. You get the support of the institution. You don't have to hustle quite so much. Personally, I don't work so well within an institution, so I've always been self-employed. But that is another possibility. If someone is expressing an interest in going in that direction, then we explore what they have to do to get into an institutional setting.

What skills do you have that make you a good self-employed bookbinder?

Curiosity. Experimentation. I've tried to learn as much as possible about as many structures and materials that I can. When someone comes in with a project, I ask them to tell me a story. By hearing that story, I get a sense of what structure, what set of materials, what relationship of binding to story the text can have. That usually leads to a project that is more successful than if I only knew a couple of different structures and tried to make all books fit into those structures. Often it's not a good fit. There are so many different ways of supporting a story, of telling a story, that we need a broad range, a good solid foundation of traditional technique and enough confidence to feel free to invent and make something custom, really specific to the story that is going to be told.

Is there anything you would rather be doing than bookbinding?

The only thing that comes close is imagining the sculpture of poetic science. I'm doing projects with a curator at the Smithsonian. We're doing videos of James Smithson's chemistry experiments from the 1790's to 1830. There is funding now to do twenty more. It's a great project. And I've been doing videos for my exhibition at Smith College; nine of the three-minute videos are of me talking about specific books. Another one is of me running my alchemical furnace, the purification of gold from the gold scraps from bookbinding. That is stuff I love. I'm a good administrator, but that is not where my heart is. I want to make things. I want to make physical objects. That is why I got into it. But I also know that as an administrator, I've created something that will help me do the work that I want to do, and bring a community of people together.

It seems to me that there is a gentle curiosity about you that will always keep you changing and doing.

I'm really only twelve years old. This is the lab I wanted when I was twelve years old; I finally built it. When I look in the mirror, sometimes I think, "Whoa, who is that guy? I'm only twelve. How did I get that white hair?"

For more information on the Garage Annex School go to: http://www.garageannexschool.com/, *and to see examples of Daniel Kelm's work, to go* http://www.smith.edu/artmuseum/exhibitions/kelm/index.htm.

Peter Geraty:
Bookbinding in an Artist's Mecca

Easthampton, Massachusetts
September 2007

Peter Geraty discovered a love for printing and binding while working at Unicorn Press during his college years. It was there that he learned typesetting, printing, pamphlet binding, and single signature binding. Desiring to work in a similar field after moving to Boston, he landed a job at a small bindery in Cambridge. He did their leather binding, learning largely from bookbinding instruction books. The owner was not that knowledgeable. Glad to leave that place, he was hired at Harcourt Bindery where he received most of his training. Those were the days when bookbinding programs did not exist in America. He trained much like the apprentices of old, learning on the job from more experienced bookbinders. He met Fritz and Trudi Eberhardt, and though he didn't take classes from them, they became friends through which he "learned an approach to their life of bookbinding."

Peter was content learning and binding books while at Harcourt. He claims that he would have been perfectly happy being a monk that just binds books—a simple life. Instead, for over twenty years he has been in private practice, now running Praxis Bookbindery, a small bindery with a few employees. His shop is located in a building that houses woodworkers, printers, printmakers, potters, and painters—an artists' Mecca. The challenges of creating elaborate limited editions in a private practice setting energize him. He calls it "a high-wire act without a net."

Bill Minter and I arrive at Peter's bindery on his daughter's seventeenth birthday. My interview is tucked in between celebrations and family gatherings. Peter has intense eyes behind glasses and dark graying wavy hair. He is calm, pleasant, and comfortable to be around. As he shows us around his bindery, I notice labels on the brightly painted equipment, written in a child's handwriting: "Eggplant" labeled a large purple die stamper; "Sunflower" is a big yellow press; "Cloudy" on a the grey press; a Kensol stamper is "Grasshopper;" and Peter's favorite, "Fly," is the paper tape dispenser, because of its sticky tongue.

The bindery is a long room filled with bookbinding equipment and worktables. At one end is a small kitchen-like area with a sink, kitchen table, and two metal folding chairs. Peter heats water in an electric hot pot to make coffee—fresh ground beans and a French press for the coffee connoisseur that he is. I am grateful. At the end of the workspace is a supply area and two small rooms—one is his office; the other is the leather paring room. Across the hall, a room houses "Eggplant," tooling equipment, and a workbench designated for tooling.

Peter's friendly and peaceful personality is inclusive and cooperative. He welcomes the ideas his employees bring to him and he shares his equipment with other bookbinders in the building. But though he enjoys the creative atmosphere where he works, he someday hopes to work at home and simplify his business. "I have often dreamed of being a monk that binds books. Go pray, do whatever I have to do, and then go bind my books. All I want to do is the work."

When were you introduced to bookbinding?

When I was in college—I was working for a small press called Unicorn Press. They published poetry. I was an art student doing lithography and etching, that sort of thing. I was always interested in printmaking. Unicorn had just moved to the area. That was my last semester in college. I worked there once a week for free, just doing typesetting and printing on the Vandercook and gradually learning a little about binding.

After I left college (I didn't graduate—I went four years and left, so I have no degree), I stayed on for two years working for them. I was basically the sole pressman. The owner, Alan Brilliant, and I did typesetting. Alan did most of it, but I did a fair amount of it too. I was doing all of the binding—the pamphlets and single signature flat back bindings. Then I moved to Boston and looked around for jobs. I was looking for anything in the book field. It didn't matter too much what it was. I loved printing; I liked binding a lot too. I could have gone either way and been just as happy doing either thing.

I started at the New England Bookbinding Company. They had been the bindery for the Riverside Press. The Press was gone by the time I came along. That is when I found Tantalus Leathersmith and Bookbinding. That is where I met Daniel Kelm. I was at Tantalus for less than a year. They made bondage stuff. I did the binding and the owner did the accouterments. I tried not to pay much attention to that. I wasn't happy there. I got a job at the Museum of Comparative Zoology at Harvard that allowed me to leave Tantalus.

I worked away, back in the stacks, doing simple repair and trying to learn to do things. Dan [Kelm] had, in the meantime, gone from Tantalus to Harcourt Bindery, so I started trying to get into Harcourt.

I was at the Museum of Comparative Zoology for a little over a year, and then finally I got a job at Harcourt. I ended up being at Harcourt for four years or more. When I first started, I was doing basic forwarding work. There were a number of men and women there. Sam [Ellenport, the owner] was more comfortable with men, especially more comfortable with them doing leatherwork.

Women were relegated more to box-making and sewing and that sort of thing. When I came, there were two people who did full-time sewing—one man, one woman. There was another woman who did all the boxes and all of the siding-up. She would trim out and put the cloth on for the three-quarter bindings. There was Joe Newman and there was Woody who had come to Harcourt on the GI bill. Woody was doing all the finishing. Joe was doing all the leatherwork. Dan was doing leatherwork and some finishing. He had been learning gilding, so he was doing whatever gilding was needed. I just filled in around the edges and did mostly forwarding.

Eventually Joe left and Karl Eberth came to the shop and did finishing. I took over most of the forwarding. Dan had moved on out here [to Easthampton]. The last year or so, I was the supervisor that sort of ran the back of the shop. I would have been content to stay there because I never really envisioned having a bindery of my own or running my own place. I just wanted a nice place to work.

I liked Sam and we got along well, but I could see it would always be a fight to change things, to make things work more smoothly. So I left Harcourt.

I was working in private practice for a couple years, working out of my apartment, for museums, libraries, and individuals. It was hard to make a living. I was doing a lot of what I called restoration. I wasn't calling it conservation. I was too nervous to call it conservation. Later, when I went to the Folger Shakespeare Library for a three month stint, I was talking to Frank Mowery about how I didn't like calling myself a conservator. He said, "Well, what is it you are doing?" I said, "Basically, what I'm doing is conservation." He said, "Then that is what you are." I got over the hump of calling myself that. I was so used to hearing of people with gobs of training and experience as being conservators. I didn't see myself as that but as more of a seat-of-the-pants person. Even now in promotion literature for the shop, I will write "conservation/restoration." I use the same techniques and materials—archival techniques, archival materials—but with restoration, I will take it further and dress it up to try and blend in or hide things that I've done—beautify the book, as opposed to just leaving it as it is.

After leaving Harcourt, I interviewed for a few jobs. I had a number of interviews. I interviewed for the first position down at the University of Alabama [book arts program]. Actually, I was hired, but six months or so before it was going to start, I decided I just could not move to Alabama. I was born in North Carolina, and I had no desire to go back to the South, especially that far south. I called them up and said, "I can't do it." And I didn't do it.

Then a headhunter called me up. I don't even know how he knew I existed. I ended up interviewing at Monastery Hill Bindery [in Chicago]. During this time, the CIA called me up, although at that time they couldn't say who they were. I think either Frank Mowery or Fritz Eberhardt had put them in contact with me. This was back during the Cold War. I had several phone conversations with the guy there. They started talking about background checks and stuff, and it started sounding like it was going to be ultra-secret; I would never be able to talk about what I did. I didn't want to go there either. I talked to Frank about this a couple years ago, trying to figure out what the job was about. All we could figure out was that they probably forged documents and hid microfilm. I can only guess at what they might have wanted. They liked me because I also had a printing background, so I could both print and bind. I guess they saw that as useful. I'm not that adventurous.

Dan Kelm had moved out here [to Easthampton] two or three years before all this started happening. Space opened up in this building. I had just gotten the opportunity to study for three months with Frank Mowery at the Folger Library, and I was heading there. Dan called me up and said, "There is an open space in this building. Do you want to come out here and set up?" I was going to disassemble my apartment anyway, so I decided to move out here. I moved everything I had—my apartment, my Vespa motor scooter, and everything—into the space, and then took off to DC. Dan went ahead and fixed up his half. Then I came back and set up the shop, and that is the way it has been ever since.

I did conservation work at the Folger. I had done some at the Museum of Comparative Zoology and in private practice, even though at that time my knowledge was pretty minimal. I had also worked in a program at the Suffolk County Courthouse for several months—a day or two a week for several odd months—where we were washing, deacidifying, and mending court records, hundreds and hundreds of documents about the Salem Witch Trials and stuff like that. We had taken over the kitchen of the jail, which had nice tile floors with drains and lots of big sinks and counter space.

I moved out here [to Easthampton] and started the shop over 20 years ago. I came into the building in June or July of 1985. Dan and I had our separate businesses but shared equipment. For a while, Dan had a board cutter and I didn't. Once or twice we even worked on the same project, but that was very rare. It was clear at that time that Dan was going off in his own direction of doing fine binding. I was more engrossed in the restoration and conservation work because I saw that as something that I could turn around by myself with a minimal amount of equipment. I could refuse to take on a job that required a tremendous amount of washing paper or a vacuum table. If I didn't have what I needed, I just wouldn't do the work. This probably went on for seven or eight years.

But as things started to get bigger, business-wise, I started branching out, and I began hiring people. That [running a business] proved to be more difficult with the conservation work—the time factor, the necessity of me not only doing my work but overseeing what was being done and making sure that it was done correctly. It was very hard to charge enough money for the work to make it feasible. So I started to figure out how to get around that. I started doing a little more outreach to get work from other places. I wasn't very successful at trying to contact small presses and in going out to libraries to get more conservation work. I was spinning my wheels. I couldn't figure out how to get beyond where I was. I could see having employees and doing strictly conservation work wasn't working. We were doing a pseudo-conservation-restoration thing. For most of the clients, that worked out fine. They wanted things to look good—we could make them look good. As I started getting more clients (the Houghton library and places like that), the demands of the client started dictating more what needed to be done. I was a bit relieved. They would tell me exactly what they wanted, and I could do it. Trying to interpret what somebody might want was more difficult, except for the book dealers and the people off the street. They were easier to interpret because they usually just wanted things to look pretty to make their collection look good. Probably because of Harcourt, there were a few of us whose names were more recognizable, so it was a little easier to find some of that work. I was able to get work, but with employees that wasn't enough; I had to go beyond that.

Somewhere around 1999, I had a website done for me by a local company. It was a sub-domain so I was within their website; it wasn't helping me get clients. But I thought it could, so I got a little more sophisticated and got my own domain. There were not very many websites out there for binders; it was still pretty early on. I started getting work off the web from all over the country. That helped. We were starting to get on our feet. The bindery, myself and one or two employees, were getting more stable. Then after 9/11, a lot of jobs we were promised just fell though. They didn't happen—these were small editions. By then we were starting to try to do editions. I was already somewhat in debt in the shop, so that just made things worse. I made a concerted effort to figure out how to turn the shop around. I started looking for edition work and doing less conservation. I lucked out. I got a flyer from a place called 21st Photography, which I knew nothing about. They were just looking to sell me books that I couldn't afford. Their prices for the books were pretty expensive, so I thought these guys could afford to have some hand binding done. On a whim, I contacted them to see if they ever wanted anything bound as a special binding. The guy got hold of me very shortly after that. It turned out that Mark Tomlinson and Sarah Creighton, two binders here in the building, were already working for the guy and I didn't even know it. They were even using some of my equipment to do the work—my paring machines and stamping machines. I was taken into the stable with them as binders. That helped solidify the edition part of the shop. They are now one of our major clients. I don't like the idea of putting too much of my work in one client because anything could happen, and that could leave us high and dry again.

We are still constantly trying to look for more edition stuff. The editions are making it easier to run the bindery. It is more efficient now. I can have people of varying degrees of skill working on different areas of the edition and making it easier to get tasks done. The thing I enjoy the most, which I find easier to encompass with editions, is to problem solve, to try and figure out how I am going to produce something. I remember years ago when I first started doing design bindings, I didn't like the designs I was doing, and I didn't really understand much about design. [Bookbinder] Don Glaister and [calligrapher and book artist] Suzanne Moore were living in the area at the time.

Don and I used to ride our bicycles together, sometimes doing 50-60 miles a day during the weekends and talking a lot. I asked him once about design. He said that one thing he tried to do, (I am really paraphrasing this quite a lot), is to try to figure out what the book wants—not what you are capable of producing or of basing the design on the skills or the equipment you have right now, but trying to figure out what design is going to work best on this book, and then trying to figure out how to produce that design. If Don ever reads this he'll probably say, "I said that?" But that is the way I try to run things here.

It has been really useful to get a book in and try and imagine what would look best for this particular book. There are a lot of other things that I have learned about design over the years, but the basic thing is to be able to look at something and decide what design would work best on that book, totally apart from whether I can actually do it or not, or whether I have either the skills, the equipment, the materials, or the knowledge to do it. Then work back from that design and try to figure out how to do it.

What I end up doing is creating a really high anxiety moment because as I start getting closer to the production of the book, I start questioning whether it is really going to work or not.

I do a prototype and so far nothing has failed, but you know how it is with prototypes—you are focusing all your energy on one book, and it may be that the way you achieve the production of that particular prototype is not exactly the way you are going to do 50 or 100 of the same thing.

Now you are doing mostly edition work and boxes. Do you still do conservation?

Yes, the conservation work comes less now from museums and more from collectors and individuals. We still get a lot of work from the website. It amazes me that someone will send me a book worth thousands of dollars when they don't know me from Adam, and then send a $1,000 deposit to start the work, and they still don't know who I am. Then I make them pay for the entire job before I will send it out. (I've been screwed too many times from sending a book out and never getting paid.) They are trusting somebody from just looking at the website. I talk to them on the phone, and I think I do a relatively good job of selling our shop to them. I think I make them feel fairly comfortable about what they are doing, but still, I don't know how or why they do that.

My website has made a tremendous difference. To all binders out there, I would say "Get thee a website and do it soon." When I first had it, it was one of the top listed sites all the time when you would go looking for it. But that was before, when there was no competition for websites. Now it is way down the list. I don't even look for it, it is so far down the list, but we still get plenty of calls. And we get a number of repeat clients. We still do conservation work but mostly for individuals and collectors.

So most of your clients are repeat customers, from your website, and for a while from when you were out there looking for work, doing cold calls?

Exactly, I did that and ended up getting some great clients. The edition stuff is where I would like to put most of my energy now. I like the conception of how to get it from start to finish—to be talking to a client before there is anything on paper. They haven't printed a page, they don't even necessarily have all of the text or all of the imagery, and in trying to conceive of how that is going to come to something that everybody likes in the end. It has been a real pleasure doing that. We've gotten a lot of good feedback from what we've turned out. Some of these fancy ones we do require a tremendous amount of work, and there is a lot of money at stake. It is one of those things where you can actually make better money doing the fancy ones than doing a more standard edition. But these fancy ones become somewhat of a beast in themselves. I'm not so sure that it is all together such a good creation because they end up becoming these fetish-like coffee table books for really wealthy people. These books will sell for $10,000 or $12,000 a book. What normal person is spending that kind of money on a book? It's ridiculous. They are beautiful to look at, but they are really overpriced, overblown, steroidal book production. But it is a lot of fun to do. Every single one is a separate challenge. It makes it much more interesting, and we finally get paid enough money that I don't have to worry about when the next job is going to show up or where it is going to come from. We are eight months behind all the time. We have been that way for years. It never changes. If new work comes in, we say it is eight or nine months before you'll get it back. It stays that way all the time.

One of the things we do that I enjoy is working for designers, doing corporate presentation material. You'll get designers who know nothing about books, who have no idea how they go together. They will come to you with a concept. I've seen other binders who would say it can't be done. That is not what the designer is looking for. Admittedly, they don't understand the kinesthetic way a book functions—it's not in their realm of thinking. That is fine; it doesn't need to be. So we will move heaven and earth to find a way to actually make that design function. It is what drives me on—can I come up with a way to make this work? Sometimes I can't because they are asking for something that only Harry Potter could do. But what ends up happening is, I get into a dialogue with them, and I explain what is happening physically and why this is not going to function exactly the way they want. I don't just drop it in their lap; I say, "If we did this, we could get it to function." Most of the time they will listen to us because we know how to make three-dimensional objects function. It gets fun. I feel a certain amount of respect coming from them because they understand that I do know what I'm doing. I can give them pretty much what they need. All of these challenges continue to inform the way we produce work here because something we learn on one job will become invaluable on another one. I work with machinists and sheet metal people to come up with concepts or to be able to fulfill concepts other people have. It's fun to try and pull all these people together to make the books work.

Is that what you like best about bookbinding—to be challenged to create new things?

Yes, easily. That is the one thing that keeps me going. I love so many aspects about it, but that is the one thing that makes me eager to come here in the morning, to try and figure it out. At night when I go home (it's 25 minutes to get home), I turn on the radio or a book on tape, and I get home and I realize I didn't hear a single word that was said the whole time I was in the car because I'd been constantly mulling over in my head how I was going to deal with what came up that afternoon, what we can do to make it work, what material might make it function better, or what technique we can invent to make it work? To me, that is what keeps it worth doing.

What about being in business? As an independent binder you get to take the jobs you want to take. Is there anything else you like about being an independent binder as opposed to working for an institution or large bindery?

I think it is taking the jobs I want. I would love to have the economic stability from working at an institution or a large bindery where I could come home and have my own little bindery at home to do the things I like to do. That is what I think I always wanted. Early on I would have just assumed I'd be staying at Harcourt for the rest of my life, but the downs and the really big ups that can happen when you are an independent person is a lot more energizing. If I was working in an institution, I'm sure I would encounter challenges in dealing with specific problems and I would find that interesting, but there is not that much riding on it. At an institution, I would have more luxury of time and the backing of the institution in order to problem-solve something. Here it is a little bit more of a high-wire act. There is nothing underneath. If it doesn't work, it just doesn't work. It is my fault it doesn't work. I feel a lot more alive.

Employees help me problem-solve too. Sometimes we will sit down here at the table and I'll say, "Okay, we have to figure out how this is going to get done." Half the people are from varied backgrounds. One woman who has been here five or six years now has a decorative arts background, doing painting and such, and understands a lot about color. I have a woodworker who produces really fine furniture, makes his own telescopes, grinds the glass lenses; he's become injured through woodworking and, therefore, has given up on woodworking, missing a couple of fingers. What he brings to the table is another way of looking at things as a very skilled craftsman. And then other people here have a great interest in doing it. Obviously, it is my show; I have to make all the decisions.

You take the praise and the blame.

Right, but the praise is a funny thing. I don't take to it well. It is nice, but I don't respond to it as well as I could. I remember years ago when we did an edition at Harcourt. In the colophon it said, "Bound by Sam Ellenport at Harcourt Bindery." I thought, "This isn't right." For one thing, he was in the office most of the time. I try to be as inclusive as I can. We usually say, "Bound by Peter Geraty and Praxis Bindery."

How important is it to you to have people working with you?

It's a good question. My ultimate dream is to scale the shop down and take it home and work only on what I want to work on, at my own leisure and speed. Financially, I don't know that that is ever going to happen. But that is what I would love to do. Employees came into this by necessity, but I also find it very pleasurable to have people involved in the shop. During the times I've tried to rebuild the shop from a much less dynamic place to where it is now and to where I think it is going to continue going, I couldn't have done that without other people. It's not that I needed hands working here, but I have had people come through the shop over the years who I think have felt invested in what goes out of the shop, who have felt that they have part of themselves in that item going out; therefore, they want to see it be good. They want input into how it is done and what changes we can make. I can't say it's exactly a collective venture since it is still my thing, but there is a lot of back and forth amongst us about how we can do things. I will set somebody on a task and they will work on it for a few minutes and then they may say, "If I did that this way and that way and the other way, it would be better." I say, "Good, go do it." I learn how to do it better from how they are doing it, especially with the repetition of the editions.

You gear up to do something and it is a one-off. You finish that one and you think, "I could have done it this way and it would have worked better." When you do two or three or four for an edition of 50 or 100 or even more of these, you think, "I could do it this way and it would be better," and all of a sudden things are moving more smoothly. I may set somebody up at a task, and they may bring an entirely different outlook to it. And then we've got a new way of doing it. If someone comes up to me in the shop with a better way, I'm all for it. I don't want to be tied to some mode of thinking that has a narrow vision to it. If somebody else has another mode of thinking that widens up that vision, then that is just fine. That goes into my experience bank. I quite like that.

Does your information come from your experience bank? You don't keep notes?

I wish to God I did. I've actually been mulling this over for quite a while now. I'm not sure I'm prepared to make a public statement or not. I've started writing an outline for a book. The book is not to be one of these things with pretty pictures that you buy at Barnes and Noble for $19.95 on how to bind a book. I'm envisioning it as a compendium. The way that I've learned what I've learned, to me, seems to be a pretty valid method for the way bookbinding is evolving in this country. I didn't have a structured education in the field. In this country there isn't, for the most part, a structured education available. I think even in Europe that is becoming less and less the case. You could go to Alabama and some other places, but you are only going to get a smidgeon of information. The way I've gathered information over the years is to work on different bindings, to read everything I could find, to take every workshop I could take, going as far as I could to get information. I don't take too many workshops now.

Someone called me up and asked, "Would you like to present at the Guild Standards?" I was flattered and I said, "Sure. I don't really know what I could show. Basically, I just do binding. It's not like I have a patented thing I do." On a stupid whim, I thought, maybe I could do edge gilding. They said, "Oh, that would be great." Then I realized that my edge gilding was modest, to say the least. I had done gilding over the years, sometimes with good results, sometimes with not great results. I knew I couldn't go into this sort of thing with something that may or may not work, especially since I was going to be in front of people. I knew Bill Minter would ask a question that would just throw me off. He did try, he did. But I read everything I could find. I used PVA; I used gelatin; I used egg glair. I had been fooling around with PVA for years but never getting consistent results. So this was the time. I started really investigating it. I read every book I could find that had the slightest thing on gilding. I came to find out that they leave out much more than they put into a book on how to do it. Sometimes I think they do it maliciously because I don't think they necessarily want you to know how to produce something as well as they could.

Or, as with teachers, sometimes when they already know how to do something and forget to impart some information because it is so built into their kinesthetic approach to something that they just don't think to say it. It's not that they are being bad; they just forgot it. I tore the place apart trying to find everything I could. I spent six solid months researching this. I got to the point where I could produce a pretty good edge, any time of day, anywhere I wanted to, on anything. The only thing I couldn't produce on at all was a telephone book. I could not get it to work, but on everything else I could.

That is what I envision if I ever write a book. As a compendium, I would want to put in many ways to do something. For example, you could gild an edge with this material or with this material, in this manner, using this technique or this technique. (I intend on making it very clear if I do this, that this is a reference work, not a "how-to." When just starting out, you really need to sew a book a particular way for a while, or make your endsheets a particular way for a while. Once you understand exactly how it functions, then go find another way to do it and see which works best for you or the situation.) Maybe you would want to gild playing cards differently than you would want to gild a book-edge.

Or you want to find two or three different ways of rough edge gilding because one book has big deckles and one has small deckles. What has worked for me over the years is to experience as many possible ways as I could of doing something in order to find what works with my particular headset and my particular skills. Then I start to hone that to my own particular way of doing it. I would have loved to have somebody give me that backbone of information from which I could work. It didn't happen. I consider Fritz [Eberhardt] as close as I ever came to having a teacher; I only wish I could have studied with him and Trudy more than I did. We aren't going to have that [these master teachers] happen in the future. I've come to realize, I am one of those so-called masters. I can only think of how much stuff I don't know.

One of the thoughts that has gone through my head, if I do this book, is to farm out certain sections of it. I would send it to Bill [Minter] or Frank [Mowery] or Dan [Kelm] or somebody else to go through it and see what doesn't make sense, and to add things. It's not that I just want to put out a book that's got my name on it. I want to put out a book that can be used by everybody. If it were a compilation of work by a lot of people, that would be fine by me. I have a certain vision of what I want it to be like so obviously in the end I would put my stamp on it, but still I think it would be really nice if there would be some central data bank that you could go to like that. I don't have the knowledge to assume I know a compendium's worth of information. No single person would know that.

You didn't mention studying with the Eberhardt's. When was that?

It was the time I was at Harcourt. Fritz and Trudy were convinced by somebody to offer a workshop on binding leather books from start to finish, including tooling—three or four weekend workshops over about a two year period. I took that. Fritz and Trudy and I hit it off pretty well. Obviously, with Fritz you have to hit it off or else. Trudy is an angel; she would be kind to anybody that walked in the door. Fritz, on the other hand, could be quite different. But Fritz and I hit it off. He knew I was serious. I think he was so tired of people who were not serious and who weren't taking him seriously. We evolved our friendship out of that. I would go visit. It was never about binding when I would visit. I didn't think that was fair. It was about drinking brandy and eating sausage and just hanging out. In the end, it is not that I learned much bookbinding from Fritz and Trudy, it's that I learned an approach to their life of binding. I could tell that Fritz was a person that was not easy to get along with. He made his own life difficult in his own ways, but I took a lot away about how dedicated and serious he was about what he was doing. I really respected that a lot. I certainly claim him as one of my teachers, though it wasn't necessarily in bookbinding. I only took those workshops. And odd calls—sometime I could call him because no matter what I did, the gold wasn't sticking. It was god-awful hot and he said, "Yes, I've been having the same problem. You just have to work faster." It got to the point where I laid the size on, turned around, picked up the gold, put it on, picked up my burnisher, and started burnishing almost instantly. It worked. Sometimes I would have a problem and call him. He would help me figure it out.

When you went to Harcourt had you had any leather experience?

At Tantalus I had done some leatherwork. But Phil Allen, the guy who ran Tantalus, didn't know a lot about it himself, so he couldn't really help. I didn't know how to pare leather. He had one of these curved blades that you stuck a razor blade in that leather workers use. It worked. The first leather book I ever did on my own I did from following A.W. Lewis' book, *Basic Bookbinding*. I didn't understand paring, so the edges weren't pared. It was an awful creation. I'm afraid my brother may still have it; I hope he doesn't. I don't ever want to see the thing again. It was so bad. A lot of what I did was self-taught.

Once I got to Harcourt, it started to gel. When I was backing books, I would take my watch off and put it next to the backer, and I would see how long it took me to back a book. I would back 50 books in x number of hours. It was the same way with the leather. I would try to figure out how to do it. I was shown how to sharpen a knife. It turned out it wasn't the way to sharpen a knife. I didn't know that, sharpening the underside of the paring knife as well as the upper side. It wasn't working that well. I got to this building [One Cottage Street] which is littered with woodworkers and found out how they sharpened a chisel which is basically the same thing as a paring knife—a night and day difference.

How do you estimate the price of a job?

That has been the single hardest factor. My job is figuring that out. There is no answer that I can clearly see. Most of my estimates these days come based just on experience. It is a little bit easier for me to estimate a conservation job. I can generally look at a rebacking and know it is going to take me five hours. At $60-an-hour, it will be $300. That is fairly simple to figure out. With these editions I'm getting better at it, especially with these intricately involved ones. But it still doesn't work. Basically, what I'm trying to do is to overcharge a bit because inevitably I miss something. One of my employees keeps trying to beat into my head that when you are stepping out into space like this with something you've never done, and your clients are asking you to push the limit, what I need to be saying to that client is, "If I am pushing the limits, I need some safety nets." That range could be up to doubling what I thought it might be. I ended up eating the costs of things too often, and I couldn't keep doing that. We don't make widgets. I kind of wish we made widgets sometimes. That is going to cost $1.99, and I know that every single time. But because we don't make widgets and people don't want us to, then I've got to come up with a way of letting them know that what we do is a little out there and we need some help with that. I have had a lot of resistance if I come back later and say the price has to go up. Admittedly so, no one wants to hear that. I had a designer one time tell me, "My boss doesn't care what you charge, but he doesn't want you to change it. So charge what you have to charge to get the job done. Don't up the cost later." It's probably because they have to figure out what they are doing on their end, so they want me to be honest to myself, so I can be honest with them, so they know what to expect. That is hard because I am trying to be all things to all people, trying to be nice to everybody. You can't do that and survive. It is not being un-nice to tell somebody it's going to take longer or cost more, so be prepared, but it certainly benefits them if they know going into it.

That would be one of the least favorite parts of being an independent binder.

I would love to have a shop manager or a secretary who says, "This is what it is going to cost."

Bill — I go to the machinist or the auto mechanic and he does the job and then I pay whatever it is. Auto mechanics at least have a book that tells how long it takes to do certain tasks, like changing the pistons on a car. They at least have a manual.

In doing this job for the Folger [Library], Richard Kuhta, who was running the job said, "We want the job done really well. You do the job and then tell us what it is going to cost." I could have gouged them. But if I did that, they would realize that. And it wouldn't help anybody to do that. But it would take a tremendous burden off of my shoulders and enable me, if I saw a better way of doing something that would cost more, to do that. There are not very many clients who will say, "I don't care what it costs, I just want you to do it well." Everybody wants you to do it well.

I get phone calls frequently from [people who visited] the website: "I've got a Bible. I want you to recover it in leather." It has gotten to the point where I realize if they say expense is no object, I know it is the

Peter Geraty's Praxis Bindery.

biggest object in the room. Once I estimate it being over $10, they say, "It is going to cost that much?!" It is crazy sometimes. I don't even want to get involved in jobs where I have to penny pinch. Things are becoming a little more comfortable in that way because our reputation is getting around enough where we are now being sought out. If they are coming here because they know of us, they want what we can do. If they want what we can do, then I'm going to charge them what I have to charge them to get that job done so that I can send my kid to college and eat and pay for the car payment. Little do they know that my wife does most of that, but I don't have to tell them that.

What else do you think is a really hard thing about being in business for yourself? Is it mostly the financial aspect of it?

The financial is the hardest thing, and its not "poor mouthing" as we used to say in the South. I don't need to be rich, but it is one of the hardest things. Fortunately, I'm married to someone who makes a real salary. She is a college professor, so we get health care through her; we pay the mortgage through her; the cars get repaired through her; the kids are going to college either because they are going to her college for free or they are going someplace else. We don't have much money as a family, but I have a certain amount of freedom that she doesn't have. That is the other thing for me, sort of tied into the money. She would love to retire, but she can't because I don't make enough money. In a way, me coming here and doing what I love to do is partially supported by my family. It shouldn't be that way.

I'm sort of equal to everybody else in what I charge for my work, if not a little pricier in some cases. It's just not out there. It will take a complete turnaround for clients to understand that we need more money. The other thing is the responsibility I feel to the employees and the anxiety I feel about getting jobs done. The finances, the responsibilities to the employees, the anxiety about getting jobs done—they are three balls I juggle equally all the time.

So is that why you have that vision of taking your work home and just doing the projects that you want to do? If you had your druthers, what would be your ideal scenario?

I have often dreamed of being a monk that binds books. Go pray, do whatever I have to do, and then go bind my books. All I want to do is the work. I don't care about anything else as far as this business goes. I don't spend as much time at the bench as I would like, but I think I spend more time than most business owners do. I can't give it up, but it does mean that business sometimes is not taken care of as well as it should be. I don't keep the bookkeeping up to date all the time; I don't do correspondence as well as I could; and there is advertising and all the other things one has got to do. What I'd rather do is just bind the books.

You said before that you could just as easily have gone into printing. Is there anything growing up that had a connection with you going in either of those directions, printing or bookbinding?

I don't know for sure. Sort of facetiously I have often told people that when I was in grade school, I used to pick the glue that had oozed out from the end papers; maybe that was a portend of things to come. Realistically speaking, no, except my dad had a little workshop in the basement, and I used to like to putter around there. I got an old lawn mower engine and wanted to make a go-cart. I didn't know enough to be able to do it, but I used to take it apart and play with it. I would watch Saturday morning cartoons, and I would be making things as I sat there watching TV—I always liked to make things. I don't think I needed to have been in the book world. In college, I was a potter and weaver and I liked those things. I wanted to be a woodworker when I was in college. I just wanted to do things with my hands; it didn't matter what. I became very aware of it when I was working at Harcourt. Sam let us come in on the weekends and do our own stuff. I had a client's book I was working on one weekend day; I started working away and I looked up at the clock at one point, and three or four hours had gone by. I couldn't believe that much time had gone by. It was one of those light bulb moments. I realized right then and there that this is what I liked doing. But as I said, it could be anything but just had to be with my hands.

In your background, you trained pretty much on the job. You learned a lot on your own with some training from the Eberhardts and some from Sam and Harcourt.

Harcourt, without a doubt, was the meat of it.

And then you came here and started working. What advice would you give to someone who has the bug to become a bookbinder and they don't know anything about it? You said they should read as much as they can and take classes from as many people as they can. What would you tell someone?

To tell the truth, when I have been asked that question now, I suggest they go to [University of] Texas or whatever, and then go work in an institution. When I went to work at Harcourt, there were seven or eight of us full-time, day-in, day-out, year-after-year, working at this place. At that time, there was Harcourt, there was Monastery Hill, and probably Kater Crafts. I can't think of any other place where you could go and work 40 hours a week doing leather bindings. That time has passed and gone. Those places don't exist as such any more. The kind of intensive, on-the-job training doesn't exist.

I have people come through this shop who will work for a couple years and maybe move on, but there aren't even many shops like mine big enough to support even one or two people. Not only did I almost move to Alabama, but I was also asked to interview for the North Bennet Street job when it opened up. I had just moved out here when they asked me if I would apply for the job. I knew I couldn't do that. Alabama and those places make me nervous because they start graduating four, five, six people a year from these programs. They've got two years of training in a smattering of techniques and styles. They can't go out and start their own shop—they just don't have enough.

You can't really ask students to continue paying that kind of money to get more training because where are they going to get the money when they are just starting out?

Yet, there aren't really enough places, like my shop or Dan's shop, where they can go after they graduate from these places to get further education. I get a little dismal in thinking what people coming through these days are going to do. Basically, I tell them to get a conservation background and try to get a job in an institution. Then maybe they can pick up other things and open up their own shop and do what they want. It worries me a bit as to what can be done. But I don't see the craft dying, that's for sure. If anything, it seems to be growing pretty nicely. So it obviously doesn't need my input on it. But I just don't see how it happens.

In running your business, do you prefer having an assistant that has the training rather than taking someone off the street?

As employees go, what I've learned over time is that the ideal employee is a skilled craftsperson who knows nothing about bookbinding, because I don't have to untrain them or retrain them; I don't have to break any habits. Some of the people I have now—I can show them one time how to do something and they will go off and do it. Maybe I'll make a tiny correction and they will go off and finish it. That kind of thing works a lot better for me than to have a binder who is trained.

Even though I like a multi-faceted approach in trying to figure out how to do a particular operation, I do have particular things I want to address when I am doing a book, and I find that people from other binderies may approach those situations differently. There are styles that other shops have evolved, just like we have evolved a style over time. You can't help it. Some things I am less willing to compromise on than others. If I get someone who has come from another shop and they've got it stuck in their head that you do things a certain way, it is a little bit of a problem.

I've often thought, had I actually been offered the job at North Bennet and taken it, how would I have run it? My inclination would be that we would do no restoration, no conservation; we would not do Coptic binding; we would not do Japanese binding; we would do nothing but straight-forward European binding, as much of it as we possibly could, because you have got to be able to fold paper after paper. You see someone take a single piece of paper and very carefully fold it, when instead you can grab three or four sheets, knock them up, fold them up, separate them out, and go zip, zip, zip and move on to the next batch—that kind of thing. It is that kind of stuff that you don't get in those programs. I can't remember whom I was talking to about this—about how precious we make all of this stuff.

When you are dealing with a book, you treat it so preciously, and all it is a book. If you start treating it too precious, you lose your own personality in the thing; you become kind of subsumed into this creation. It is my own particular way of thinking about it, right or wrong. I think if you treat it more like a book and less like a precious object, it is probably a little easier to get the job done. So every corner is not turned absolutely perfectly and gone over like a mother hen. Maybe this is a result of the fact that I have to produce. I can't put an extravagant effort into a single book, although I might like to at times.

For more information on Peter Geraty, and to see examples of his work, to go http://www.praxisbindery.com.

William Minter:
An Inventive Mind

Woodbury, Pennsylvania
September 2007

He is one of the old guard of bookbinders, dressed in a button-up shirt, tie and slacks, clean-shaven, grey hair combed back. Bill Minter stands straight and tall at over 6', head slightly tilted. I am grateful to call him one of my best friends. I have driven to his place in rural Pennsylvania where he will join me to drive out east, accompanying me as I do more of my interviews. It is fall, and fresh apples and pumpkins are plentiful at roadside stands. The air is crisp, and leaves are beginning to turn vibrant. Bill's red wooden barn blends into the dairy farm countryside, but instead of farm equipment and cows, his barn houses his generous-sized bookbinding shop where I conduct his interview. He has been busy working on multiple projects when not running his three boys to school and activities, so things are in mild disarray. Remnants from jobs just finished lie scattered on tabletops and floors.

His shop possesses character—old intricately carved wooden arches, architectural relics, from a printing company where he started his apprenticeship in Chicago, grace the entries into various work areas. Rolls of bookcloth are tucked between sturdy ceiling rafters. An old granary is Bill's office that also houses a large fireproof closet with a safe. Vast open space is packed with equipment, sinks, worktables, and storage drawers, and is flanked by rooms dedicated to inventions that Bill has developed and sells.

As we talk, he uses hand gestures to impress upon me the comments he makes. His hands are strong and still youthful looking. Bill is very knowledgeable and embraces any opportunity to share what he knows. When instructing, he not only gives details on the subject at hand, he often adds all sorts of additional interesting and valuable information. His inquiring mind continually invents new equipment, new products, and new ways to improve upon what already exists.

A master bookbinder/book conservator who established a successful and well-respected business in Chicago, he agreed to move to rural Pennsylvania to the hometown where his wife wanted to return. Arriving with the bindery and all their belongings, it was his first time he set eyes on their new home in rural Woodbury, hours away from a metropolitan area—a contrast to the constant stream of work and students in Chicago.

Though the cornfields and dairy farms are pastoral and picturesque, and people are good, hard working folks, business is tougher for a bookbinder in Woodbury, PA. Artists and craftsmen do not populate the area. Now a single father to three sons, and running a bookbinding business, he perseveres. Bill is committed to continue living and working in the area where his children thrive.

The ultrasonic welder for polyester film encapsulation that he invented in 1980 and builds in his shop, is still in demand throughout the world. His skill level and attention to doing the best work possible continues to place him among the best bookbinders/book conservators in the country today. And he continues to invent.

How did you get started in bookbinding?

Mechanical drawing and architecture had been an interest of mine in high school. Since I was the only boy in our family, I had been encouraged to go to college. Two days after getting on campus, I realized that I needed a part-time job. Fortunately, a job was available in the audiovisual department, where I worked with photographic equipment, film projectors, slide projectors, and even a printing press, where we printed poster signs. I was really intrigued with photography, but I couldn't get a degree in audiovisual communications because that was a graduate program. The closest thing associated was graphic arts, so that is what I chose. Strangely enough, I remember as a kid going into a print shop and just loving the aroma of ink and the machinery. In fact, I distinctly remember that I wanted to build a printing press.

Somehow ink had gotten into my blood even though my father was a construction worker. So, while working in the AV Department, I was taking various graphic arts courses, such as setting type—both foundry type and hot metal type—and all the wonderful things involved in that field.

After a period of time, I became a staff photographer for the university. Part of my job was to take pictures for the newspaper, as well as for the yearbook. In my junior year, I was named photo editor for the yearbook. My senior year I became the editor-in-chief. A man, who became a very dear friend, was my supervisor. He gave me wonderful advice and direction. I graduated with a Bachelor of Science degree in Industrial Technology, with a concentration in Graphic Arts. I was thinking of going to graduate school for audio-visual communications, but I couldn't afford it.

As my senior project, I decided to design and print my résumé. The design was unique—a four page folding sheet of 11"x17" paper, with photographs on the front cover with all the typical resume information on the inside. I had used my skills from graphic arts to dress up my résumé. In fact, the university used my résumé as an example for other students as something they might want to do to get an edge up on their competition for a job. My supervisor-friend saw an ad in a magazine called *Advertising Age* for an editor, writer, and photographer for the employee newsletter of a Midwest corporation. He suggested it might be a good job for me. The job was at The Cuneo Press in Chicago. I am sure that I got the job purely on the résumé that I had created.

After about three months of working for the company, [master bookbinder] Bill Anthony became my supervisor. On a couple of occasions, he needed a little extra help to get a couple of projects ready. One of the projects was the four-volume set of the first edition of *Audubon's Birds of America* for Northwestern University. We had to clean-off dirt and remove excess glue that was on the spine area of all the individual sheets of paper. The Audubon is called a double elephant folio, but the plates are not folded sheets and are actually single sheets that are roughly 26"x40". The bindings were basically a glorified perfect binding. There was all this hide glue on the spine edge of the sheets that we had to chip away.

Here I was, six months out of college, working on a very valuable book. I also helped with a couple of other less-notable projects. Bill had worked on a 1565 German ophthalmology book. There were some missing areas of alum-tawed pigskin, so he had put new pieces of tawed pigskin on the corners and a couple of other areas. He said, "Here, I want you to retouch this." I do not recall that he gave me a lot of direction. The only things we had available were watercolors and Dr. Martin's aniline dyes. So there I was retouching this white leather so it matched the original 400-year-old alum-tawed leather that was a very wonderful beige, brown color. He had a great deal of faith in me. I was helping out as need be and at the same time trying to take care of *The Cuneo Topics,* the employee newsletter. Within about six months of Bill becoming my immediate supervisor, our work areas were combined into The Cuneo Studio. On one occasion, the executive secretary for the president of the company asked Bill how "this Minter kid" was working out in the studio. "He's doing quite well," was Bill's reply.

It was now about ten months into my employment when in April of 1971, Bill Anthony sat me down and said, "I would advise you to make a commitment to either writing or photography or bookbinding, because you can't spread yourself too thin." Now, my writing skills were pretty dismal—I barely got through college English. I could take a decent picture, but I was not overly creative in that respect. I could take the necessary pictures for a magazine, but bookbinding was a better option. I realized that I really enjoyed working with my hands and working with my brain. I liked that combination, and I instantly knew what to do. That was the greatest advice that had ever been given to me.

Hook, line, sinker, I lived and ate and slept with bookbinding for many, many, many months and years. We published one more newsletter after that time. The company was sliding. Bill left the company a year-and-a-half later to join up with Elizabeth Kner. The main reason The Cuneo Studio even existed for so long, even though it never really made any money, was because William Randolph Hearst had visited the company back in the '40's, and the last point of the tour was to go through the Fine Binding Studio, as it was called at that time. He told Mr. Cuneo, "Any company that maintains this interest in the traditions of the book is the company that I want printing my magazines." I learned this after Bill had left. I took over as director of the studio, but I had only had a year of experience with Bill at that time.

So, I was left at Cuneo by myself. At one point, after I took charge of the department, I went to Mr. Cuneo to tell him I was interested in moving the facsimile of the Gutenberg Press from the 4th floor, where it had been tucked away in a corner, to where it really deserved to be in The Cuneo Studio. His 85-year-old eyes lit up with joy. The press was moved up to the studio within days of my suggestion. In fact, I asked an artist to do a drawing for me. It shows the Gutenberg Press very prominently at the front entrance of the studio. I feel that the front entrance to any business really needs to show professionalism and the quality of the work that is being done inside. The Cuneo Studio was a wonderful place, with all the great architecture. In fact, I have some of it here. I acquired these wooden archways in my shop from The Cuneo Studio when it closed down in 1977.

I had started my apprenticeship with Bill Anthony in April of 1971. Bill left The Cuneo Studio in December of 1972. I had worked with him for one-and-a-half years, side-by-side. I have wonderful, wonderful memories of working within five or ten feet of him on a daily basis. As a young kid, I was constantly asking him questions, "Why do we round a book? Why do we back a book? Why do we sew it with thread?" He always had an answer. Sometimes it was, "Purely tradition." There was an almost constant dialogue going on between us. During 1973, I was seeing Bill regularly, once a week for dinner, and I was showing him the projects that I was working on.

The former head of the Fine Binding Studio was George Baer, a German-trained binder, who had been there prior to Bill Anthony. George had had a heart attack and wasn't expected to come back to work, and they brought in Bill. But George did return, so then there were two binders with hardly enough work for even one. George Baer retired about the same time that I started at Cuneo. George had been teaching a Saturday morning bookbinding class at The John Crear Library. Bill took over the classes when George retired, but he didn't really want to teach the class, so the two of us went to the Crear Library on Saturday mornings, where we were both teaching.

You can just imagine having ten students and two binders walking around—one who knew what he was doing and the other one who didn't but was trying to show that he did. It must have been confusing for some of the students. However, it was a wonderful opportunity for me to hone my skills as a binder. Sometimes there was a mistake, and I got the added advantage of learning how to correct it. Bill would always say, "The mark of a good craftsman is his ability to correct his mistakes."

After a short time, Bill started up a class on Wednesday night, in addition to the Saturday class. I had those two opportunities to see him and show him what I was working on. I admit that I did not take full advantage of that one-year stint; I was getting paid, but there wasn't a lot of work for me to do. We were not getting that much corporate work from the other departments, though we had an annual project to do: *The Cuneo Christmas Book*.

I didn't go out and hustle work because I didn't know how. I didn't know enough about going out to the book dealers to tell them I could restore their books—the simple fact being that I didn't have enough experience. Since I was getting my salary during that one-year period of time, I could easily have been cranking out as many things as I could. I knew that I couldn't continue that way.

During my year by myself at Cuneo, I took a trip to Europe. I must have been the boldest kid in the universe. I had never been out of the country, much less out of the state of Wisconsin, where I was born. I got on a plane and flew to Rome, went to Florence, then Ascona, Switzerland, and the National Library in Paris; and then I went to England and met Bernard Middleton. I met with Bernard Middleton in his home in Clapham, and in our discussions, I realized I was not a book restorer. I was a book conservator. He is the greatest book restorer there ever was, and there was no way I could ever reach that level, nor would I ever want to reach that level.

He did things so perfectly that the average person, even an expert, would have difficulty discerning whether or not a book was a 20th century binding or a 17th century original; he is a true master of the field. Our Cuneo calling cards said, "Bookbinding and Restoration." When I got back, I changed the word "Restoration" to "Conservation." We were certainly doing a different style of work.

About a year later, Bill and Elizabeth needed another person. Bill asked me to come to work for them. He said the work they got in was pretty mundane. It was doing financial reports, and I would be responsible for those because his part of the business was growing. He realized he couldn't run a business as a fine binder. There just wasn't enough demand in the 1970's for "fine" bookbinding. There were the occasional limited editions, but I am going to guess that even the private presses in the US were slowly gearing up and weren't yet doing what is being done today. Bill realized that the only real way to make any money as a bookbinder was to do book restoration (and conservation), so he was slowly getting in more of that work and building a reputation. There was enough restoration work for him to do. Elizabeth had the bread and butter job in the financial records for stock transactions—huge books, side sewn.

Fortunately, there was another young woman, Eugenie, who did most of the tedious work. She just loved it; it was her calling to deal with getting everything fitted together. There were times when we would be making 120 cases at a time. The three of us could crank out 40 cases an hour, all by hand. Bill could paste these huge pieces of cloth, pitch the boards, trim the corners, and start turning the edges; then I finished turning them, and Eugenie would nip the covers and stack them. We were cranking them. It was a real bread and butter sort of thing. As it turned out, more and more restoration work came in.

While working with Bill, we were doing some bookbinding, some limited editions, and some conservation—all types of work—but nothing with elaborately designed fine bindings as he had expected when he moved from Ireland to the USA. There were so many opportunities to learn. Occasionally Bill would take on limited edition work. It could pay the bills, but as Bill would later explain, one of the reasons he took on the jobs was so that I could get experience. I remember we had to hand round and back 300 books for the University of Hawaii. On a couple of occasions, we did send out some aspects of the job. We also bound 300 spring-back record books for the Little Sisters of the Poor. Bill wanted to do it in the traditional way. We did 50 that were hand-sewn, using leather to line the spine and the traditional spring-back board that grips the spine of the book, and then covered them in imitation leather. After we had sewn the first 50 by hand, Bill sent out the other 250 and had those machine-sewn. He brought in some of these jobs partly so I would be able to get more hands-on experience. Even Don Etherington says you've got to "make 4,000 cases if you are going to learn how to make cases." You can't just make one or two, or even 50 in a year. In having to do 100 or 200 in a few days, you really learn how to use the bone folder, how to work with the materials. I think it is one of the things that was really driven home to me.

As bookbinders, we have to understand the materials that we work

252 Pamela Train Leutz

with. When we work with these materials, we know, or we should know, that we can only push them so far and then something is going to happen. Obviously, we all know that if we put a piece of paper on one side of a board, in order to balance that, we have to put another piece of paper on the other side. We also have to be careful when using different types of adhesive. And in some cases, we have to be aware of different materials because they will react differently. During my apprenticeship with Bill, a lot of that was driven home. A certain amount of learning was available, too, by my asking questions and understanding what he was saying about these things. He had experience working with vellum and working on different-sized books. It is one thing to work on a book that is 6"x9" and another to work on very big books and boxes. Everything comes from inside of us, as to exactly what we should do when we are putting a book together.

I worked with Bill for what I call a seven-year informal apprenticeship, though one of those years I was not working side-by-side with him. I had always wanted to be a partner with Bill. I was still not earning very much money. Bill and I, along with Eugenie, were doing the production work. Elizabeth was basically in the office doing bookkeeping and secretarial work. At one point, Bill said that he didn't want to have another partner. In 1977, there was a small incident that made me say to myself that I should consider going into business for myself. It was really a bold decision. The Newberry Library was the other facility in Chicago where I could have gone, but at the time I felt that wasn't where I wanted to go. Paul Banks had left there; John Dean had left there. I was involved with some real estate in Chicago and didn't feel like I could leave the city, so I thought I could set up a business in the basement of the apartment building where I lived. So for about six months, I secretly acquired equipment and materials and created a space where I could start my business. Around Christmas of 1977, I gave my notice. Bill asked me to stay on for a full month until he could find an apprentice. David Brock was that person. Bill had this wonderful ability to interview somebody and somehow know that they would be great bookbinders. David Brock and then Mark Esser were selected by Bill and taken on as apprentices, and [they] have committed their lives to book conservation. It is wonderful that Bill's legacy has continued.

During that last year working with Bill, we were asked to work on a special set of brittle paper magazines for the Art Institute of Chicago. We knew about encapsulation at that time, but the thought of encapsulating 12,000 sheets of paper with double-sided tape would have been a horrendous job, and a horrendously expensive job. During that time, I learned about the possibility of using ultrasonics to seal polyester film. I had suggested this approach to Bill, but he was a little reluctant to get involved in machinery. I don't think he or his business could have supported the development of the welder. He gave a proposal to The Art Institute, based on us purchasing a readily available piece of equipment that really wasn't designed for our particular purposes. The project never got off the ground. But it sure put a bee in my bonnet.

In 1978, after I left Bill, I established my own business working in the basement of the apartment building. I didn't have a lot of work, though I fortunately had established a long waiting list of people who wanted to take bookbinding classes. It is wonderful to think back on that time, realizing that there was such a building momentum of interest in hand bookbinding. I had a guy who wanted to take classes who was a steel salesman. He only did sales to pay the bills; he really loved calligraphy and binding books. When I went into business for myself, teaching was my bread and butter. I had classes in my basement on Monday, Tuesday, and Wednesday nights and Saturday mornings. I had five students at a time down there. I was running around from one student to the next. Some of those people have become lifelong friends, and some of them have gone on to become noted book conservators. Other students of mine also took classes from other people, and they too have stayed in the field. I've had students who were in the library science program. I would like to think that people who get a library science degree would have taken at least one twelve-week session of classes, three hours a week, learning how a book is bound. There were times when I would get a phone call from someone who was interested, and I would tell them that we had classes once a week, three hours a night, for twelve weeks, and the fee was $150 for those twelve weeks. They would ask, "How long before I become a bookbinder?" I would say, "Well, Paul Banks once said that if you take classes only three hours a week, it is going to take you 150 years to learn how to become a bookbinder." I still agree with that statement.

I'll say, even now with 37 years of experience, that I'm still learning, and I'm going to be learning until the day I die. There are so many interesting and wonderful challenges. Every single book is different. All binding is a challenge, don't get me wrong, but with conservation we get one chance, really one chance, to get it right. Obviously there are times that after ten or twenty years, a book will show signs of failure because something was not done right. For me, unfortunately, I sometimes go off the deep end and try to find the best materials that might be available. I don't want to think that the work that I do will fail. I recently heard that some books that were bound 25 years prior by another binder were coming back to be restored. I would like to think that the work that I'm doing is going to last for at least 100 years. In fact, I would like to say that it will be 200 or 300 years before that item is really going to need any work, primarily because I am very particular about the materials that I've chosen. Also, I try to understand the materials that I'm using and the structure or the technique that I'm using. I think too often some people will thin the leather far too much in order to get that fine, dressed sort of appearance. But as a conservator, I'm always striving to get the maximum amount of strength from the materials that I have available to me.

As you look around, you will see bookcloth of lots of different colors. As cloths and papers have been available, I have purchased the variety because when I encounter a book, I would like to be able to pick and choose the right material for the book. After tours of cloth-making facilities, I now realize why some of the cloth that is available is pure garbage. So much of the cloth tears as easily as a piece of paper. That disappoints me greatly. I still have the old materials, some of which are far better than new.

So have you been an independent bookbinder/book conservator in private practice ever since you left Bill Anthony? You also taught a lot and were an esteemed binder in Chicago. How long were you in practice there?

I set up my business in Chicago in 1978, and in 1994 I moved with my then wife to her hometown in rural PA. We packed up everything. We thought we could get my studio and all of our household materials into a 65' long moving van. Much to our amazement, my business equipment filled the entire van. All the benches and everything were knocked down to the smallest degree. There was only enough space on the back-end of the truck for one dresser.

So I had all this stuff moved out here. My then wife found this property. I had not seen it until we bought the place and moved here. Fortunately this barn was available. Initially, I set up the business in the basement of the house and worked out of there for about a year. Much to my displeasure, I learned that many of my Chicago clients were not interested in sending work to me out here, so it was a very difficult time.

I knew I couldn't continue working out of the basement of the house, and the barn was available. I started making the renovations. This is really a wonderful space now. All of the beautiful wood that was available is still visible, and the original granary was converted into an office. A chicken coop on the other side has become a dirt room where leather is pared. Another room has been added to take care of the welder. I've been here for 13 years now. It is good.

But I understand that it's more challenging having a business in a rural area. It seems very secluded out here, not like some rural areas that are close to a big city where there is more art and related work going on. How do you get clients? I understand that some came with you from Chicago. What about the others? Do you call on them? Do they just know of you?

There are a couple clients who continue sending me work out here. I've tried making inroads with some local universities and special collections, but that hasn't happened. Fortunately, I'm only two-and-a-half hours from Washington, DC. I've received some good work through my dear friend, Frank Mowery, at the Folger Shakespeare Library. Also I'm in contact with the National Park Service, and I did some work for the University of Maryland after a small flood in their collection.

As we hear from a lot of our colleagues, the work has been purely word of mouth. I'm old school, and I've relied upon that. I've been advised on numerous occasions to have a website. While that is desirable and something that needs to be done, it hasn't been done. It would probably be of benefit to me. I do have a young man helping me build a website right now.

Over the years, I have had a couple people come in and work with me over the years. Everything around here is very family-based—a rural community of stable families, many dairy farmers—so there is not a great opportunity to get apprentices. If I was to have an apprentice, say from North Bennet Street School, they would have no after-hours life available here. There are no museums, no libraries, and no place to socialize, within a half-hour drive. It would be wonderful to have an apprentice. I desire it; I almost need it, someone that I can train. Unfortunately, the welder has taken over much of my time, along with a couple of other things that I've developed, like the eraser crumbs.

Tell me a little bit about your sidelines you have going. I think of you being an idea person, an invention person, as much as a book conservator. You come up with ideas and take off with them. Can you tell me some of the things you have created?

The ultrasonic welder [which encapsulates documents safely in Mylar] is now 27 years old. The first one was sold to the Library of Congress in 1980, delivered in 1981. The second one was a year later, and for a number of years after that, I sold ten a year. The one that is being delivered next week is number 160. In total, there have been 190 machines delivered to all parts of the world. I have a machinist who fabricates some of the parts; the electronics package comes from another supplier; and other little bits and pieces come from other suppliers. Because of the special nature, almost like hand-bookbinding, there is no one who can fabricate some of the parts for me, so I end up doing that myself. Everyone I've talked to about making those parts, want to do 100 or 500, so just needing to do one or two, I do that on my own.

The eraser crumbs is something I developed in 1993. At a conference there was mention of an Italian cheese grater that was used to make eraser crumbs. One of our fellow conservators said, "Bill, you are in private business. Rather than our institution spending $1,000 on this machine, why don't you buy the machine, grind up erasers and sell us the crumbs?" My oldest son has basically been taking over that for me. I'm thankful he is available for that.

I've also been developing a number of tools and techniques. Because I don't have a website and those things aren't advertised, they haven't shown any return. For example, for the board shear I've made some modifications on the clamp to improve the safety. There is also the board-crimper that is available to us; it has a treadle that is a hazard and a danger, and I've made some modifications to that.

I've also been playing around with "the Force" for keeping things in alignment when using the stamping press. I've been working on a binder for spiral bindings. I've developed a way to wash a bound book, and I've been looking for the materials to perfect that. A myriad of things—I love to develop those things.

I have also developed a modified ring binder. As binders, we occasionally encounter books where the ring style may be the ideal way to handle the book, but we can only get the rings in standard sizes, and there is no way to make a modification. I've taken the standard screw post binder, and I've adapted it to the ring binder so that the bookbinder could make any number of rings on any dimension; it is adaptable. It is another one of my pet projects waiting to get out to the public.

One of the things I tell students, apprentices, and even my son, is that part of the joy of doing this work is the challenge of making it easier to do. I admire Tim Ely's improvement to the sewing frame. I've actually used that sewing frame in a completely different way on another style of book conservation that I needed.

What is it that you haven't achieved yet in bookbinding that you would like to achieve? What is your ideal scenario for your business?

This doesn't necessarily answer your question. One of the difficulties of running a business is that you have to make some money. It would be very nice if we could do this work and, while we enjoy doing it, not have to worry about the financial aspects of it. I enjoy the challenges; I enjoy the different types of work that come through the door. On one occasion, I was called by the Library of Congress to work on some pieces. I was asked, "What are the specialties of the shop?" I said I didn't really have a specialty. I enjoy the different types of challenges that come through. Unfortunately, because of my obsession with doing it right and giving the very best treatment to the item, I tend to go overboard trying to come up with the best technique to take care of the item. And I spend excessive time and excessive money on materials—time and money I don't get compensated for. If I didn't have to worry about the money aspect of it, a large burden would be lifted.

At one point, when I was first getting established, I had these grandiose visions of having an operation similar to Sam Ellenport at Harcourt Bindery, where there might be four or five or ten people who are here, with one person doing just forwarding, and another person doing just tooling, much like the olden days. Or, maybe like Don Etherington's current facility where there are experts in particular areas.

When an item comes in the door, it can go to that particular individual. I guess if I had any one goal right now, it would be to have a facility that could be a training facility, a learning facility, a sharing facility where there would be a couple of people working together to take care of the books. We would be willing to take on the unusual project and not worry about paying the bills.

What about projects that you would like to do?

I want to do an *Audubon's Birds of America* again. When I left Chicago in 1994, the University of Chicago decided to have some work done on their Audubon, but I missed out on that opportunity. About eight years ago, the University of Pittsburg wanted to have their Audubon treated. I consulted with them, offered them some ideas on how to bind their copy, and helped them design an exhibition case. It was a four-volume set, as they are traditionally covered in full-leather. As part of my proposal, I developed a modified miniature screw post binder, something neat that also provides the ability to change pages. I need to share it with the world; I think it has potential. The University, however, decided to go another route and utilize a folder that the Library of Congress developed. I thought my design for the folder was a little more conservationally sound, but the pricing caused the project to go elsewhere.

You talked about your skills. You are good at working with your hands, and you are good at working with your brain, and in putting the two together. And I think you have an inquiring mind. Are there other skills or talents you have that make you a good bookbinder?

I have a talent for developing things. I certainly don't feel I am artistically creative. Give me a design, and I will do my utmost to make it work. I've developed a talent and find great satisfaction in engineering things. If it wasn't for the financial aspect of it, it would be nice to continue to evolve and develop in those ways, constantly be faced with new and unique challenges to keep the creative juices rolling, not so much in the design—other people are more creative in that. I enjoy the physical aspects of the challenge.

You come back often to the financial thing. One of my questions is what is your least favorite part of being in private practice as an independent bookbinder. Finances are always a worry. Is there anything else you dislike about it?

I would like to not worry about the financial consequences of freely giving my time. I love when people have a question of me, and I can help them solve a problem or a question that they might have. Give me a challenge that involves the structure of a book; give me a new possible technique; open up a peephole to a possible new material or technique. I get excited about that. I want to learn more. Simply walking through a hardware store or through an exhibit of materials, I think, "How can I use that?" Reading *Popular Mechanics* magazine, "How can I take and use that information?" As Bill Anthony said, "There is nothing new in bookbinding. It's just a modification on something someone has already done." One of my favorite programs is James Burkes' Connections. We are always building on something else. While we might think something is new, like the laser, there had to be something else before that. I enjoy the aspect of seeing a new material or idea and thinking of how we can utilize that in our work to make our work easier, to make our end product better. Anytime I've come up with an idea, my main drive is to make it better. I'm constantly challenging my brain. Unfortunately, that one-hour operation turns into something that takes a lot longer because I've gone off the deep end with some of these other things. If I had just stuck to the point, the job would have been done more efficiently. But I love that aspect of bookbinding. I enjoy the part of receiving something that is in pieces, new or old, doing all the work on it, and coming up with the finished piece. If I didn't have to worry about the amount of time it was taking, and consequently the amount of money it was costing, that would be the ultimate.

Is there anything you would rather be doing as a career than bookbinding?

I can't think of one. It is wonderful to have a desire to use the brain, and have talents available, and convey them to hands, and use both things in that particular way. Fortunately, in America, we have this opportunity to make changes from one type of work to another. For us as bookbinders, we have the opportunity to use our creative ability, to use our hands to do something that is very satisfying.

Is there anything else you want to add?

I think it is important that we continue to share our experiences and our knowledge with other people. Bill Anthony was given an opportunity to leave private practice and go to work at University of Iowa. He wanted to train people and also not worry about the financial aspects of things—to be able to share with apprentices and students in the fields of bookbinding and book conservation. I think that we need to develop a way in which people who have a certain amount of training can train with others. The Guild of Book Workers Standards of Excellence conference is one opportunity for us to get together, but another could be to meet with somebody in their shop and discuss aspects of the work, share our experiences, and then come away with new information. One of the true beauties of hand bookbinding is that while some people would look at it as competition, that doesn't seem to be a major concern in hand bookbinding.

What advice would you give to someone who is interested in pursuing bookbinding as a career?

I think the best way is if they can take a series of classes from one person. In Chicago, I was teaching three classes weekly where students came to class for three hours, once a week. At the same time they were taking classes, they should have been doing work on their own, and reading. They would come back to class and show something that they had done, and what they had read, and knew what they needed help with. So that three-hour time with the instructor was jam-packed with as many questions and answers as possible. I had this opportunity in Chicago, after working with somebody for a period of time, to say to him or her, "If you are interested, I will put you to work." I didn't pay them a lot because it was still a training situation. Then after a period of time, they gained more experience. After maybe a year working at the bench in different sorts of areas, they could gain more experience.

North Bennet Street School is available. I've known a number of people who have taken those courses. It's wonderful because it is structured to start with very simple bindings and progress through the various stages, until they are washing papers, deacidifying, mending, and doing other treatments. And then that person who has had this training goes into the workplace, usually to an institution. At the Library of Congress and some other institutions, there are internship programs, but it is rather different in an institution than it is in private business.

One of the sorry things about the field in the US is that there is no conduit for someone who has some training to go to work for a private person, because there is no supplemental funding available. It would be wonderful if some foundation existed that would provide a stipend for postgraduates to work with a qualified, independent hand bookbinder for a period of time. The independent bookbinders usually can't afford to pay more than a little bit, but there would be this beneficial exchange.

For an independent bookbinder to take on an apprentice, the money is a very difficult aspect. If the normal shop time for a business is $60 an hour when the person running the shop is doing the work, to have someone in training may cost $120 an hour—two hours of shop time to do one hour of work, because of the training that is going on during that time. It may even be more than that if the student makes a mistake or takes six hours to do an operation that would normally take three hours, and the master is there teaching along the way. It

The big red barn that houses Bill's bindery.

becomes a real financial burden. It is not an ideal situation to learn in a private business because one has to do the binding jobs that are in the shop at that time. In an institution, there may be a wide variety of projects to have an intern work on. You can do a multitude of items and really learn very well on those things. In private business, whatever job comes through that door at the time is what we have got. The training is limited because you may only have one item. But at the same time, because you are in a profit-making business, you have a responsibility to make money. The end result is that you learn the process much better because you have a noose hanging over your head, making you get the job done in a reasonable amount of time. And at the same time, you cannot cut corners. There is this mechanism going. You've got to keep the engine going. Consequently, the end result is that you learn the material in a much better way.

It sounds like you are saying that an individual should get an education and then get a job at an institution, since it is difficult for a private practice business to afford to bring them in. Though in an institution, they wouldn't learn how to run a business. What about the business aspect? What is the reality of having an independent business?

That is the big question. During my training, nothing was ever said on estimating the time and charging for the time. I remember on one occasion when Bill Anthony, who also did not have training as a businessperson, became in charge of quoting the prices for the shop. I remember him saying, "Whatever the hourly salary is for that person, the business needs to take in double." That is what he thought was necessary. I discussed this with Carolyn Horton in NYC, the preeminent conservator in the US at that time who was also a very, very good businesswoman. She said you needed three times the salary to cover the entire overhead—lighting, heating, insurance, rent, all of these things that are really mind-boggling.

For the binder who is working from his dining room table and charging $35 to restore a Bible, there is no reality [of making a living] with that sort of thing. They are operating from their dining room table and are not thinking about insurance and heating and lighting and all of that. But when you are running a true business, you have payroll taxes and other things to deal with, and it can become overwhelming. That three-times-the-hourly-salary is more realistic and in some cases more, due to other factors. When you bring someone in to work with you, they are producing, and they are helping to pay the overhead, but if you have to train them from the start, then it becomes an extra burden. One of the other things I learned is that when you hire somebody, and say they are getting ten dollars an hour, it is actually costing you fifteen dollars an hour because of the social security taxes, Medicare and health insurance, and other things.

It makes it difficult to be a small businessperson in America.

One of the great things about America is that we can do this. There are hurdles that have to be overcome, but it is not impossible. We are in a fortunate time when we can hang up a shingle, and we can do the work. We don't have to get a certificate to bind a book; we don't have to be recognized by the local craft guild, as happened maybe a hundred years ago in England. They had to go through a very structured organization. They couldn't just open up a business. They had to abide by the guild rules.

I've had million dollar books in my hands that I worked on, and the only thing the owner of that book has had to go on was my reputation—being honest, doing a good job. They bring me their rare book, or their family Bible, where no others are available. I know some of my colleagues have a contract that spells out the condition of the book when it came in, the proposed treatment, and a disclaimer, the insurance that is charged, an extra rider if necessary—a formal, legal contract. For me, I give the person a quotation; sometimes it is just purely verbal. I may write out a receipt with the proposed treatment and the amount that I've estimated, but I don't do a contract. Basically it is a handshake sort of arrangement—the old fashioned way.

What are some good things about being in business as an independent bookbinder?

The customer comes through the door with their project, and for me at least, they tend to have some unusual requirements. I enjoy the different challenges that come up. Maybe it is because I have an inventive talent or that I am not afraid to take on something that is a little outside of the ordinary. Giving a quotation is always difficult because every book is different. It's a cliché, but to a certain extent every book *is* different. That is one aspect of it. The other end of that rainbow, so to speak, is being able to deliver that project to the owner and see the pleasure that they receive from their finished project. Yes, they are paying a bill, but there is a great deal of gratification from delivering it to an individual. I'm going to guess that in an institution, the finished work goes to the curator. I can imagine that if you give it to the curator, they are pleased with the work, but they have such an abundance of other materials that it goes in among this huge collection, and the next day it is lost in a maze.

Whereas, the private individual is going to have it out, show friends, and share it with relatives. There is an ongoing appreciation that they have a book restored. We've got the challenge, and we've got the gratification. I think the independent bookbinder doesn't necessarily have his business just to get his paycheck. There is so much satisfaction with the work that we are doing; it's kind of a love of our life. We have the great pleasure of taking a new book or an old book, something in pieces, and we have this wonderful opportunity to take those pieces and bring it all together, almost like a sculptor takes a block of stone or a clump of clay and molds it into something that is beautiful. We're taking something that not only is beautiful, but we put it in our hands and work with it and get other sorts of pleasures from that.

An objects conservator once told me she would take an object, do whatever treatment was needed, and then it just sat there or went on exhibit or what have you. She never really realized how difficult it was for a book conservator because not only are we conserving the object, but the object has to also be functional.

Sometimes the book can be quite fragile where the paper is easily torn. We have a lot of different things that are going on with our work—the detail, the functionality, the handling. We have to know our material: the paper, the cloth, the leather, and the structure and engineering. It is work, but it can be fun at the same time.

Gabrielle Fox:
Exquisite Miniatures

Cincinnati, Ohio
October 2007

Delightful miniature design bindings with tiny gold-tooling and vibrant leather onlays that wrap around the covers so that colorful designs flow onto the inside covers. That is the image I have of Gabrielle Fox's bindings. I first met Gabrielle when she gave a workshop in Dallas on binding miniature books. Gabrielle is a good teacher—well organized, patient, encouraging, experienced at breaking down the bookbinding process into achievable steps.

Gracious and femininely attired in a skirt, blouse and apron, Gabrielle meets me at the door of the Cincinnati home she inherited from her English mother. The years she spent in England are reflected in her slight accent and English way of saying things. Gabrielle offers a beautiful smile. She is tactful and polite.

Her home is furnished with antique French pieces that belonged to her family. Over the fireplace is a domed mirror in a quirky ship motif, not French, but a favorite of her mother's. Handmade quilts drape furniture throughout the house. It is a house that holds memories.

After a quick glance around the house, we go upstairs. There are two bedrooms and a bathroom. One small bedroom is Gabrielle's studio. Her husband, Andy, has handily arranged the space so that equipment can be moved on wheels into either the hallway or the other bedroom to create more room in the studio when needed. Things are tightly organized; a miniature press and plough perches on a shelf above a huge, beautifully handcrafted wooden press and plough, contrasting the type of bookbinding work Gabrielle does. Daylight from two windows provides adequate work light. The top of flat files serves as workspace on one side, while a custom-made bench with storage below, and shelves above, provides additional workspace. Gabrielle stores bookcloth and other supplies in a storage facility in town that she can access when necessary. She should write an article about bookbinding in small spaces.

She hoped to make writing her career. Instead, while working in the special collections department of a library, she was introduced to book conservation. She found the work interesting. Having family in England, she decided to pursue a bookbinding education there where she could get good training. She studied and then worked in England before returning to Cincinnati where she is the only book conservator/design binder in the area. Gabrielle has also included writing in her bookbinding career. She is the author of *The Essential Guide to Making Handmade Books*, published in 2000. Her life has come full circle.

How did you get into bookbinding? I read about your background and studies at Guildford College. How did you initially get interested?

From the time I was five, I was told that I should go into writing, which is why I am really intrigued with this project you are doing. My father was a journalist and an editor in labor newspapers and publications. I grew up with a lot of people who wrote, so I always assumed that was what I would do. I was a senior in college, and I got an article published. Do you remember when newspapers used to have their own Sunday supplement? Well, I had a feature piece published in the Sunday supplement. It was pretty good going as a student. One of the young men that I interviewed took exception to it and started phoning me up in the middle of the night and saying he knew where I lived and he wasn't happy with what had come out in print. It was an article about Native Americans in this area, and it was at a time when it was very political. When I interviewed these people, I had to meet them in clandestine places and I couldn't use their real names half the time. The editor edited it with a slightly stronger slant, which is what editors do—I knew that. But this young man was going through a very serious personal crisis. The end result was that I thought, "Maybe I am not tough enough to be a good journalist."

I was working in special collections at The University of Cincinnati library at the time. I started looking around. There was a woman who had been hired as the first person to do conservation rather than just in-house binding at the university. Her name is Chiara Renaldo. She had studied with Jean Gunner in Pittsburgh. When I talked to her about getting training in bookbinding and conservation, she said, "Really, there is nowhere to study right now here in the States. If you have family in England, that is what you should try and do." That was 1978. I went to England and studied full-time for two years. It was a personal challenge because everything I had done previously was in academics and writing, and I really was known as one of those people who, given the option, would just go upstairs and finish reading a book. I am not a practical person. I think it is pretty amazing that I am still doing this because it is not my basic nature at all. It is sometimes a struggle for me to work out a practical problem that others would think perfectly obvious. Being married to a practical person has helped a great deal.

At the very end of studying in England, I met Andy. We carried on a long-distance relationship. He worked for the telephone company, so that [the long distance calling] was possible. In the end, we got married. We spent the first ten years of our marriage in England. When I left, I had what they referred to as a .5 position which was a full-time job but only half of it as the head binding instructor, Senior Lecturer, at Croydon College of Art and Design, just outside of London. The program had been reduced in size so there weren't many people going through intending to be professional binders, but there were a lot of people in the art department who wanted to make this a major part of their work. It was nice being in a regular teaching position. I really do miss that now. I taught at a lot of other places too. I did what I do in the States, where I go somewhere and do an intensive three-day workshop.

We came back here to Cincinnati in 1990. When we moved here, I had a job lined up with a printer who had done binding. Remember those huge big ledgers—that was his specialty. But there was trouble with the business, and I realized that I was going to have to find another way of earning a living, so I set up my business again. I set up in the basement of a used and antiquarian bookstore near the university area, called Duttenhofers. I was there for about ten years. In the early '90's, I commuted to Lexington, KY where I worked part-time as Binder-in-Residence at Transylvania University. I decided I needed to move on, so I got a studio not far from here in a square, in an older residential area. I had a studio that was quite nice there for about five years. It was on the street, above an antiquarian bookstore and nice stationary store. The owner of the stationary store and I did a lot of projects together. I taught in my studio there. When my book was published, *The Essential Guide to Making Handmade Books,* I had a big signing in her shop, The Natural Paper Co.

In 2000, we started the Cincinnati Book Arts Society. The goal of the four initial founders was to establish a book arts center. We began to realize this wasn't going to come together as we had hoped. One person, a printer who was in town, decided she was going to go under completely, and she picked up and left town, getting a teaching position in Massachusetts. The other two people had other jobs. I stayed involved as long as I could. I realized when my lease came up that things weren't going too well, so I moved here into our spare bedroom at home.

In England, I had been set up in many different places. Several people gave me space. I started at the end of the kitchen in the one bedroom apartment we owned. Then someone lent me living room space for a while, and then someone gave me space above an old stable block out in the country. It was gorgeous—not much heat, but the views were really great!

Are you glad you moved back?

I miss England a lot. Andy loves it here and would never move back. There are a lot of reasons why both of us feel the way we feel. I think it might be a little easier for a self-employed bookbinder in this country than in England. On the other hand, there is a longer tradition and a concentration of clientele in England. If you can survive, you can do quite well in England. There is a high fall-out rate. I was in a graduating class at Guildford of about ten or fewer. I came back to the States for two years, and when I went back to England, more than half had already decided to move on to do something else. It is very difficult to get the business going. I think it is easier to get going here in the States.

I miss not being able to get on the train and go to London and see what other people are doing. I could go in and really see what that 16th century book was supposed to look like. I used to hang out at the Victoria and Albert Museum whenever I could. I was out in the countryside between the sea and London. For any lectures I wanted to attend, I got on the train or drove up. I really miss not being closer to people doing what I am doing. I don't particularly like being the only specialist in my geographical area. I would like to be challenged a little more than that. I have to be careful; working on my own, I can slip into some bad habits or forget what [quality] I am aiming for because people don't know any different. The only people who are doing anything to do with the book, on a similar level here, are letterpress printers. There is a whole community down in Lexington, KY. An individual named Victor Hammer nurtured it. It is almost like a school of letterpress printing in Lexington, KY, so I find that I do a lot of projects and work with them. That keeps me working on a certain skill level and challenges me. I do like to work alone, but I also like teaching a lot. I loved it in England where I was teaching part-time and working on my own part-time. I think that is a really good combination. I had to be careful to keep them both part-time. Sometimes it doesn't balance out too evenly, but it is a good way to do things. Also, without other people in the field nearby, the challenge of teaching can keep me on my toes. Students will come in and say, "Why aren't you doing it this way?" And I will look at it and think, "Why am I not doing it that way?"

Do you have them come here?

I do, but not as much as I did with the studio I had before this. I can only get two in here. Andy has been brilliant. That big press behind you is on wheels. The cutter is on wheels, and I can kind of extend things into the bedroom. It works. The light is good. It is all right.

In some ways, I really love it up here, but it has been a challenge organizing it. I do have a storage area about a half-mile away where I put things. Eventually I would like to have everything in the house, but I have to move family things out of the basement first.

Did you ever think about working for an institution?

Yes, I did. When I first went into bookbinding, that was my intention. When I went to England, it was with the idea of getting a good, firm background in traditional binding and then going into conservation. It was in the early days of conservation in institutions in this country. I came back and was the first conservator/hand binder at the University of Cincinnati. Chiara Renaldo had just set up the department and gotten an NEH grant for it. She then left town because her husband went on in his profession. It was very exciting and quite a challenge. I set up the bindery. That is what I was doing for two years before I went back to England.

In England the pay [at institutions] was so bad that it would only cover my lunch and train fare, so I had to just set up on my own. I was living out in the countryside in England, with no job nearby. I would have had to commute to London.

If there had been a conservator job in Cincinnati [when I returned], I would have taken it. But there wasn't. We came back to Cincinnati because my mother was very ill. Then my father became very ill. We ended up staying in Cincinnati longer than we thought, until they both died. By that time, we had been here about eight or nine years. We considered moving to other parts of the States, but it didn't come together and we ended up staying here.

Are you glad you are an independent bookbinder in private practice?

Yes, I am. But being back in the States as an independent bookbinder, married to a man who is also self-employed, is becoming quite brutal when it comes to health insurance. I know that the national health system in England is far from ideal, but what it takes to be responsible [for your health] in this country is a big chunk out of your income. If I had a real job, I wouldn't have to worry about that in the same way. Realistically, I am doing something that is manual labor, and that leaves me open to more health problem possibilities than a lot of people our age. I have to be very careful about that.

Is there anything else that is a downside of being in business for yourself?

Well, actually I don't really like dealing with money very much. My brain doesn't click that way. So I have found it quite a challenge dealing with customers, when it comes to the pay.

Is it difficult to give customers the price up front? Or to collect?

I've only had one or two bad experiences with collecting. I have a very strong feeling that if I do the work, they are going to pay. I have pursued it legally if they haven't paid. I think within the community, at least locally, they know that if they don't pay me, I will at least make their life a living hell. I feel strongly about that. I've always been pretty straightforward about what it is going to cost because I don't think anyone needs surprises in that sense.

The part that I find the hardest is selling my design bindings to dealers and collectors. For a lot of them, haggling is part of the experience. I could haggle for someone else, but to haggle on my own behalf is almost like I have to have some kind of out-of-body experience. "This is Gabrielle's and ...." I've found that difficult.

Another thing I found funny, along the same lines, are dealers who think they can challenge me to do what they ask—to do something which isn't actually kosher. "Yes, I can take two first editions, that have seen the trials and tribulations of age, and make them into one perfect copy, but I don't actually think that is ethical." I remember when I was younger, they would say, "Well, Gabrielle, aren't you good enough to pull that off?" thinking they would appeal to me on that level.

There have been times when someone has turned up with something which I'm not quite certain belongs to them. Cincinnati and the book community here is a small world. I try to take care of the situation without sending up too many red flares, in a quiet way.

What about the advantages of being in business for yourself in private practice?

It is a new challenge every day, which is very exciting. It can be tiring, but it is very exciting. As I said, I'm not really a practical person, so I'm not very good at editions or multiples. Just through default I've ended up working on very special, individual items, both in my own work and in conservation and restoration work. Each is an individual challenge, and I really enjoy that.

It's interesting because you've been at it for so long.

A lot of it is the nature of the work that comes in. I'm in an area, geographically, where a lot of different things come in, instead of the work going to a dozen of us [bookbinders]. There are other binders in the area, but they don't specialize in the area of fine conservation and fine binding that I do.

Do you get many Bibles?

I get Bibles, but I don't do them. I really only do Bibles as a favor or for a good customer that has a Bible as well. A lot of the Bibles that come in here are the huge Germanic, heavy board Bibles. I decided I wasn't going to be keeping them around, especially in this space. They come in and take over the whole room.

Who are your clients, and where do they come from?

All sorts of clients—most are special collections and university libraries; the next groups are private collectors of both antiquarian and new books; and then there are those people that have one precious book they want conserved.

How do they find out about you?

Word of mouth. I've never advertised. I took a listing in the yellow pages, and that brought me more trouble than it was worth. I was obviously on a list that people would call who had to submit so many applications in a month to get unemployment compensation. There aren't that many places to apply for a job in bookbinding.

I spend a lot of time educating people who call to inquire [about getting a book bound], and then they decide it is too expensive. I'd much rather do that kind of educating by going to libraries and doing a presentation or doing the community projects which I do.

That is a way of advertising.

I will do those things. Sometimes I will be paid; sometimes I won't. That was also part of getting involved with setting up the Cincinnati Book Arts Society. I do really love teaching. This business is like converting people to another religion. There is all this stuff about books not being important anymore, and it's not true. I hear that from a lot of librarians. I've been aware of it because of my association with academic libraries. For example, the nature of my work is going through a major shift because a lot of the academic libraries' budgets for conservation work are being slashed. It is quite often because a new dean wants to spend the money on the computer side of things. Money is going into that. What is happening, in my experience, is some of my regular academic clients can't afford to have the books conserved, but they have other budgets that allow them to buy new bindings. It is shifting in that direction.

What about your website. Does it bring you work?

It is beginning to. I only got that up within the last year. I've been in Cincinnati long enough that anybody who wants to find me will find me, but I also realize that it would help people find me. When I was in a street traffic area, it was easier to find me.

What kind of relationships do you develop with your clients?

I develop some interesting, intense relationships with clients in a very good way. To a lot of the collectors I deal with, this is their treasure; this is their baby; this is how they relax; this is what they look forward to; this is their time out. Once I've worked with them for years, I am associated very closely with their collection. It is a nice place to be. They will get to the point where they are far enough in their own collecting that if there is something they can't get a perfect copy of, they will call and say, "There is this, this, and this wrong with it; do you think you can sort it out?" So I participate. I have become interested in subject areas I never dreamt I would be interested in because of that. I have two clients who collect early medical books. I learned a lot about medical history and the publishing associated with it. It's been really exciting. It's an area I don't think I would have looked into otherwise. I enjoy that.

It seems similar to writing. You get exposed to things by doing articles. You are doing it in a different way.

Yes. That is part of what I really love about being self-employed as a bookbinder. I meet extraordinary people from all different walks of life. The assumptions that many people make about who collects what are not as set as people think. A lot of people are serious collectors. It's a very serious part of their life, and it doesn't always jive with their socio-economic status. It is a priority for them personally.

Did you have other jobs besides bookbinding?

When I went to England, I decided I wanted to teach a lot more, so I went back to do a City and Guild Certificate in Adult Education. The person that I was studying with had to come and evaluate my classes. I was teaching bookbinding at that time. But he didn't understand bookbinding, and basically I don't think he liked the idea of having to observe a three-hour class. So he said, "We have to find you something else to teach so that I can evaluate you more critically. You used to be in journalism. You can teach Communications to nannies and nursery school teachers." So I did that part-time for three or four years because it paid quite well. Actually, it was kind of fun because it was so different from what I had been doing. It was a two-year course in a technical college.

What happened was that anything the other instructors didn't want to deal with ended up being in Communications. It was a time when the AIDS issue was coming to the forefront. I would have thought that would be in Health Sciences, but somehow it ended up in Communications. Most of the students would go on to work in private situations, and in a lot of those situations there is still a gentlemen's agreement when working as a nanny. You wouldn't have a written contract at that time, but there were certain things that you needed to sit down and discuss so there wouldn't be any misunderstandings. After I had done it for a while, I had people coming back and telling me what really happened after they got out there working. They were stories in which you could laugh at the end, nothing really tragic.

But there was one young woman who went to a job in Spain and found out it wasn't a little child she was to care for; it was a boy who was mentally challenged. His family took her passport and was really holding her prisoner. She tied sheets together, climbed out the window, and ran to the police station. There were also some who went off with rock stars and flew all over the world in private jets. There were all sorts of stories. I really enjoyed it. That is the other job I had. Also, when I was a high school student in the summer, I worked in the public library in Films and Recordings.

Is there anything in your childhood that might have suggested bookbinding as a career?

There is one thing. At an early age, I started making my own notebooks. I didn't like the notebooks you could find. I kept a regular journal. Still to this day, my time out, the thing I have a lot of fun with in bookbinding, is playing around with new materials to make my own journals, experimenting with something that I'm not sure is going to go quite right.

Is there any direction you would like to go that you haven't or something you would like to achieve in the field but you haven't?

I would really like to come back full circle to writing. I enjoyed working on the book, *The Essential Guide to Making Handmade Books*; I would like to do more writing. I remember now looking back—I went into bookbinding for the reasons I did, but I remember someone who was a journalist that I admired saying, "To be a good writer you have to learn something that you've never done before." The examples he gave were like: learn a different language, or learn a skill that is completely foreign to you. And when you can write about that, you are a good writer. When you can explain that to someone else, then you have honed your skills. I would like to do more writing. And I do miss not teaching on a regular basis.

Is there any project that stands out in your mind as the most fabulous thing you've ever done?

I've had one or two incredible challenges, technically—two bindings in particular. They were both commissioned for a presentation. One of them required [that] a metal plaque be incorporated into the front cover so that it could be removed for display. It was possible, but it was complicated by the fact that the text was going to arrive about two days before the full-leather binding had to be finished. I had to come up with a way to make the binding, working on approximate sizes that were given to me, and then get it together. I remember waiting for FedEx to arrive, and when the book did arrive, some of the pages were smeared

The press in Gabrielle's studio.

because the ink had been wet when they shoved it in the box. But it was for a major event, and it had to be there for the presentation.

The other big challenge was one of those projects that grows. It was a memoriam book for a church in Kentucky. I worked with a local calligrapher on it. I suppose it is not the largest book I've ever worked on, but close to it, about 20" by 15", with carved wooden boards that were inset on the front and back boards, as well as the spine. The first set of boards that arrived was warped, and I had to ask the woodcarver to do them again, which wasn't easy. Technically, it was an incredible challenge. I enjoyed those projects, but I learned that I should charge a lot more! You have to take into consideration the time for the planning. And you have to incorporate into it the possibility that something is going to have to be purchased again.

I try and tell myself that even when something comes in that might have challenges, I still like what I am doing—I really love what I'm doing. I don't want to hate that book. I have had the experience that by the time I was done, I was so angry, because the financial situation had become pretty serious, that I wanted to fling it out the window even though I really enjoyed the work.

If you put a fair price on it, you wouldn't have hated it?
No.

How do you do that? When a client comes in with a book they want you to do, do you give them a price right then or do you say, "I'll get back to you on it?" Or do you give them a range?
If I can see fairly clearly what the problem is, then I can give them a price. If I can't, I say, "I have to have a closer look and then get back to you." I always give an estimate and tell them, "If I get started and I find that there's a lot more work involved than I expected, I will contact you before I continue any further." But that is easier said than done, because if you started to excavate already, you are not able to give it back to them in the same condition as it was when they handed it over. If I've learned anything, it's that the people who can afford it often are not willing to budge. In the early days, coming back to Cincinnati, I told a client that the work turned out to be much more difficult, and he refused to pay me more for it. I learned my lesson then.

So you give them one price, not a range?
I give them one price. Often there are options, and I give one price

for each. What have you found in interviewing others? I'm willing to learn.

It varies. I find that people want this discussion to take place, about pricing. Many bookbinders are frustrated about pricing.

Was it Sam Ellenport [from Harcourt Bindery] that did that survey about 17 years ago? I remember something about it shortly after I came back from England. I think it was Sam who sent out a survey with questions like, "What would you charge for this job?" Of course there can be a difference in materials. Black leather is different for different folks, but there was enough of a description that we were close to being on the same page. I think it was done anonymously. Replies came back with estimates ranging from $10 to $1,000 for the same job.

We've [bookbinders] never been very straight up with one another about that. It is a really important thing. The program where I studied in England is no longer in existence, but I know that towards the end of it, they were really working with students like that, on a practical level. When we all headed out after our studies, I would say a third of the people went out of business because they went straight out, took out small business loans, bought all the equipment that they needed, and then they just couldn't cover their debts. That is when you need to charge the most, and you don't have the skills to warrant those fees. I have spoken to several people who specialize in small business, and the advice they give does not work for us.

One of the most frustrating things is talking with clients who want wholesale prices. They assume as a professional you get wholesale prices on your material. I don't order enough materials to get that break. Occasionally I do on a big job, but on the whole, I just buy a few skins here and a few skins there. In our business, what we get is good service from vendors.

What advice would you give to someone who thinks he/she wants to be a bookbinder—as far as being realistic about making a living and about the education and experience he/she needs?

I'd say that if they have the opportunity, they should go and study in a college program. I think [institutions in] the States still want diplomas more than other countries. If you have that when you are starting off, it gives you credibility. The other reason is, I think it is good to learn with other students when you first start. You see certain things you aren't so good at but someone else is, which gives you a sense of your skill level. And also I think you see that certain things that seem impossible aren't; that you have to approach them through a different point of view. I think you learn a lot of that when you are learning with other people. Also, don't go out and buy everything at first. Set up and see what work is coming in, get the equipment you need for that work, and go from there.

Would you say you can make a living in private practice, or would you suggest the aspiring bookbinder work for someone?

It is a bit like acting—keep your day job. But at a certain point you have to take a leap of faith if you are really going to do it. There are things you can do to bring in some income that can compliment it, but at a certain point, just like writing, you either are doing it or you're not. I think other people may disagree.

What are your gifts or abilities that make you a good bookbinder?

Attention to detail. Also, I'm feeling much more comfortable with my own work; it's a sense of balance that only you can develop. There are a lot of skills you spend a lot of time trying to be really good at. At a certain time, it begins to click and you feel a sort of freedom with it, and you can start playing with it, or experimenting. I feel I'm just getting to that point. You learn the basics, but the individual has to grow into it. There are certain structures or formulas in bookbinding that just don't apply to every textblock that comes through the door. There is a sense of learning that and the balance of it. I think I have a good sense of that balance, and that my books actually work.

Is there anything you would rather be doing than bookbinding?

I'd like to write more.

Tell me about the miniature books. I think of you as the miniature book expert.

It happened by chance. I was teaching bookbinding in England, and one of the students came in with a serious book collection. It was one of those three-day, residential workshops. She brought in her miniature books and asked if I would help her work on her collection. She said that whenever she took them to workshops, the instructors turned their noses up and said, "They're not real books. We might get to it by the end of the weekend." And they never did. I was intrigued with it. She introduced me to the dealer, Louis Bondy, in London. I went to see him to ask if he had any books with really nasty bindings that he would sell to me at reduced rates. Then I would go off and mess with them. He started giving me some work to do. It went from there. When I moved back to the States, I wanted to go back to England and still be involved in the binding community.

For purely practical reasons, miniatures were a good thing to specialize in. I could pop them in my suitcase. I could even pop the equipment in my suitcase and go back and teach a weekend course. It is a challenge with the detail work. Maybe that is where I get the balance thing. Balance in miniature work isn't just scaling everything down. There is a different balance. There is a whole theory of teaching binding based on miniatures. You learn sensitivity to materials and balance by working with miniatures. Those theories you can apply to big books.

I don't think there is any book written on this subject. I think you need to write it. I think that is your book.

I'd love to do that.

For more information on Gabrielle Fox, and to see examples of her work, go to http://www.gabriellefox.com.

Karen Hanmer:
Melding Book Arts and Bookbinding

Glenview, Illinois
October 2007

When I arrive at the home and studio of Karen Hanmer and her husband, Bob, they are finishing lunch. Their suburban home in Glenview, IL is in a lovely area where McMansions are popping up, suffocating the neighborhood. Their two-story frame house is snuggled between two of them, one with a huge boat deposited in the narrow space between their houses. A piece of heavy white paper covers the window in the door that would otherwise look out at the enormous vessel. A tour of the house includes a visit to the basement where Bob has built an extensive model train system. Though their house doesn't rival the size of the McMansions next door, it is spacious, with an upstairs addition Karen and Bob built in 1999 that is Karen's large bookbinding studio.

As we enter the studio, I am attracted to a vintage 1950's dress that decorates a wall. A fox fur is draped around the neck. Jesus and Mother Mary icons adorn the room. Whimsical art objects reflect quirky, creative Karen. She shows me a flag book she created with pictures of Elvis and names of his songs. Though she made it as a sample to show students, she entered it in an art contest at Graceland and won a trophy.

An inheritance Karen received funded cabinetry as well as bookbinding equipment, tools, and supplies that were once part of Rebecca Shaffer's bindery. Her studio is a bright space with two walls of windows, one wall of cabinets, and a large closet to accommodate a four-foot sink and a guillotine. The space easily accommodates her Jacques board shear, a sturdy backing press, book presses, a large Epson color printer, a computer, a large worktable, flat files, and other drawers for book board. Bookshelves flank the walls near the two comfortable chairs where we sit.

Though her artists' books and book designs have a playful element, Karen is very serious about what she does. Using well-honed organizational skills, she orchestrates regular mailings, promoting her work and keeping it in the public eye. She even has an agent who takes her work to libraries to sell to special collections. She visits heads of special collections to learn what kind of work they collect. She visits libraries and archives to thoroughly research subjects that will become part of her artists' books. She exhibits her work, and often wins awards for her artists' books. She travels around the country giving workshops. She stays connected.

Karen Hanmer adds a dimension of fun to bookbinding—her bindings suggest a let's-not-take-ourselves-too-seriously attitude. By rigorously studying traditional bookbinding and mastering techniques and styles that she applies to her artists' book pieces, she has been instrumental in melding book arts with bookbinding, two factions of the book world that have historically not been closely associated with each other. Her artists' books set her apart from most book artists by her skill at folding together unique and interactive designs with high quality craftsmanship, creating books that are not only artful, but function well as books. She has incorporated her economics background and business experience into a career in book arts and bookbinding. And she moves ahead in her career in a very purposeful, yet gracious, way.

What was your first job? I know you graduated in economics.

I don't know what I thought was going to happen when I graduated. I guess I thought I was going to go to business school. I got married and got a job as an office manager for a marketing research firm where I answered the phone, ordered the pencils, made the reports look pretty, did the bookkeeping and taxes. I did all the support for the office, the loftier and less-lofty tasks. I never liked it, and finally I couldn't stand it any more. I'd think of getting another job, but then I'd always think, "Well, I already have a job I don't like and at least I'm used to it," and I didn't know what else I could do. Finally, I emailed everyone I knew, "I don't want to be here for another 14 years, working for this guy's kids. Can you help me?"

I had always done photography—I was exhibiting a little bit but not selling any work. (It was a long time before I realized I could actually sell my work, not just exhibit it.) Someone I knew from a cooperative gallery where I was a member who was a photo-researcher said she thought I would be really good doing what she did, and that she wanted an assistant. So I worked for her for a year; then I worked for an educational publisher for three years doing photo-research. I really loved it. But then the company was bought and left the Chicago area and moved to Austin. It was the end of 2003, and I had been making books for six years. I was only working part-time by then, so I wasn't making that much money anyway. We decided I wouldn't get another job working for somebody else again.

You said you were making books. How did that happen from your photography?

In photography, you press a button on the camera and then this electronic stuff happens inside the camera to make the image. I didn't feel very much a part of the process, so I was trying different things to feel more physically connected to what I was doing. I started taking pictures of myself using a pinhole camera, because it kind of felt like I was the camera, hand-holding for long exposures and operating the shutter by removing and replacing a piece of lightproof tape. I was coating sand paper with photo emulsion and trying other things to make my process more tactile.

By 1997, PhotoShop was available, so if you wanted to do something with text and image together, you didn't have to run between several different enlargers to get it all in the same image. You could just sit down at the computer and do it. I needed to learn PhotoShop for a project, so I got a designer friend to show me the basics.

Then I started making some calls to see who could teach me to do the bookbinding I needed for the same project. I didn't even know bookbinding was what I needed. I went to a lecture by a printmaker who also made some books. I called her, and she suggested some potential binding instructors. Then somehow I found Scott Kellar, but he didn't want to take beginners. I was able to persuade him to show me how to make this thing (folio with prints inside) that I wanted to make. I told him that if it didn't work out, I'd leave the class. From the beginning I really liked binding. I liked how it physically felt to do this, to make this kind of work, to be so physically involved. The viewer could be physically involved as well. As an artist, I want people to feel something. I believe if I can get them to feel something tactilely, that will induce them to feel something emotionally.

I don't show these first books now because I'm not so happy with them, after all this time. They were a starting place. There are ten of them; they were made for an exhibit. I realized in April of 1997 that this was the work I wanted to make, and the show was in July. I was really hustling to figure out how to do it all.

I really liked how it felt making books. Now I can't imagine having just one image on a wall, with no layering of imagery and no opportunity for the viewer to interact with the work, that people just look at as they walk past.

You are good at promoting your work.

When I inherited some money from my father, I was able to get my website professionally designed. My husband, Bob, designed the first one; he is a computer guy, but he's not a graphic designer. The website was functional, but it looked kind of clunky. If you are a visual artist, you can't have this clunky visual thing representing your work. The look of the website has to reflect the look of your work.

Now you are hooked on bookbinding, right?

This past April was ten years since I started studying with Scott Kellar. I feel like with ten years, I finally have some legitimacy, but I am horrified at how much I haven't learned. For the longest time I wasn't interested in traditional binding. I just made my artists' books, and in class I would fiddle around and cut pieces to make boxes.

Until you started taking classes from Scott and learned more traditional things?

Until I started working more seriously on bindings in class, instead of on my artists' books projects. Scott isn't terribly interested in artists' books, but he has been a really good sport, and has helped me with a lot of problem solving for my more interactive artists' books. You have seen his designs. His geometric designs are lovely.

One of the things I noticed on your webpage is that you like to make things into games and puzzles, an interactive dimension. I think that sets you apart from most other bookbinders.

My binding skills are not to the point where I have been able to do that in a fine binding yet, but I'm working really hard to learn.

How did you initially learn book art?

I began as a photographer. Then I took some weekend classes at Columbia College, before the masters program there got popular. People from the community could take these workshops from people like Daniel Kelm, Hedi Kyle, and Julie Chen. Now those classes aren't available to people in the community because there are enough graduate students to fill them. It is a real loss for the community.

Then I started going to PBI (Paper and Book Intensive) too. The classes at PBI cover a wide variety of topics, and also, it is really fun and a great way to meet other serious bookmakers.

How do you find the exhibits that you are in?

From the book arts listserv and various organizations that I belong to. Also I used to subscribe to Art Calendar. I would answer calls for entry for art exhibits open to any media, or to universities that were looking for exhibition proposals. I wasn't looking specifically for book opportunities at first. Initially I was trying to get known in Chicago. You'd think since I live here, that would be easiest, but it was like I was beating my head against the wall. I've done a whole lot better since I've been focusing on book arts nationally instead of the general art scene locally.

Do you sell any of your pieces?

Yes, but not so much through exhibits. Mostly I sell to university library special collections.

How do the special collections know about you?

I send a mailing with postcards of new work each year to all the special collections I've found that might be interested, and to many of the book people I know. Then I send a follow-up email to the collections. It is getting more effective each year.

It seems like a good marketing plan. Do you make a very good living?

I'm beginning to break even. It will be better this year because I finally have all the supplies and equipment I need for my studio. It is amazing just to be selling so much of my work. I also have a dealer,

Vamp and Tramp—Bill and Vicky Stewart in Birmingham, Alabama. They spend a lot of time on the road, going around the country, showing work to special collections, at book fairs and to private collectors. They take a commission, so it is less money for me, but I couldn't visit all those special collections, and I certainly wouldn't want to spend every vacation for the rest of my life making these visits instead of relaxing or learning something new. And I wouldn't want Bob to spend all of his vacations sitting on the curbs outside of special collections.

Where else have you gotten your bookbinding education besides Scott Kellar and Columbia College classes?

I'm studying with Monique Lallier through the American Academy of Bookbinding in Ann Arbor. I have taken a couple of classes from Priscilla Spitler. She had a weeklong bookbinding intensive in March of 2005 and a long weekend in February of 2006 (fine binding class and finishing with onlays).

Taking class from Scott is great, but he has a room full of students all working on their own projects. He will help each person for a few minutes, and then he needs to help somebody else. I can get into a lot of trouble before it is my turn with him again. Still, I do not know how else he could teach a group of people of different levels and interests, and I'm grateful to have him here. Taking an intensive where everyone is working on the same project and there is no interruption in the instruction is a great luxury.

I find myself working mostly at home now. I am used to my studio, and I'm not competing with the other people for equipment or space. Then I bring books I'm working on to class to talk over with Scott. That seems to work pretty well.

What are the aspects you find most challenging about being a bookbinder?

Paring. I'm better now that I use the Scharfix [paring tool]. Paring has been my nemesis. In Priscilla's class, I tore the leather and there wasn't time to fix it. I couldn't start paring a new piece of leather and keep up with the class, so we had to move on. So I made a design of an onlay in the shape of a spokeshave adjacent to the tear.

Now that you've got this far, what are your aspirations, your ideal scenario?

I want to learn new things. I've been printing all my artists' books on an inkjet printer. It is not ideal for everything. I am looking into different printmaking methods for the next book so I can keep learning techniques. I shouldn't do the same thing over and over again just because it is all I know how to do.

I'd like to spend more time doing research for my artists' books projects, maybe go somewhere where they have documents about something I'm interested in. I'm interested in the history of science and cultural history. I'd like to go to a library and spend a couple months looking through original documents to get text for the artists' books projects.

As far as the bindings, I've always been okay with design, although it may not be to everyone's taste. Many binders tell me that design is the hardest part for them. I enjoy it. Sometimes it is really hard work. For my *Ficciones* book for the last DeGolyer exhibition [2006], it took me months to come up with the design. I think my designs are distinctive and playful. Instead of binding fine letterpress literature, I often pick texts that are on offbeat topics and sometimes pretty lowbrow. It would be great if people would come to know my style, [if] people would come to me for commissions. That would be really cool. I guess everybody wants that. I can imagine being known for my design one day; it would be really, really great if my craft got so good that people would know me for my craft as well.

People who know my artists' books think they are well-crafted, and I seem to be somewhat known for that in that arena, but I don't know if it is because my craft really is so great. Artists' books have a reputation for having horrible craft. I don't know that that is always fair, but I wonder if I have a reputation for having a high level of craft because it is not awful rather than because it is magnificent. The book arts programs seem to be more like printmaking programs with the binding as an afterthought—like the thing to cram their prints into. There seems to be limited emphasis on developing binding skills. It seems so wrong. I can't believe what a snob I've become. But then a mentor told me I was just "developing a healthy connoisseurship."

I am disappointed that people who take workshops at book arts centers sometimes seem to view them as entertainment, and they only make books in class and never on their own. I teach these classes sometimes, and I am entertaining. I just wish more of the students were serious. But I would hope that the people who want something more are aware that there is something more and that they can find it somehow. To study with Scott, to study with Priscilla or Monique, to study with someone who actually does know so much, is such a privilege. We are so lucky to have these skilled binders and teachers. To study with a couple different people is important. [For example] maybe there is something that Scott does and I just can't get the hang of it. And then I see how Priscilla does it—well, my wrist does turn like that—I can do that.

What would you suggest to the aspiring bookbinder that is interested in pursuing bookbinding as a career?

Find yourself some kind of community so you aren't working alone—so you are getting feedback and knowing if what you are doing is good or bad. Have a mentor who may not necessarily be your instructor. Priscilla is kind of like my bookbinding mom. Scott is local and is a great problem solver. Peter Verheyen is a good friend and has really been a mentor also, and has provided a lot of opportunities for me.

Try to find a teacher who actually knows what they are doing—but then you have to get to a certain point before you know if your teacher knows or not. See work whenever you can. Get critiqued on what you are doing. What is a corner supposed to look like? What is a head-cap supposed to look like?

I've started commissioning a fine binding every year so I can support the field. How can I expect people to buy my books if I'm not willing to buy any? Also, it is a teaching collection of well-made books. I can refer to them and see, "Oh, this is what a head-cap is supposed to look like; this is what a hinge is supposed to look like." Plus, to have these really fabulous objects! Compare what you are doing with what other people are doing so you know what you have to learn. I don't know how people can learn completely on their own. I've not rented any of the Guild of Book Workers videotapes, but I don't know how people can learn from a video if they have not seen a well done, completed object in person.

Some people have told me they have done the CABBG home study program [a series of bookbinding lessons on video tape, put out by a bookbinding organization in Canada]. I guess there is an option where you can send your physical books in to be critiqued. I think you need somebody who is more skilled than you are to check-in with pretty frequently as you are learning.

What about working? I know you haven't been out in the field working—you work here. It is interesting how you market with your mailings. Would you have any advice for anyone who wants to make a living doing this?

I don't really have that kind of advice. I'm still trying to figure it out. I will tell you that since jurying the Guild of Book Workers 100th Anniversary exhibition, I've been really intrigued with edition binding. It is something I'd never thought about before.

Scott does mostly conservation, so that is the kind of work I usually see. There are people out there who have skills similar to my skills, better, hopefully, some of them probably not, and they are supporting themselves making books that people actually want—and will pay for. It's amazing.

I send out my mailings and I exhibit my work, and I hope the work will sell. Sometimes it leads to an invitation to teach instead.

Do you like teaching?

I like to teach a handful of times a year. It helps me clarify what I'm doing and why, and is an opportunity to travel to new places and make new contacts. I'm not as passionate about teaching as some people are.

Priscilla is fabulous. During the Fine Binding Intensive, not only was she teaching us, but she also prepared our cabins and arranged for our food. When students were discouraged, she would encourage them. She explained to me that it was very important that I, personally, continued to bind because the field really needed me. I had so much to contribute. I'm sure she told that to all twelve of us. She was very motivating and very kind.

Is there anything in your childhood that would have suggested that you would be interested in bookbinding or book art?

There was something in my childhood that got me interested in photography, but I didn't have any special affinity for books. Even now. I enjoy reading very much, but I can't say I want to be surrounded by books. I'd prefer a handful of books I really love. Maybe several handfuls.

I see you as needing to be multi-stimulated. That is a good thing. Perhaps that is what sets you apart as a book artist.

How do you feel about including a book artist in your interviews?

I think it is good, especially since you have such a strong interest in bookbinding.

I was ready for a different challenge. I'm really, really enjoying it.

What are your favorite things about bookbinding?

I like sewing, and I like coming up with the design for a binding. And making boxes is pleasant. I enjoy doing that.

Not everyone can do the design well. I think that is a gift you have.

It really helps that I am usually binding a text I selected on a topic I have a strong interest in. It is harder when it is for a competition with a set book that I don't feel any connection to.

What are your least favorite parts of bookbinding?

The things I'm not yet skilled at, head-caps and paring. I have finally gotten so I'm not horrible at paring. Last year I decided if I couldn't get better at paring, I was going to quit making leather bindings. Then, I began the American Academy of Bookbinding program with Monique Lallier and learned how to pare with the Scharfix. That's working a lot better for me.

The aspects that I don't like are related to my frustration at my skill level. And then there is all the paperwork I do related to sales and exhibitions of my artists' books that takes me away from working on new projects. But I'm really good at doing the paperwork, and it makes a difference in sales and being readily available for opportunities.

Do you like being self-employed as an independent book artist/binder?

Yes, though it is hard for me to think of myself as "employed." I have started to turn the corner since I am beginning to make some money. It is great to have the flexibility to do whatever I want, whenever I want to, but it makes it easy to become overcommitted. What was my hobby, has become my job. It is kind of hard to have leisure time. I'll come up to my studio to work after dinner, and all day long on the weekends. I am always up here doing something. Shouldn't I be relaxing after dinner and on weekends?

That is a common thread—everyone works really hard. Who are your clients?

Special collections librarians, and sometimes individuals buy my work.

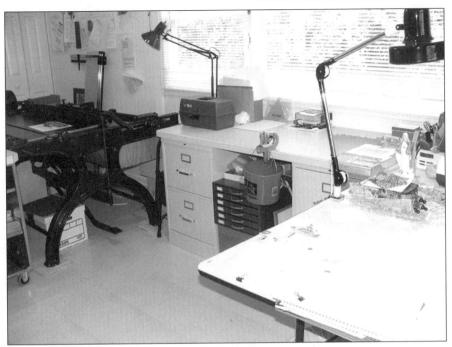

Karen Hanmer's studio.

Who do you send your mailings to?

I send them to special collections and to other book people I know, because you never know who knows whom. I like to let friends know what I am doing, but I try to keep my business separate. I don't need to be sending everyone I know my promotional materials. But it is hard to keep it separate since so many of my friends are binders or artists.

Do you develop any special kind of relationship with clients?

A few librarians have helped me figure out what special collections people want. It does not affect what I make, but it does affect what information I provide, or what time of the year I send my mailing. There are a of couple librarians I will show work in process to get feedback because they see lots and lots and lots of books. They are a great resource. And I will ask to see work from their collections— examples of a particular structure or printmaking method, work by artists I'm interested in, or historic books on a topic I'm researching.

One thing that is appealing about what you do that I haven't thought about before is that you work like a journalist—you get to go and research subjects that you like and then make them into something cool.

That is why I like to bind whatever interests me, rather than whatever fine press book in sheets is available.

What are your gifts and abilities that make you good at what you do?
I have a good (and quirky) design sense and attention to detail. I'm interested in a lot of different things. Someone who read my bio on my website emailed me, "Your books reveal the kind of deep and wonderfully devious thinking of someone educated in a discipline other than fine arts." With my liberal arts background, I studied other things instead; so all my interests bring something else to the artwork.

A lot of my work is playful; even if the subject is somber, maybe the structure will be playful. That sets me apart a little bit. Priscilla's designs also can be playful—that's something I really like. Seeing her work and the work of some other people that have nontraditional designs made me realize, "Oh, fine binding does not have to be stuffy and boring after all." Imagine me starting off as a book artist in the Guild of Book Workers ten years ago!

How long have you been in the Guild?
My first year to attend Standards [the Guild of Book Workers annual conference] was 1999, in Chicago. I wanted to join some kind of professional group. The Guild was not a great fit, but what else is there? People in the Guild have been very welcoming and encouraging. When they saw I was serious and wanted to learn, it didn't matter that I was a book artist, as opposed to a fine binder.

Do you go to Chicago Hand Bookbinders?
Yes, but the group has really changed. The fine binders are all gone. The members are less serious. Making books is a less important part of members' lives than it used to be. It is a big loss for our community here.

The Midwest Chapter of Guild of Book Workers doesn't have an organized local presence in Chicago. I keep thinking I'll get something going, but I have my hands full being Exhibitions Chair for Guild. Even though it is a lot of work getting the next Guild traveling show organized, I am enjoying the job.

Last year for practice, independently from the Guild, I curated a small traveling show of work from ten binders who submitted two bindings each [*The Book of Origins: A Survey of American Binding*]. I thought, "If I am going to screw up, then I'll just have a handful of exhibitors angry with me rather than the whole Guild."

I went through all the steps of getting six venues, writing proposals and doing PR, and having the show travel across the country for a year. I learned a lot and even raised enough money to produce a catalog.

Is there anything you would rather be doing than doing what you are doing?

I tried to think of something since I knew you'd be asking this, and I really can't think of anything I'd rather be doing.

For more information on Karen Hanmer, and to see examples of her bindings, go to http://www.karenhanmer.com.

Don Glaister:
An Idea-Driven Approach to Making Books

Vashon Island, Washington
July 2008

I walked off the Fauntelroy ferry that took me from Seattle to Vashon Island and found Don Glaister standing next to his Subaru—tousled, wavy white hair and robin-egg blue eyes. He could be one of the now middle-aged hippies that settled on the Island in the '60's to escape the draft and ended up staying. He says he feels at home among these folks, and shares their liberal, freethinking attitudes.

He takes me on the long route to his house so I can see the coastal view. It is woodsy with hairpin curves. I see occasional glimpses of the sound. We arrive at the contemporary home that Don shares with his wife, Suzanne Moore, a calligrapher/artist/bookmaker. I meet Roscoe, a young, energetic white dog that resembles a small German Shepherd. The contemporary house has plentiful windows on both the living area on the top floor and in the basement that opens to ground level. The stairway to the basement divides the lower level into two studios: one side for Suzanne, the other for Don.

I get the opportunity to look at the last two limited-edition art books that Don has created. His sold-out edition of Brooklyn Bridge books feature unique airbrushed aluminum covers and pages. He has already sold half of the edition he is currently working on, a book that includes drummed, filled pages engineered to support intriguing collages of sailboat motifs. The two editions are very different, but both are innovative, creative structures that blend art and skilled bookbinding structures, producing visually and texturally intriguing and pleasing books.

Educated as an artist, Don was disenchanted with his art career when he was confronted with the politics of the art world. He decided to pursue bookbinding after taking some classes in San Francisco. His teacher assured him it was a profitable career, and so he traveled to Paris to learn more. After his return to the States, he began teaching and doing commission work. He discovered that it was difficult to earn a living. Even though his work is well respected and his design bindings are original and marketable, he has sometimes struggled financially.

He and Suzanne moved from the west coast to the east coast, to the south and to mid-America before deciding to settle on Vashon Island, off the coast of Seattle. "We thought, what are we doing? Waiting around for retirement or something? Let's go and do what we do and live our life and hope we can pay for it. That is why we are here; moving to a situation seemed to not be working for us. We decided to move to a place that we wanted to be, and make a situation. So that is what we did. And that is this place."

Living on groovy Vashon Island with his wife, the companionship of a dog ("Dogs make us happier people," claims Don), doing the work he enjoys doing, Don seems to be living fully in the present. One thing he would like to do is to share what he does with an apprentice who gets what he does and who is really interested in learning about idea-driven work, soul-driven work. To teach someone who can run with it.

What made you interested in bookbinding?

I went to graduate school and got degrees in painting and sculpture. I went to San Jose State. When I finished graduate school, I had an advanced degree in painting and sculpture, and I wondered what I was going to do with that to make a living. I got a full-time job at the Stanford Museum of Art. My job was to design shows, hang shows in the print and drawing collection. Within the print and drawing collection were books. I wasn't terribly interested in the museum; it was just a way to make a living while I was working weekends and nights in my studio making sculptures. It wasn't going well. I wasn't selling work. It was hard to live. I was frustrated with the museum job because it was taking all my time, but it wasn't paying me a lot of money. Things weren't balanced very well.

I quit my job and thought I would make a go of the art business and get a part-time job to feed myself. It came down to two part-time jobs. One was a job at the Palo Alto city dump that paid pretty well. I really wanted that job. I would take money from people as they went to the dump. The other job that was available was at the Stanford library, mending books. I didn't really want that job because it didn't pay as much. I just needed some dough so I could work in my studio. I didn't get the dump job—bummer. I did get the library job.

I started mending stack books (nothing like conservation). Because of my experience with books that were really fine at the museum, I knew that I was doing really awful things to these books. I didn't quite understand the difference between a stack book and a fine book. I just knew I wasn't doing those books any favors.

About the same time, I was starting to get disillusioned with being a painter and sculptor. I didn't understand how to make a success of it. I could do it. It seemed to me it was not so much about the work as it was about where you lived, who you knew, how you could get shows—things like that. It wasn't about the art. I didn't know how to play the game. I was frustrated. I was unhappy with the path I had chosen, but I was sort of interested in this other thing I was doing at the library. I started asking some questions about book conservation. Nobody knew anything at the library. I went from one person to the next, trying to find information about doing the right thing for these books.

I ended up talking to Stella Patri in San Francisco who was a book conservator and taught people book conservation. She was a terrific woman, probably 70 years old when I first met her. She asked me, "Are you a bookbinder?" I said, "No, but I want to learn conservation." She said, "I won't teach you. You have to be a bookbinder first, then I'll teach you conservation." I said, "Fine, how do I become a bookbinder?" She said, "My studio mate, Barbara Hiller, teaches people bookbinding. You could study with her."

So I called up Barbara Hiller (whom Eleanore Ramsey also studied with. Eleanore and I took classes together). I talked to Barbara. She was a really infectious person. She was a terrific teacher because she would get you excited about stuff. I use almost nothing that she taught me in terms of techniques, but she got me so excited about making books. She had studied in France. After I started working with her, I wanted to go to France. That was all there was to it. She said that is where you learn. After six months studying with her, I knew that was what I wanted to do. It took me three years of saving money, but I finally did it. I went and got my old job back at the museum. I needed money because I was going to France. My wife at the time had a job, and we saved money and didn't spend anything. We lived in Paris for a year, and I studied bookbinding privately with two bookbinders, and she went to the Cordon Bleu Cooking School. It was cool. We came back to Palo Alto, and I opened up a studio.

What kind of binding did you study in Paris?

[Fine binding.] I forgot completely about conservation after studying with Barbara. I wanted to do fine binding. I didn't even know there was such a thing before I met Barbara. Barbara showed me books and exhibition catalogs and books people were doing in her classes. It was cool. I knew how to make my hands work and my eyes work and manipulate materials. It was a good fit. I asked her, "Can I make a living at this?" And Barbara answered, "No problem!" She always seemed like she had enough money. I didn't know anybody else who was a professional bookbinder. It wasn't until after I came back from France, maybe after she died, that I found out she had private funds (a big trust fund). She didn't live like she had a lot of money. Now I know that there is no way she could have lived on the money she made from students. If I'd known, I wouldn't have done it.

When I came back, I set up a studio and lived just south of Palo Alto in Mountain View, CA. I converted a two-car garage into a studio. I started teaching and taking commissions. I would take any book that came in the door—cookbooks, Bibles, boxes. Part of the French training that I've now gotten away from is the idea that there is a separation between fine binding, edition binding, and book repair. I never learned to do a case binding until I was 50 years old! That's the truth! I'm not particularly proud of it; that's just the way it was.

I worked at the museum again for about six months, just while I got my studio started. I was married, and my wife had a job. I was teaching all the time in my studio, and I was making enough money for it to make sense. I couldn't have done it at first without both of us working. We couldn't have lived off her salary either. We did all right.

We were there for two or three years. The marriage ended. I left that house and moved to Palo Alto. Then I was on my own. I had to make it work financially. I had a little studio that I rented and a miniscule apartment. I just kept making books. In the beginning, when I first came back from France, I didn't want to make art with these books, but instead be a craftsperson, a bookbinder. I didn't want to be a book artist. I was still gun-shy about the politics of art. I didn't want anything to do with it. I wanted to be the guy to execute the designs that somebody else would do. I didn't want to be the artist. I'm not saying that it was a really good idea—that is just what I had in mind.

I came back from Paris in 1977. In 1978, there was a bookbinding exhibition in San Francisco, one of the first of my generation that we, my generation, could participate in. I think it was called "Hand Bookbinding Today and International Art." Because I had studied abroad, I was invited to be part of the jury of this exhibition. I got sucked into this book as art thing even though I thought I didn't want to do that. Because I was on this jury, I got excited about the exhibition and I bought a book, designed and made a binding, and I liked it. I liked the idea of designing it. That idea of not making art with books didn't last too long. When I finished the book, it was juried in, and I sold the book. That got my attention. "I can make money at this! Barbara was right."

I had this strategy that I would always have a design binding that I would be working on, even if I had to go buy the book myself. And I would continue along doing the family Bibles and the teaching and other stuff. I think I only had to buy that first book. When I sold that book to a dealer in San Francisco, he gave me another book to do, and it continued like that. It was only one book at a time, but it was enough to make me understand that I could sell them and people liked them.

I learned a really important thing from doing one book at a time. I would take the commissioned book to the dealer and get the money, and nobody else would know anything about it. Only the dealer or the few people he showed it to would see it. That didn't do me any good except to the one person who bought it. The first book was in an exhibition, but after that no one saw my books.

Just by accident I discovered a new strategy. Every time I finished a book, I would take it up to San Francisco and show it to anybody I could, mostly book dealers since they were the ones commissioning design bindings. I would say, "I've just finished a commissioned binding, and I'd like to show it to you. I just want to show you what I've been up to." So the whole business of money—is it too much or too little—was all gone because I was not selling it. There was no commitment. They would say, "Sure, I want to see it." I would show it, and these guys would say, "How much is that?" They wanted it. They wanted to do a deal. "No, you can't have it. It belongs to someone else." It would make them nuts. They didn't like that. Dealers and collectors wanted it. Sometimes a guy would say, "How much are you getting for that?" I'd tell them and they'd say, "That's too much." I'd say, "It's a done deal. It's not too much. I got it." It was great. The coolest story was, I did a book for a dealer and before I gave it to him, I took it to this other dealer. I didn't play or name drop but he asked whom it was for. I didn't want to lie to him, so I told him. He said, "That rascal! I've got one of those (another copy of the same book). See what you can do with this one." There is this competition. Nobody wants to be the dumb guy that didn't buy something when they should have. I don't quite understand it, but I do know that when people can't have something, and they are collectors, it does something to them that is good for me.

I built the business by doing my work and just exposing myself to as many people as I could. And I tried to get into every exhibition that came up, especially ones that had catalogs or some kind of record. As you know, there aren't that many of them. It doesn't happen all the time. In San Francisco, the Hand Bookbinders of California had an exhibition every year. It was a small thing, but it was the only thing. There was always at least that show. It was an open show so you had all kinds of books.

I was in the Bay Area, living a modest existence. I decided I needed to get out of town for a while for divorce reasons. I had this old 1965 Karmann Ghia. I wanted to go on a car trip. I made plans to travel the perimeter of the country to give workshops and slide shows to make a little money, but also to give me a reason to do it. This was 1982. I took three months and drove 11,000 miles around the country in my Karmann Ghia. I had a little backing press, a couple of finishing presses, and some gold-tooling equipment, like the itinerant bookbinder. Just before I left to go on the trip, a woman from San Francisco who was studying lettering called me. Her studies had stopped for a short time, and she wanted to learn to put her lettering in books. Our old friend, Stella Patri, told her that if she wanted to learn bookbinding she should look me up. She came down to Palo Alto on the train. It was Suzanne

Don Glaister's bindery.

[Moore]. We talked for quite a while. It wasn't going to work out because I was leaving the next week on the car trip. A couple days later, she called and said she would be in Seattle in three months and asked if I would be near there then. She was looking for a ride from Seattle back to San Francisco. I said, "Sure, here is where I'm going to be. I had addresses and phone numbers. Three months later, I walked into my friend's house in Seattle, and the phone was ringing there. It was Suzanne. We got together and drove down the coast together. That was it. We started living together as soon as I could convince her to move out of the city and move down to Palo Alto. We lived in a basement apartment that was big enough to hold my studio. Suzanne got a job at Stanford at the special collections library.

Did you teach her bookbinding?

No, I never did. The bookbinding that she knows (she binds most of her own books) she learned through osmosis and from other people. We never had any lessons.

At some point we couldn't stay in Palo Alto any longer. Silicon valley was developing, and it was getting more and more expensive—not only expensive, it wasn't our people. There weren't artists around.

We would go to parties, and we would be the token artists. Suzanne is from Wisconsin. I was born in California and couldn't imagine living anywhere else besides Palo Alto. She opened my eyes to the fact that there was something other than the Bay Area in the world.

I went cross-country skiing with her for the first time in my life. I had never been to the snow before. I lived right there and I never went there. She helped me get out of that jingoism that I had going. On my car trip, I had gone through the Pioneer Valley in Massachusetts, more specifically Easthampton and Northampton, MA. Back in Palo Alto, I remembered the Pioneer Valley, and I thought we might like living there. I told Suzanne about it and about all these book people that live there. On my trip, [bookbinder] David Barbeau had a party for me and invited bookbinders and printers and book people. I knew them all by reputation but had never met any of them. It seemed that they all lived within walking distance of each other.

We figured out a plan. We went to Massachusetts in January, and I taught two workshops. Our reasoning was that if I can stand it (California boy, right?) in January, then I passed the winter test. It was goddamn cold! I wasn't prepared for it. But I did pass. I bought more and better clothes. I bought real insulated boots, and that did it. We went back to California, and that spring we moved. We finally landed in Ashfield, MA, about 45 minutes from Northampton. As wonderful as all those people are, we didn't want to live right in the middle of them. We wanted to see them when we wanted to. The move was a really terrific thing to do. It was wonderful to be among those people, and they are still really close friends. Peter Geraty and his family were here last weekend.

We bought this wonderful Victorian five-bedroom house. It was terrific except it had no heating system. We bought two wood stoves and burned 12-13 cords of wood a year and froze our butts off. We worked and lived there. I thought if I could make a living in Palo Alto, I should be able to make a living where it is cheaper to live doing the same thing.

I wasn't very sophisticated about my market research. A big part of my income in Palo Alto was teaching, but I found that teaching was not really an option in Ashfield (nobody wanted to take lessons). People already knew what they were doing. We were among peers. Also, I lived 45 minutes away from Northampton. The teaching thing was out the window. I thought that would give me more time to work. So I started making work.

It was a really fruitful, fertile time. I went to my studio every day and worked, uninterrupted, until I dropped. I got work somehow. I worked with a couple dealers in Boston. One is Priscilla Jervalis who is still my dealer, along with Joshua Hiller (rare books) in Washington. Those are the two people I work with now. I've known and worked with Priscilla forever. She got me work. She would get me commissions. She would commission work herself. Suzanne and I went to the San Francisco book fair just after we moved to Massachusetts. Priscilla was there. She was the only person there that had books that were interesting to us—a lot of French bindings, gold tooled books, interesting work. We went to her booth and it said, "Boston, MA." That is how we met her. We are friends and have been doing business for a long time. We were both born on the same day and year.

I had a lot of work. I was okay. Suzanne started making books. She had studied lettering and had a degree in printmaking, sort of parallel to me. We both have fine arts backgrounds and studied classical tradition. Then we took the classical traditions and fine arts and combined them in different ways. We lived in that place three or four years, then moved close by in a barn that we renovated. We lived in that area from '84 to '96. We both did a lot of work. There was nothing else to do. Suzanne was on the road a lot and taught. I did a little of that too. It was a very prolific time. There was work, and there was money to pay for the work, and we had time to do the work—until the whole thing fell apart.

There was a recession in the mid '90's and it was really difficult for us. I eventually got a job at the Northeast Document Center, which is in Andover, MA, way east of where we lived. At first I only worked three days a week, so I would stay with a friend two nights and then drive home after the third workday. The schedule was terrible. At first I just made boxes. Then the friend that I was staying with, Deb Wender [who also worked at the NDC], got a new job there. Her former job as book conservator opened up, and I took it. It was a full-time job, so Suzanne and I moved to Salem, MA.

We rented a little apartment and tried to sell our house in Ashfield but couldn't. It was awful. That is where I made my first cloth case binding. People thought I knew how to do all this stuff, and I did know how to do a lot, but I didn't know how to do some of what I needed to for that job. Joe Newman was the chief book conservator. I had known him for a long time. Joe said that if you know how to take books apart and put them together, you know a lot about being a book conservator. That is why Stella Patri wouldn't teach me book conservation until I became a binder. Then you've got something to work with. It was something like that at the doc center. I rebound books, washed pages, mended pages, mended bindings. They were very interesting books, some killer books. It was important work. I got paid, and I got health insurance. It answered a need, but it took all day to do it. All my bindery stuff was in storage. Of course they had anything I needed at the document center to do my own bindings. I did two or three books while I was there, after hours and weekends. But it was hard. You can't get any rhythm going, and you are tired. I didn't do very much during the three years I was there. About a book a year.

I was grateful to have that job. It saved our butts. It was interesting, and the people were great. Deb Wender was a great boss and continues to be a good friend. It was all good except it wasn't my work. It wasn't who I am. At first when you get a new job, every day is exciting and everything is new. I learned how to do all these things, and I was decent at it, so it wasn't frustrating. It was good. But at some point, I wasn't learning as much new stuff, and it was slowing down. Since it wasn't the kind of work that I had my soul into, it started to be less exciting. It wasn't my work. I wasn't doing any art. I was less excited about the job, not unhappy, but the fire had cooled a bit. At that time, the University of Alabama was looking for a bookbinding teacher for their book arts program. I heard about it. A flyer went around the document center. I gave it some thought. I thought I could maybe get the job, but going to Alabama and moving and so on sounded crazy. I went home and told Suzanne about it. She thought it was crazy too. We gave it a day or two to think about it and talk about it. It ended up that I applied for the job and got it, and we moved to Alabama.

I stayed in Alabama for two-and-a-half years, but the situation wasn't a good fit. After two years, Suzanne got a job in Cleveland to be the art director of the hand lettering team at American Greetings. She left Alabama to do that job, and I stayed another semester before leaving to join Suzanne. I planned to go back to being a maker again. We found an industrial space in Cleveland and built a studio there for both of us. Suzanne had this very responsible, full-time job, so the amount of her own work that she could do was small. She thought she could do weekends and keep her hand in it so we both had spaces. I had a little bit of work. While I was at the document center and at Alabama, I was kind of out of circulation. I wasn't getting much work. The recession had dried things up a lot. But Suzanne had this killer job, making good money with benefits and vacation and stock options. That part was good. For her it was like for me at the document center. Everything was new and groovy, learning new things, getting paid. But it was really hard, a big job. I think she did a really terrific job.

I had a couple of bindings that had been commissioned and more trickled in. But over time, my work has become more and more complicated to make—visually complicated. It is taking longer and longer to do the work. Over my whole career, it has become more and more difficult to make these books. The more I make art out of them, the more I want to experiment, and that takes more time.

I learned gold-tooling in France. When I came back to California, I did a lot of gold-tooling on books for the first ten years. That is time intensive, but you can draw the pattern, you stick it on the book, tool through the paper. You make a drawing, and you know what that book is going to look like. But now, there are layers and layers of stuff, and painting and all kinds of things other than gold-tooling. It is harder and takes longer.

For example, I am working on a book right now that I made a model for in an attempt to shorten up the process, kind of like the tooling patterns did. It has layers made out of different kinds of materials—board and plastic and things—and still I come to the place right now on the real binding where I take the parts and put them together like it says on my model, and it doesn't work right. It is not right. It had to be changed, so I've changed it. But it has taken me a week to change it, to figure out what is wrong and why I don't like it. Here I have all this work in it. I'm not going to throw the thing away or tear it apart, so I have to use what I've got but alter it in a way that I like. It is actually going to make it better, but it all takes time. I couldn't get paid for that time.

There is a ceiling to what I can charge. I could only charge a certain amount of money for a book, but the books were taking longer and longer to make. It was a problem. How do you make this work? People thought the books were so terrific, but I couldn't really make a living making them. At some point I thought, this isn't a profession, this isn't working. Suzanne had this great job, killing herself doing it, working long hours, learning. I was spending a lot of time too and not making enough money.

I thought I should either get a job or go back to school. I didn't know what I should do. I thought I would give it one more shot. Maybe I could make multiples, an edition of artist books. As I was saying before, you make a book, sell a book, and it is gone. You start all over again. At least you are selling the book, but there is no momentum. It is too hard to make that work. What if I had a bunch of them? I could design it once, spend a bunch of time making them, take all the time I needed, but I would have more than one to sell. So I made the *Brooklyn Bridge* book [the end of 2002]. It took 18 months to do the Bridge book and about six months before that to figure out how to do the Bridge book. I hired the printing of the poem and the title page [from] a guy who prints license plates and things like that. I hired a woman who had been a student in Alabama, Melody Carr, to help me bind them. It was an edition of 60, 50 for sale. I didn't know if people would buy those kinds of books. But Suzanne bought me the time by working at that job. That was about two years of me not making money. As it turned out, the Bridge book was very popular and sold very well. The experiment really worked, so I am back in business. It was close!

How did you market the book?

I went to Priscilla. She helped me sell it, but she also helped me, along the way, to think about it. I took some sketches on metal to her and we talked about it. They really didn't have anything to do with the way the book ended up, but to talk about making a book this size with painting on it [helped]. She knew I could paint, and she knew sort of what things would look like. How many of these do I have to make? How much can we get for them? How do we do it? We had one meeting like that. I was about ready to get into production, and I was talking to her on the phone. She asked, "What is the text?" I said, "There is no text; it is just images about the Brooklyn Bridge." She said, "There has got to be a text." I said, "Why? I don't want text. It is a book of images." She said, "These are books. Librarians buy books. Librarians buy books that have words in them. Get a text." So I thought, "Oh man." I was all ready to go. I looked at different texts that I might be able to use that would fit and finally thought, "I can do this." I wrote a poem. She was absolutely right. It was a marketing thing, and it is a way better book for it. It holds it together. She sold some books. Joshua Heller sold quite a number of books. I sold probably two-thirds of them myself. I bought plane tickets and took the book to places. I talked to people that I knew in libraries and private collectors. As a design bookbinder, I never had anything to show these people because everything I did was on commission. Institutions like that don't commission. They'll buy something if it fits into their collection, but that is really iffy. My work was known to many private and institutional collectors. They had seen my work in exhibitions or catalogs, but I never had any way to do business with them.

With the Bridge book, I finally had something to sell them. It was great. I really enjoyed it. I enjoyed talking to people about my work. They would ask questions. I would ask questions. It was fun. People liked the stories about the book. It gives them a connection to the work that they wouldn't have otherwise. I sold a bunch on the West Coast, a lot in Massachusetts. I had all 60 done when I started selling them.

With my current book [sailboat theme] that I am working on, I am making them in thirds, 20/20/20. It is an edition of 60, and I have sold half of them, almost all of those I've made. This book is different. One thing interesting to me is when I sat down to do the second book I thought of the great ride of the Bridge book. I thought, "Why did people buy it?" I will just use that formula and make sure I follow it. But the reason I think that people bought that book was because they had never seen anything like it. Well, you can't do it the same way. So this is a different kind of book. It is actually a bigger book, in terms of the meat in it. Visually, there is more of it, more pages, a bigger idea. It is more expensive, and it is taking a hell of a long time to make. People will have to work harder on this book because there is more stuff there. I can't do it the same. If I did it the same, nobody would buy it and I wouldn't be happy with it. So the marketing of it is a little different. I enjoy marketing—talking about the stuff, meeting people. Maybe all those years working in the studio, sending the stuff off and getting a check in the mail with no contact with the people that end up with the work, makes me enjoy this part of it.

What made you leave Cleveland?

Life is short. Two things: Suzanne wasn't doing her own work. She was invited to work on the Saint John's Bible, a huge deal to be invited to do that. She accepted. She was doing huge illuminations for that on weekends and nights and also doing her full-time job. It was too much. Because she was making decent money and I was selling the hell out of the Bridge book, we had some cash. We got out of debt, and we had some dough. We thought we could go somewhere. We had gone to a situation in Alabama that turned out to be not what we wanted. We went to another situation in Cleveland that turned out to be not what we wanted. Moving to a situation seemed to not be working for us. We decided to move to a place that we wanted to be and make a situation. So that is what we did [2005]. And that is this place.

Suzanne's college roommate lives on Vashon Island. We have been visiting her since we lived in California. We knew about the place but never really thought about it much until we were in Cleveland. It took a lot of work to get here. Trying to buy a house across the continent is difficult. The market was really hot. Houses would be on the market for three days or less. We decided that based on the *Brooklyn Bridge* experience and the fact that I had a lot of binding commissions to do, that I would do both—I would do my edition books and commission work too. Suzanne had a lot of work if she just had time to do it. Life is short and people die. Suzanne's brother died at 60; her mother died; my mother died. All this happened within a year while we were in Cleveland. We thought, "What are we doing? Waiting around for retirement or something? Let's go and do what we do and live our life and hope we can pay for it." That is why we are here. We got lucky and made some money at a time when we needed to. We probably had no business buying this house, but we did it and somehow it is okay. It is working out. What else am I suited to do?

Do you like being a book artist?

I do like it. There is something very good about being an artist of some kind. I've designed architectural things. I've worked on buildings. But making art is what I do. I like it, but it's not a question of liking it or not liking it; it is what I do. As a bookbinder, the art is in the form of a codex. When I am working on buildings, it is in the form of rooms. When I was at the document center, I was commissioned to work on the design of some buildings in Aspen, Colorado. I did drawings, concepting. An architect in Aspen put it together in a form that builders can use, and it got built. I don't see making books and making buildings as way different from one another. A painting is different. It's a surface. A book is a place. You can put something in it. You have to interact with it for it to work. Like a building. A building is nothing if something is not happening in it or around it.

Is there anything you would rather be doing than what you are doing? Is this what you want to be doing?

I enjoy doing it. I don't know what else I would like to do. If there was something else, I guess it would be to be an architect, to make buildings. The reality of being an architect, I think, is different than my idea of it. I don't think it is like I think it is. I wouldn't want to worry about anything but just drawing and have someone else make it work. I don't think that is what architects do. You'd have to be somebody like Frank Gehry to do that. It wouldn't be as much fun as this. The money would be better though.

Do you have any projects you would like to do or something you would like to achieve that you haven't done yet?

There are two things that I hope someday will happen. I have gotten really good jobs. I've been commissioned to do terrific things. There is no book job that I can think of that I've been lusting after. I've been able to get the most interesting jobs I can imagine. What does bother me, and what I would like to fix, is the sense of financial ease that I don't have. I don't mean being rich, I mean knowing I can make it through "x" time to live. If I knew that I could keep working hard and I would make enough money to just live, I would be so happy. We don't live that extravagantly. If we had to cut back, there isn't much we could cut. I would change that if I could, if I could have some kind of security about my work. I don't.

The other thing I would like, and this could happen, I would like to be able to teach somebody about what I do and have them really take off with it—someone that is hungry and really wanted to run with it. I haven't found that person yet. It would be nice to have one or more people that would really get it and want to take their own direction, but I could help them do that. A lot of people who are interested in books and book arts are technique driven. They want to learn techniques. I am not so interested in that. Technique is important because things fall apart if you don't have technique down. But what people do with the techniques, those are the things that are important to me. I would like to be able to talk to somebody about that, to have somebody respond to that kind of approach to making books—an idea-driven approach as opposed to a technique-driven approach. I haven't found that person. I've taught a lot of people, but I haven't found that person. That would really make me happy.

What do you tell people who want to become book artists or bookbinders? Where should they study? What should they do?

I don't know, man. I don't emphasize technique, but I am a good craftsman. I know how to make things work and build books. But that is not what I'm focusing on right now. People respond to good craftsmanship, even if they don't respond to other things I might be doing. They can see a corner and get it that it looks good, or a head-cap that looks terrific. People understand that. I know that my work has a little bit of staying power with people because it is well crafted. It is a hook. It has to be well crafted in order for it to hang together, but it is also a marketing tool. People can say they don't understand my work but they say, "Wow, look at that." That can give them a little bit more time. Sometimes they like it and they don't know why they like it. Craftsmanship is really important. It is important to me, but I've got that. Now what do I do? That is what it is about for me. What do you do with it? So what?

I would tell them that craft is important. They have to learn how to make books. I would not suggest, necessarily, that they go to an institution to learn it unless a degree matters. I wouldn't say don't go, but I wouldn't say go. I would say studying with a person is better in my opinion. I had a painting and sculpture teacher in graduate school that I worked with two or three days a week as his studio assistant. I learned more just being with that guy and working in his studio and working on his stuff than I probably learned in all the rest of graduate school. I learned more about how to be and how to live, how to think about your work, how to make mistakes and what do you do about it.

It is an attitude. Not the technique. The technique you can learn and you've got to learn, but this guy, Sam Richardson, he lived in a track house—a wife, three kids, this whole middle class thing going—and he was, and still is, a working class kind of guy. That is how he approached his work. He went to work every day in the studio about 8:30, took a break in the morning, lunch, the same time each day. That is the kind of guy he is. I didn't learn that from him, but I learned to work hard, really hard. He could compartmentalize things. He could work in his studio, and his kid came in with a scraped-up knee, and he would be a dad and take care of that. It was really wonderful to watch. His wife was important to him, and his work was important to him. He was really focused. I learned to focus because of him. I'm really a focused person. I don't think you get that from taking classes at a university.

If you want to teach and you need a Masters degree, then you've got to go get it. But otherwise I wouldn't. I would find somebody and make them teach you something. Beg them. Pay them. Whatever you have to do to get instruction in technique. And hanging out with artists is a good thing. Book people, print people, papermakers, everybody is really focused by specifics. That is valuable.

What do you consider are the personal characteristics that help you succeed as a book artist?

I am focused. I can stay focused for two years on a project. I don't think I have any gifts. I can work hard. Like Chuck Close says, "Inspiration is for amateurs; the rest of us just show up and get to work."

For more information on Don Glaister, and to see examples of his work, to go http://www.foolsgoldstudio.com.

Don Etherington:
A Bookbinding Father Figure

Summerfield, North Carolina
March 2006

I call Don Etherington the father of modern bookbinding in the US. A thread ties him to almost all of the great bookbinders currently working in America. Trained and apprenticed in England, he rose through the ranks, working with Roger Powell and teaching bookbinding at the Camberwell School of Arts and Crafts and then at the Southampton College of Art. He was persuaded to move to Washington, DC to work in a book conservation program being developed at the Library of Congress, and from there he was lured to the Harry Ransom Humanities Resource Center at University of Texas in Austin where he had the opportunity to set up a conservation center. He has influenced many peoples' bookbinding careers—people who apprenticed with him, those that he hired and supervised at the institutions where he worked, students of his private teaching, and those whom he mentored and advised.

We sit in his office/library at the home he shares with his wife and fellow master bookbinder, Monique Lallier. His bright eyes peer out from under bushy eyebrows. He is smartly dressed in slacks, a button-up shirt, and a sweater vest. He is charming and suave. I think of the romantic story of him meeting Monique at a bookbinding conference in Finland where they fell in love. He proposed to her in Helsinki after knowing her for only ten days. More than 20 years has passed since that day.

I first met Don in Dallas about 25 years ago when he came to teach a leather-binding workshop. We were to have our books sewn, rounded, and backed, and our leather prepared before his workshop. Our skills fell quite short—our textblocks were not properly prepared. He practically had to start us from scratch. I remember his frustration as well as his patience as he tried to make sure each of us finished a nicely bound leather book.

I continue to see him each year. He and Monique attend the Guild of Book Workers' annual Standards of Excellence conference. Don was instrumental in forming the Standards; his mission was to create an opportunity for book workers to gather and learn techniques and skills that would raise the standards of bookbinding in America. His presence at the yearly meetings inspires beginning and novice bookbinders alike.

As I hear him talk, I recognize a businessman's mind at work, more economically driven than most of the private practice binders with whom I have talked. He would like to do everything possible when conserving a book, but he realizes that to run a business, only the necessary, contracted work should be done; but the work has to satisfy the clients.

He has both a business and a private practice, and he excels at both. The design bindings he continues to do independently are the full monty. He holds nothing back in creating superbly designed and crafted bindings. And he understands what it takes to keep a business alive so that affordable bookbinding and book conservation services can be available to book collectors, institutions, and the public. He has spent decades striving to raise the standards of bookbinding skills in America. Out of a hundred crafts, for no particular reason, he chose to study bookbinding. He immediately loved it. He went on to significantly influence bookbinding in America.

Thank you for agreeing to allow me to interview you. Even though you are not exclusively a private practice bookbinder, I would enjoy hearing how your career in bookbinding developed. You have been influential to so many of the people that I interviewed for this project. I understand you began bookbinding when you were thirteen.

I picked it out from a list. In those days, when you were eleven years old, you had to take the eleven-plus exam. If you failed, you were placed in the failing stream. I achieved a free pass, which allowed me, at thirteen, a second chance. You either went to academic or tech school.

I opted to apply to a tech school. They send you this list of a hundred crafts. I don't even know why I chose bookbinding. Bookbinding was my first choice—jewelry and engraving were my other choices. I opted to apply to the Central School of Arts and Crafts in London. I had an interview and showed my portfolio of a decorative alphabet. I got accepted. Six of us got accepted to bookbinding.

Interesting, the very first day I started school in bookbinding, I came away absolutely enamored by it, and I've loved it ever since. My background didn't do anything to make me more attuned to it. My only vague connection was that my father was a house painter and was doing the inside of Hatchards, a very famous rare bookstore in Picadilly. I remember the bindings in the window. It is a big stretch though the only connection I can think of. But I feel very lucky for it. Not many people can say they are happy with what they chose at such an early age.

Actually [in tech school] you have to continue your academic classes. You do some bookbinding in the first year; and in the second year you do half bookbinding; and you do more in the third. The Central places you with a company where you begin a seven-year apprenticeship. I still have the books I did while at the Central. I ended up doing five bindings over a period of three years. In your third year, they start deciding what you are going to be apprenticed at—a finisher or a forwarder. I was to be a finisher. When I first started at Harrison's and Sons I was told, in no uncertain terms, to fuck off when I started to ask questions of the people whom I thought would be training me. The owner of the company agrees to keep you employed for seven years. I was working 45 hours a week for $3.00 per week when I first started. At the end of my apprenticeship I earned $22 per week.

I had to do two years of national service, in the Air Force. I was able to continue my education, so during those two years I left the base two days a week and continued my studies at the Central School of Arts and Crafts. When I got out, I finished my apprenticeship and passed my exam (in bookbinding, printing, and design). I thought teaching was the only avenue to do design binding and still make a living. So when I finished my apprenticeship, I went to Camberwell (I was about 21 or 22 years old) and applied to teach. I was told, "Young man, I think you need more experience."

I applied for a job at the BBC. There I got a job restoring music manuscripts in the music library. Then I went to the British Library. I asked Howard Nixon, head of Collections there, if he could help me in developing my restoration skills. I would buy decrepit old books and work on them and show them to him. He was planning to introduce me to booksellers in the area.

Meanwhile Roger Powell told Howard that he wanted an assistant and asked if he knew of anyone. Howard recommended me, so I had an interview with Roger. I was working at the BBC at the time I was talking with Roger Powell. Working with Roger is what, in a sense, changed my life as a bookbinder, to begin a career in conservation.

Within a year, I got a call from Camberwell College of Art. They asked, "Would you teach one day a week?" I said I would love to. I went back to London for one day a week. Then, soon after they asked if I would like to work one day and one evening. After a few weeks, they said, "We would like you to work two days and two evenings," which was wonderful because it was good money. I stayed overnight at my mother's and traveled back and forth to the south of England. I can't remember how long I did this.

Southhampton College of Arts contacted me and said they were trying to set up a program in bookbinding and design and asked if I would be interested in setting it up. "Yep." So I left Roger to set up a program in Southampton. The day-release students came from the printing and binding industry. I taught trade bookbinding to boys like I was when I began. It came full circle.

I was a member of the Design Bookbinders and would go to London for the meetings. I was Treasurer for a while. Then in 1966, after the Florence flood, I was asked if I would go help train the Italians. I said yes, and so I went back and forth to Italy. I did that for a couple years. In 1970, the director of preservation at Library of Congress asked Peter Waters to set up a conservation program there. I was asked if I would come to Library of Congress as Training Officer. After I visited Washington, DC on a scouting trip, I agreed to this move.

Polly Lada-Mocarski, who was very involved in the Guild of Book Workers back then, was one of the ones included in the Washington discussions about Standards of bookbinding in the States. In 1980 she asked me if I would be interested in going to Texas to set up a conservation program at the Harry Ransom Humanities Resource Center at the University of Texas in Austin. I ended up there. I was attracted to the opportunity to build a program from scratch. It has been a remarkable success and continues to flourish. Polly was active in supporting book arts programs like the Creative Arts Workshop, Yale Conservation Center, and the New York Center for the Book.

How did the Guild of Book Workers Standards of Excellence conferences get started?

I had brought up the subject of there being a qualifying standard in the field of bookbinding and discussed this with a Guild of Book Workers committee. They thought I should be the one to send out a survey to the membership asking their opinion. The members replied with a resounding no.

We gathered at the Folger Library to discuss what to do to answer the needs of standards. It was a lively discussion. That is where the Standards of Excellence conference idea was born. I became the chair of it and continued for six or seven years until Bill Anthony took over. I think Standards has done a good job of raising standards of bookbinding in America. It has been remarkable.

Did you ever have a private practice?

While I was in Washington, DC, I always had a private practice, in addition to the institutional work at the Library of Congress. Though I didn't make my living off of that in Washington, DC, I did a lot of work. I think I could have made it as an independent.

What motivated you to start this business?

Jack Fairfield. He owned Information Conservation, Inc. (ICI). We talked many times about problems in large libraries that could be handled by commercial institutions rather than in the library.

So there was not a conservation part of ICI when you came. You developed it.

Yes, I was not young then—it was a challenge—I thought maybe I should give it a whirl. We started in 1987 with three people. You have to have a certain mindset to be successful in the business in bookbinding.

What do you think that is?

You can't totally forget that it is a business. You can't get caught up in doing all the things we all wish we could do. You have to come up with the best solutions and start doing it.

A lot of conservators don't have the business mindset. I was lucky to have both. I was always trying to come up with ways to become more efficient. I think it worked out pretty well. I still think it is tough, especially in book conservation. In paper conservation it is not so difficult.

I sold my part of the company, Etherington Conservation Center, in April 2005, and now it is Etherington Conservation Services. It is a small change, but it reflects that it is not just conservation, but includes the addition of digitization and scanning services. It has changed a lot from the beginning. It was basically just three of us in those days. We were lucky that we had a couple of big contracts doing a lot of repetitive stuff at that stage—encapsulation, boxmaking, etc. That was good because the people weren't skilled. I trained them. It was easier to do repetitive stuff. That got us settled. Over the years we would do work that was relatively more skilled. Now we have a higher percentage of work that requires higher skills, which is fine, but we don't have the same percentage of people to do the work yet. The amount of work is greater than the number of highly skilled conservators to do it. There is not the number of people available who want to live in North Carolina and who want to work all day, nine hours a day. I understand.

I am in the same position as when I started. I am not an owner any more. I got to [age] 70, and I thought others needed to carry on the business. We have no guarantees in life, and I was concerned about the employees, if anything bad happened to me.

How did you get clients in the beginning?

I was relatively well known 18 years ago. We never did a lot of advertising. It was mostly word of mouth. You can't be blasé about that. You can't sit back and think the work is just going to come in. We made telephone calls. Sometimes I think we still should. But right now we still have a backlog. It would be silly to bring in work that we can't turn out in a reasonable amount of time.

Where does most of your work come from and what kind of work is it?

Most is special collections and rare bookwork, mostly from institutions east of the Mississippi. We have four people who conduct paper conservation. That area hasn't necessarily grown that much. There are a lot of paper conservators, but not so many book conservators. It is a funny thing, but customers are happy to pay for a work of art but not for a book that requires the same amount of time and skill level. But we do have a base of customers now. The biggest change is that the level of work we do is of a much higher level now. We have had a good balance for many years, both in technicians' work and conservators' work.

I have worked at SMU for many years. In the past few years the Bridwell Library has been without a book conservator. Do you think a library of that size would be better off sending work out to a company like yours, or hiring a conservator?

Logically and economically it is better to send them to a place like this. There are a lot of libraries that can't afford their own conservator. It is purely economics. What we could do for a library for 30 or 40 thousand dollars is enormous. If they don't have a conservation librarian, they feel they are behind the times, like they have to keep up with the Joneses. I've worked at institutions. It works on a big scale. It may sound crass of me, but it is crazy for an institution to set up a lab for one person.

It is a sad reflection that in this country that there are only three large book and paper labs in private practice. There is more work out there than you can shake a stick at. People are not aware of the economics of sending work out for a collection. I coined the phrase, "collection conservator." I think having someone like that in an institution is important. They understand conservation and manage it and control what needs to be done. You organize it but don't set up a conservation treatment lab for one person. There are now a couple places that advertise a collection conservator.

What advice would you give to someone who is interested in making bookbinding a career?

Be rich. I've loved what I've done all these years. I've been lucky and happy. But if money is your focus, you shouldn't do bookbinding or even book conservation. If you enjoy working with your hands, and doing what we do gives you fulfillment, then you can get by. It comes down to a personal decision.

It is a little better in this country than it used to be. We now have North Bennet Street School and the American Academy of Bookbinding. There are a lot of courses around the country, and things are a lot more positive to get good training. That was not the case 30 years ago. But there is still no degree-granting program in this country, even for book conservation, which is pretty sad. Graduates from North Bennet don't have enough experience in conservation to be conservators. University of Texas offers a certificate in conservation as part of the Master of Library Science degree, but not a degree. It is a tough life. They need to work for a company like ours, Library of Congress, or for another institution where they can be trained. They can join the AIC (American Institute for Conservation). It's not easy. They've really got to work for it. Still it is much better than it used to be.

To have a successful career you generally have to be a conservator. Don Glaister [design bookbinder] is a good example of the exception. He does wonderful work. I think it helps that he does some multiples. Most design bookbinders can only do it as a side job, part-time. In conservation there is a potential for a career path. But in my perspective, salaries are not very good. Rare book conservators are a rare species. They are hard to find.

I think of you as kind of the father of bookbinding in the States. You seem to have touched the majority of people working in the field today, either through your jobs at Library of Congress, University of Texas, your private teaching, or your leadership and involvement in bookbinding organizations.

I don't know about that, but I've been doing it for a long time, about 60 years. I've trained a lot of people in England and here. I am still teaching. I've been very fortunate, enjoying what I've been doing for over 30 years here. I don't really consider it work.

Reflections

*T*he world of bookbinding is appealing—the people, the unique and imaginative bindings, the written words. Bookbinders are mechanics, engineers, designers, craftspeople—they require imagination, creativity, intelligence, problem solving, and passion.

Most of the successful bookbinders I spoke with have had to work very hard—to be "a little bit crazy." They weathered hard financial times, persevered when learning opportunities or jobs were scarce, and remained totally committed. Many of them have taken a variety of jobs to make a living—teaching, general bookbinding, restoration, conservation, box-making, edition work, tool making, machine or equipment production, selling bookbinding supplies or their own decorative papers.

But considering the harsh economics of bookbinding, I didn't hear anyone express the desire to do anything else. However, the majority of them voiced their frustration about feeling unable to charge a fair wage for their work. Unlike a plumber who charges per hour at the end of the job, a bookbinder is usually expected to give a firm price up front. The need to do extra work is often not discovered until a book is disassembled or the unique structure of a book is begun. Clients often can't understand why getting a book rebound or restored would cost more than buying a new book. And so bookbinders regularly attempt to educate the public about what bookbinding involves and why it is valuable.

Though some of the bookbinders I interviewed are living entirely on their bookbinding income, the majority of them have a partner who contributes a second income, and often provides insurance benefits to help them continue their careers as bookbinders.

Several of the independent bookbinders I interviewed would welcome having an apprentice work with them, but financial reasons prevent this from happening. Unlike the old days in Europe, contemporary young people generally do not want to commit seven years of their life training with a bookbinder. The bookbinder cannot afford to bring in a student, spend valuable time training him to do work that would take far less time alone, and then lose him when he wants to move on. A number of the bookbinders I interviewed would like to pass on their skills to apprentices, but they need funding to subsidize the training. Instead, many of them teach bookbinding, either in workshop settings or in regular weekly classes. There is a common sense of responsibility among bookbinders to share their knowledge and skills.

Each of the independent bookbinders I interviewed had an awakening to bookbinding, often caused by a significant, pivotal event. All were intrigued with the work, drawn to it, and committed to it. The majority of them studied intensely for many years before venturing into private practice. In addition, most of them prefer that life—setting their own hours, taking the jobs they want to take, avoiding office politics, enjoying creative freedom. Jim Croft, the bookbinder in rural Idaho, takes this freedom to an extreme level as he lives the old way with only limited electricity powered by solar panels, a wood burning cookstove, and outhouse facilities.

The world of book workers in America is still relatively intimate. As I listened to people's stories, I noticed their frequent references to each other. Bookbinders are interconnected, almost like a family tree, through their training, work, collaboration, or friendships.

I realize I like bookbinders because, like me, they find satisfaction in creating things. Money, material things, or fame does not drive them. They emit an energy of joyful living.

Bookbinding makes my life interesting. In creating a design binding, I gather information much like a writer collects research. All the pieces come together—the story, the typeface, the illustrations—and an idea develops as a small ripple that expands and grows. In creating a design binding, I have the opportunity to give birth to a physical expression of how a book affects me.

So what did I discover regarding bookbinding as a possible career for me? For now, bookbinding will remain my avocation; other sources of income will sustain me financially. But bookbinding is my passion, my sanity, my expression, a vehicle to connect with others in a positive way in this world. Bookbinding is an extension of me. It is therapy. And teaching bookbinding and working side-by-side with other binders is bliss.

The bookbinders I interviewed are a testament to the continued life of the artist/craftsman. They exist and they thrive even as they work hard and continually educate people about the value of their work. Many of us would like to choose that life but are unwilling to take the risk. Fortunately, there are still people keeping the old, fine arts and crafts alive.

ॐ   ॐ   ॐ

Index